Aspects of Phonological Theory

ASPECTS OF PHONOLOGICAL THEORY

PAUL M. POSTAL

Thomas J. Watson Research Center

International Business Machines Corporation

Yorktown Heights

Harper & Row, Publishers

NEW YORK, EVANSTON, AND LONDON

ASPECTS OF PHONOLOGICAL THEORY

Library of Congress Catalog Card Number: 68-10142

To Susan

CONTENTS

PREFACE

Let the term 'modern linguistics' refer to the field roughly within the period 1930–1960. Then it is unanimously agreed that one outstanding feature of modern linguistics in both Europe and America is the development of a new and special conception of phonology involving the 'discovery of the phoneme' and the application of 'phonemics' to an extremely wide range of languages. We may say, in other words, that despite a wide variety of far from identical formulations, there has arisen within modern linguistics a fairly coherent and extremely widely accepted doctrine about the nature of the phonological aspect of language.[1] It is difficult to say exactly when this view of phonology became firmly established, but its entrenchment as the dominant view in the United States surely dates back at least twenty-five years.[2] The

---

[1] This essential unanimity excludes Great Britain where a rather, though by no means completely, special development took place. For some discussion cf. Langendoen (1964a, 1964b) and Chapter 8.

[2] I am inclined to agree with C. F. Hockett (1951:339) that the first really complete statement of this position was his article 'A System of Descriptive Phonology' (Hockett, 1942). It must be emphasized, however, that almost all of the ideas typical of post-1942 autonomous phonemics were being discussed much earlier, in L. Bloomfield's *Language* (1933), in Y. R. Chao's famous paper on non-uniqueness (Chao, 1933), and in many European works such as Trubetzkay's monumental study (1939), as well as a number of others. In my opinion only one fundamental point basically differentiates Hockett's 1942 statement from these earlier works: the refusal to allow the relevance of *word boundaries* in phonology. This last final step toward a wholly consistent autonomous phonemics completely independent of grammar was one generally taken only in America, and then not by all, leading to the well-known 'grammatical prerequisites' dispute, whose substantive basis was just this point. Notice, however, what an extremely limited aspect of 'grammar' was being advocated even by those, like K. L. Pike and his associates, who supported 'grammatical prerequisites' (Pike, 1947, 1952). By 1942 essentially everyone agreed that properties like morpheme boundaries, morphophonemic alternations, grammatical categories (Noun, Verb), etc. were necessarily irrelevant to phonology. This left only word boundaries to argue about. In other words, the 'grammatical prerequisites' insisted upon by Pike in the late 1940's and early 1950's amounted to only a small percentage of the kinds of nonphonetic, grammatically determined properties which systematic phonemics now insists are relevant for phonetic interpretation (cf. Chapter 6). For further discussion of this point cf. Postal (to appear b).

ideas we are referring to are embodied not only in dozens of mongraphs, manuals, texts, and hundreds of articles within linguistics, but, especially in America, have found their way into the literature of other related fields as well. Most notable of these are anthropology and psychology, where the discovery of the phoneme is often referred to as an outstanding achievement of the 'behavioral sciences' due to linguistics.[3] Within the domain of its original acceptance, the doctrine under consideration ruled essentially unchallenged from sometime within the late thirties until the late fifties.

I shall refer here and throughout to this dominant conception of phonological structure as 'autonomous phonology' or 'autonomous phonemics,' considering this terminology preferable to that of 'taxonomic phonemics' which has been used on the recent past.[4] Although there is a close historical and theoretical association between the view that linguistic structure must be discoverable by procedures of segmentation and classification (hence 'taxonomic') and the view of phonology to be designated, this aspect is not, from the present point of view, what is essential. What is critical to the dominant view of phonology over this quarter-century period is the belief that there is a separate phonological level of linguistic structure which not only can but must be characterized in total independence of grammatical or syntactic information. What is *excluded* as necessarily irrelevant to phonology includes word boundaries, morpheme boundaries, morpheme identity, morphophonemic alternations, Surface Constituent Structure, etc.[5] In short, this view of phonol-

---

[3] Cf., for example, the psychologist John Carroll's remark in Carroll (1953:35):

"The formulation of the theory of the phoneme takes its place as one of the more significant intellectual achievements in the social sciences."

[4] The term 'taxonomic phonemics' was proposed in Chomsky (1964a). The newer usage 'autonomous phonology' is suggested by comments in a review by C. F. Ferguson (1962) and Chomsky's discussion of this review (1964b).

[5] The reference to 'Surface Syntactic Structure' here is motivated by the fact that within the theory which has developed in the framework of generative grammar there are two distinct aspects of syntactic structure: Deep Structure, which is highly abstract and relevant for semantic interpretation, and Surface Structure, which is a labelled bracketing of the actual phonetic form of the sentence. No one has ever suggested that Deep Structure is relevant for phonology (although this is of course logically

ogy holds that there is a level of phonology, henceforth the level of autonomous phonology (phonemics), which requires reference to only two sorts of facts: phonetics and the difference betweeen repetition and nonrepetition among utterance tokens, i.e. between free variation and contrast.[6]

The beginnings of a steadily more basic and thorough rejection of the doctrine of autonomous phonology grew out of the 'revolution' in linguistics initiated by the development of so-called 'generative grammar.'[7] Very quickly it was seen by those working within this new framework that the kind of phonology required as part of an explicit description of sentence well-formedness is not at all compatible with the form of phonological description countenanced by the official phonemics (of any brand) of the previous quarter century. (Lees, 1957; Halle, 1959.) All successive work in generative grammar has strengthened this conclusion.

In the last six years or so, autonomous phonemics has come under increasing criticism from the point of view of work in generative grammar.[8] Advocates of this approach have claimed that language contains no level of structure with the properties

---

possible), but recognition of the phonological relevance of Surface Structure was in fact quite traditional before its elimination by modern linguists. For some discussion cf. Postal (1964a). For the Deep-Surface distinction in its most recent formulation cf. Chomsky (1965).

[6] Only Bernard Bloch in a series of papers during the late 1940's and early 1950's (1948, 1950, 1953) attempted the further step of eliminating appeal to any kind of facts besides phonetics. Bloch tried to show that the notion of contrast was itself definable in terms of phonetic properties and their distributions. It is generally agreed that this attempt was a failure (although I think that the really crucial objections to this approach have never been explicitly stated). But the usual inference, namely, that therefore contrast must be defined in terms of *semantic properties* is a non sequitur. For some discussion cf. Chomsky (1964b).

[7] For some general discussion of this development, its underlying ideas, contrasts with previous views, cf. Chomsky (1961a, 1961b, 1962, 1964b, 1965, 1966, to appear a), Chomsky and Halle (1965), Katz (1964, to appear), Katz and Postal (1964), Lees (1957), Postal (1964b, to appear a, to appear b).

[8] Chomsky (1957a, 1957b, 1962, 1964b, to apear a); Chomsky and Halle (1965); Chomsky, Halle and Lukoff (1956); Hale (1965); Halle (1959, 1960, 1962); Halle and Chomsky (to appear); Keyser (1963); Keyser and Halle (to appear); Lees (1957, 1961); Postal (1964a, to appear b).

of autonomous phonemics and that the first significant level 'above' the phonetic is not this artifact, but rather a level which has been called <u>systematic</u> phonemic. This kind of structure is akin in important respects, though by no means in all respects,[9] to what followers of autonomous phonology refer to as <u>morphophonemic</u> representation.[10] That is, this latter is a level <u>in which</u> choice of representation of forms is based on considerations of morphophonemic alternations, word and morpheme boundaries, morpheme identity, and Surface Syntactic Structure, as well as on considerations of phonetics and contrast. Criticism of autonomous phonology has, however, only been a peripheral aspect of more substantive work on phonology within generative grammar: work which has created, and steadily revised and enriched,[11] the theory

---

[9] The *similarities* between systematic phonemic representation and more traditional 'morphophonemics' seem to be well recognized and understood. Both involve representing morphemes with abstract base forms (one for each morpheme except in cases of irregular suppletion) only indirectly related to phonetic structures by a complex chain of rules: both fail to meet the conditions required for autonomous phonemic representation. But the *differences* between current systematic phonemics and the older morphophonemics have not been as well understood, and these are many and crucial. For example, in the latter the minimal elements are morphophonemes which are unanalyzable segmental entities. But in the former, systematic phonemes are complexes of binary properties. Further, in the latter, the class of morphophonemes is arbitrary, i.e. morphophonemes are ad hoc and the set of all such elements is not constrained within linguistic theory. But in the former, the class of systematic phonemes is constrained to just those which can be constructed from the binary projections of a fixed set of phonetic features plus a set of universal combinatorial restrictions. Hence choice of a universal phonetic theory immediately constrains the class of possible systematic phonemes. Finally, in traditional morphophonemics the representation of a form was in general given exhaustively by a string of morphophonemes. But in systematic phonemics the systematic representation of a form consists not only of this, but of the Surface Constituent Structure of the form as well. In short, the input to the phonological rules is identical with the output of the syntactic rules. Many other important differences exist as well, some of which are mentioned below.

[10] For some discussion of more traditional views of morphophonemic representation cf. Swadesh and Voegelin (1939), Lounsbury (1953).

[11] It would be difficult to exaggerate the extent to which ideas are constantly undergoing revision within this framework. As far as one can see, however, all of these revisions seem to share the property that the resulting theories are less similar to those of the structural or descriptive linguistics

of systematic phonemics as part of an overall theory of language including syntax and semantics.

The present volume is intended as a contribution to the continuing discussion of the relative merits of autonomous and systematic phonemics. It maintains the dual aspect of previous phonological work within generative grammar. That is, it is concerned both with criticism of autonomous phonology and with construction of a more adequate theory congruent with the goals of generative linguistic description and with known linguistic fact. The two separate studies of this work consider highly disparate aspects of language, arguing in each case that systematic phonemics is supported and autonomous phonemics disconfirmed by the facts of the relevant domain.

Part I is concerned with a variety of synchronic matters bearing on the relative adequacy of the autonomous and systematic conceptions. In Section I we begin with a study of the fundamental notion contrast/free variation which has not been extensively discussed in terms of generative grammar and which is often brought forward as an argument in favor of the existence of a level of autonomous phonemics. It is shown how such arguments are fallacious, and the way in which a generative linguistic description explicates the notion of contrast without a level of autonomous phonemics is described. We consider certain common variants of this kind of argument, showing that they are equally fallacious. Certain implications of the fallacious character of the arguments given for autonomous phonemics in terms of contrast are discussed, and the basis for the unsound conclusions is pointed out.

In Section II we turn to a consideration of real arguments against the assumption that there is a level of autonomous phonemic structure in language. We review a fundamental argument against autonomous phonemics which was first developed by M. Halle, survey similar kinds of cases, and consider an attempt by advocates of so-called 'Stratificational Grammar' to avoid the

of the period 1930–1960 than were the ones which came before. Hence these revisions can bring no comfort to defenders of modern 'taxonomic' linguistics. This is notably true, for example, of certain crucial revisions in phonological theory having to do with the notion of Marked and Unmarked values for phonological features, which have taken place recently. These are discussed in Chapter 8.

negative conclusions of Halle while maintaining the basic tenets of autonomous phonemics. It is concluded that this attempt is a necessary failure. More importantly, however, discussion of these topics leads to an account of the Naturalness Condition, which is, it is claimed, a fundamental constraint governing the relations between phonetic and phonological structure. It is shown how stratificational phonemics violates this condition and how its conceptual foundations are chaotic. This latter issue involves a positive discussion of the correct interpretation of phonetic structure which has generally been badly misunderstood. Subsequent chapters in Section II deal with nonphonetic properties in phonology (that is, the role of various types of grammatical information) and with rule ordering. In Chapter 8 we turn to rather revolutionary ideas proposed recently by Chomsky and Halle which amount to a substantial revision of systematic phonemic theory. Fundamental features of the newer version are discussed and briefly justified. All of these chapters also continue to yield criticisms of autonomous phonemics in both stratificational and nonstratificational variants. Finally, in Chapter 9 we present two new kinds of arguments against autonomous phonemic theory, arguments which are in certain respects even more damaging than the original kind discovered by Halle. One of these arguments is concerned with the notion of contrast, relating back to the issues raised in Section I. Most significantly, it is shown that the situation is the reverse of that claimed in the fallacious argument of Chapter 1. That is, this argument claims that the facts of contrast show the need for a level of autonomous phonemics. But in Chapter 11 it is pointed out that these facts actually reveal the exact opposite.

In Part II attention is directed to the domain of diachronic phonology, and we investigate the nature of so-called 'sound change.' In particular we consider the truth value of a classical view of the nature of sound change which, while predating the development of autonomous phonemics, is closely linked to it theoretically, factually, and historically. It is concluded that this widely accepted Neogrammarian position is false and that the theory of sound change must be based on a more flexible and abstract conception of phonology within the framework of systematic phonemics. More generally, it is concluded that sound change, like other aspects of language and language change, is an essentially *mentalistic* phenomenon and that a major aspect of the error of autonomous phonemics and its historical corollaries is the futile attempt to maintain an antimentalistic methodology. In dealing with this question we consider in great detail the recent attempt of C. F. Hockett to formulate an antimentalistic theory of sound change within the general framework of a nonmentalistic interpretation of autonomous phonemics. It is argued that the overwhelming inadequacy of this attempt is directly related to its failure to recognize the mentalistic nature of linguistic phenomena. Most crucial in this discussion is the argument that phonetic description, often considered to be physical and completely free of mentalistic 'bias,' is in fact an account of a mentalistic domain, namely, the system of instructions which determines the ideal behavior of the speech apparatus.

A special feature of the present volume should be noted. The greater part of the empirical evidence brought forward is from the Northern Iroquoian languages, mostly Mohawk. This is the result of intermittent investigation of the Montreal, or Caughnawaga, dialect of this language over the last six and a half years. I shall report more fully on this work in a forthcoming monograph of which this study can be taken as a preview.

The general debt which I owe to M. Halle and N. Chomsky for my ideas of phonological structure needs no emphasis since it is obvious throughout. But I would also like to express my appreciation for their detailed help with the present study, which has greatly improved the final form of the manuscript. I am also indebted to J. R. Ross for his detailed and persevering criticisms of earlier versions, which have materially improved the finished product. Remaining errors and deficiencies are, of course, my own. I am also very grateful to Mrs. M. Lahache for checking all of the Mohawk examples.

PART I

Autonomous Phonology:
Pro and Con

1

A PURPORTED JUSTIFICATION FOR AUTONOMOUS PHONEMICS

THE BASIC ARGUMENT

It must surely be recognized that the majority of linguists in the United States, Europe, and no doubt elsewhere are far from convinced of the inadequacy of autonomous phonology. This is manifested in both the continued widespread utilization of the autonomous framework for the description of particular languages and for the discussion of theoretical issues, and in a certain number of explicit attempts to defend the framework against its generative critics.[1] There are obviously many grounds for this

---

[1] I am aware of the following explicit defenses: Marckwardt (1962), Hill (1962), Householder (1965) and Vachek (1964). But these are obviously merely symptomatic of wider dissatisfaction or disagreement with the critique. Cf. for example the many comments after Chomsky's paper to

continued faith in autonomous phonemics, cognitive and otherwise. I suspect, however, that an important motivation which
leads many to continued acceptance of this conception of phonological structure is to be found in a certain initially rather per-
suasive argument, an argument lying close to the heart of the way
autonomous phonemic representation has traditionally been justified and introduced to students, nonlinguists, etc. The argument

---

the Ninth International Congress of Linguists (Chomsky, 1964). For criticism of the first of these papers, cf. Chomsky (to appear a). For criticism
of the third, cf. Chomsky and Halle (1965), which is devoted entirely to its
analysis. The fourth paper by Vachek consists of a critical account of the
antiautonomous phonology part of Chomsky (1964a, 1964b). Vachek's argument needs little discussion, however, since it has a quite uniform logical
structure. In each case Vachek accepts in effect the correctness of the analysis of particular examples suggested by Chomsky, agrees with Chomsky that
these cases are incompatible with the various principles of autonomous
phonemics which Chomsky was criticizing, but then accepts both the particular analyses and the general principles these refute with the remark that
these merely show 'fuzzy points in language.' Obviously this invention of a
new terminology for counterinstances to linguistic principles has no empirical
or substantive relevance. That is, if one is allowed to save theories by
christening the cases which overthrow them 'fuzzy points,' then no theory
can be falsified.

I of course do not count as defenses of autonomous phonemics such empirically and logically contentless remarks as the following (Hockett, 1961:49):

"It is also for empirical reasons that I believe we should reject any proposal
to replace the phonological stratum—reasonably regarded as a 'bridge' between the grammatical stratum and that of articulation—by something else.
Certainly it is possible to delete all reference to phonology from a description of a language replacing morphophonemic and allophonic statements by
more complex rules that describe directly the programming of morphemes
into articulatory motions. The trouble with this logically possible procedure
is just exactly that it leaves out the phonological stratum, which on empirical grounds I believe to be objectively a part of language design. Part of
the evidence (or basis) for this belief is my continuing conviction, with
Smith and Trager—and despite charges of irrelevance from Chomsky and
Lees and expressions of skepticism from Pike—that the phonological system
of a language can be discovered and described without any critierial use
of grammatical facts. No other imaginable intervening stratum between
grammar and articulation has that property."

These comments involve an almost total distortion of the position of systematic phonemics. Obviously no one, certainly not Chomsky, Lees, Halle,
etc., has ever proposed mapping morphemes directly into articulation. Such
an idea does not even make sense (at best one could talk of mapping morphemes directly into phonetic representations, again something no one has
ever seriously suggested). The real question is not the existence of phonological representation but its proper character. It is, to say the least, not
obvious how Hockett's, Smith's, and Trager's *conviction,* continuing or other-

to which I refer revolves around the notions of contrast vs. free variation or repetition. It is worth stating and discussing in great detail because it is completely fallacious. That is, it in no way does what many appear to believe it does, namely, justify or provide support for the existence of autonomous phonological representation vis-à-vis systematic phonological representation. The argument does not, in other words, show the need for the former.[2]

---

wise, can be part of the *empirical* evidence for autonomous phonology. Notice also that the last sentence in Hockett's comments is both irrelevant and far from obviously true since phonetic structure might very well have them, and indeed if autonomous phonemic structure has them, phonetic structure necessarily must also. Similarly, I do not count as a challenge to the generative criticism of autonomous phonology C. F. Ferguson's discussion in his review of Halle's *The Sound Pattern of Russian* (Ferguson, 1962). Ferguson, extraordinarily, dealt not with the counterexample proposed by Halle in the book being reviewed (for discussion of this example cf. Chapter 3 of this text) but, instead, with an example given by Lees (1957:389–390) which, however, Lees had previously retracted as incorrect in a work to which Ferguson referred (Lees, 1961:62–63). For discussion of other inadequate aspects of Ferguson's discussion cf. Chomsky (1964b) and Part II, Chapter 10 of this text. Nor obviously can one count as serious protest such substantively empty assertions about systematic phonemics as the following by H. A. Gleason (1964:79):

"To achieve efficiency in this function or functions, various shortcuts are taken. For example, the phoneme is by-passed by a set of rules which go directly from morphophonemes, alias 'phonemes' (and roughly our morphons), to phonetic specifications. Such shortcuts inevitably complicate other possible functions of a grammar, or render them impossible."

Neither in this article nor anywhere else does Gleason even attempt to give a single fact or argument to support a claim that systematic phonology complicates or renders impossible any known function of a linguistic description. Notice, however, that, in contrast to the quote from Hockett's 1961 article, Gleason at least gives a reasonably accurate account of what he opposes, namely, descriptions in which systematic representation is connected to phonetic representations by a set of rules with no intermediate autonomous level of structure.

[2] I assume of course that the need for the latter level of systematic representation is unquestioned, although this, of course, deviates as much from modern linguistics as the assumption that autonomous representation is not needed. Indeed the elimination of morphophonemic representation from both the practice and theory of linguistic descriptions is one of the most striking and incredible features of the development of post-1940 linguistics. Thus the comment by Hockett (1961:42), "Morphophonemes . . . are *artifacts of analysis or conveniences for description,* not elements in a language," is perfectly typical of the prevailing attitude. Cf. first part of Chapter 8.

Given any utterance token in any language, all linguists assume in effect that it may be correctly represented, independently of any further knowledge about it, in a <u>narrow phonetic transscription.</u> However, modern linguistics has, at least since Bloomfield's time, been tortured with a kind of intellectual schizophrenia by phonetic representation. On the one hand, every linguist recognizes that a discrete, segmented, correct phonetic representation is an absolute prerequisite to any work in phonology, and linguists are contemptuous of nothing more than inept phonetics. Yet at the same time, a priori methodological assumptions about antimentalism, etc. have forced linguists to the conclusion that phonetics must be the direct description of some *physical* reality, either articulatory, acoustic, or both. Yet it has been known for decades that neither articulation nor the acoustic signal has the discrete, segmental properties which phonetic representations manifest. Hence phonetic transcriptions seem to the modern linguist to be something at once descriptive of no reality, not part of any serious description of the world, and yet strangely absolutely necessary for all phonological work for which accurate, instrumental representations of the actual signal or its articulatory causes have proved largely useless. It is surely no accident that in just those areas where the phonetic representation of the facts is most undeveloped and most controversial, as with intonation, there is least agreement about phonological interpretation, even among those who accept similar theoretical views of phonology.

Modern linguistics is thus burdened with this never-resolved inconsistency and remains to this day on the horns of the dilemma that on the one hand linguistic descriptions require phonetics both as a basis for phonological description and as such (for description of allophonic variation, dialectical differences, historical change, etc.), but methodological assumptions do not permit any such description to be part of linguistics. The obvious solution to this problem, namely, the traditional realization (Saussure, 1959:11) that phonetic representation is not a direct description of speech signal or articulation but rather part of a theory about the instructions sent from the central nervous system to the speech apparatus is, of course, intolerable to the modern linguist because it is mentalistic. And the horror of that is learned at the linguistic cradle. Rather than give up this a priori methodology, the modern linguist has, for various reasons, preferred to keep the inherent and insoluble inconsistency about phonetics, often trying to disguise it by making phonetics in some way seem merely like a practical aid to field work; rather like having a sharp pencil or an empty notebook. I return to this issue of the mentalistic nature of phonetic representations and its rejection by modern linguists in Chapter 5 and in Part II, Chapter 13. It deserves a special study. In the rest of this section we ignore these difficulties about the interpretation of phonetic structure.

Assuming then that a large set of utterance tokens are represented phonetically, these may be placed in sets[3] whose members either do or do not bear the relation <u>noncontrastive</u> or <u>repetition</u> to each other. This is, for example, the relation which holds between phonetically different versions of the English word 'awful' spoken with or without initial glottal stop, or between phonetically different tokens of the English word 'pit' spoken with final released, unreleased, or even mildly aspirated stops. Of course the exact basis or nature of this relation is and has been quite controversial. There is, for example, a large literature dealing with the question of whether this basis is semantic, a conclusion which many linguists have seen as self-evident. We need not be concerned with such questions here, and for present purposes the notion may be considered primitive. All linguists are agreed that there is such a notion, and working on any particular language there is, in practice, almost complete agreement on the assignment of utterance tokens to contrasting or noncontrasting sets.

Taking a set of phonetic representations which are descriptions of utterances that are repetitions or noncontrastive, one will in general, of course, find *distinct phonetic representations* as members. Furthermore, a phonetic difference which is associated with a contrast in one language is not necessarily so associated in another. That is, given a pair of utterances [bin] and [pin], both of which occur in two different languages, it is not necessarily the

---

[3] No doubt most linguists would immediately argue that these sets are disjoint. They would argue, in other words, that noncontrastive is a <u>transitive</u> relation, i.e. one such that if it holds between an utterance *a* and an utterance *b*, and between *b* and an utterance *c*, it necessarily holds between *a* and *c*. However, this claim is not at all obvious and involves empirical assumptions far beyond what are necessary for our present argument. We return to this issue in the latter part of Chapter 9 where it is shown that the fact that autonomous phonemics directly entails the transitivity of contrast permits new evidence to be brought to bear on its truth value.

case that these pairs are either free variants in both or contrastive in both. Hence from phonetic representation alone it is obviously impossible to infer whether two utterances in a language are or are not repetitions. Since the specification of this kind of basic fact is properly seen as necessary for an adequate linguistic description, the modern linguist versed in autonomous phonemics has concluded something like the following. It is necessary to set up for a language another kind of representation of utterances besides phonetic, namely, autonomous phonological, whose goal is just exactly to represent all and only those phonetic features which distinguish free variants from contrasting utterances. And upon such representation are imposed many conditions which include the following:

(1.1) Given two identical phonological representations, the utterances they represent, that is, the phonetic representations they are associated with, may or may not be *identical* but are necessarily not *distinct*. That is, the associated phonetic forms must be free variants or repetitions.

(1.2) Given two phonetic representations which are not free variants (repetitions), and are hence necessarily not identical, their phonological representations are necessarily distinct.

Conditions (1.1) and (1.2) are fundamental conditions for any theory of phonology and are accepted by all variants of autonomous and systematic phonemics. On the other hand, autonomous phonemics also insists on the converses of (1.1) and (1.2) which are respectively:

(1.3) Given two phonetic representations which are free variants, their phonological representations are necessarily identical.

(1.4) Given two distinct phonological representations, the phonetic representations they are associated with are necessarily distinct.

But as pointed out by Halle (1959:21), systematic phonemics while accepting conditions (1.1) and (1.2) rejects the converses (1.3) and (1.4) which turn out to have no justification and many intolerable consequences. Conditions (1.1) through (1.4) as a whole seem to me to be an absolutely uncontroversial reconstruction of assumptions which lie behind modern autonomous phonemics, so much so that I will not attempt to justify them textually here by quoting instances of them from the literature. But cf. the quotes from Lamb, Lounsbury, and Hockett in this and the following two chapters.

Conditions (1.1) through (1.4) are necessary for phonological representation, the autonomous phonemicist would claim, just exactly so that autonomous phonemic representation can indicate the difference between free variation and contrast not necessarily indicated by phonetic representation. For now, although it is impossible to determine from the phonetic representation of pairs of utterances whether they are in free variation (just because some but not all distinct phonetic representations may be repetitions), this is always immediately determinable in a mechanical way from their associated autonomous phonological representations. For regardless of their phonetic structure, two utterances are free variants if their autonomous phonological representations are identical, and not otherwise.

Furthermore, vis-à-vis either systematic phonemic or morphophonemic representation, the advocate of autonomous phonology would claim that the above facts definitely show the need for the intermediate[4] autonomous phonological representation. For systematic phonemic representation is such that of the above four conditions which characterize autonomous representation, only (1.1) and (1.2) are necessarily met. Conditions (1.3) and (1.4) are not necessarily met because two distinct systematic representations may both be mapped onto the same phonetic string (i.e. so-called <u>complete overlapping</u>,[5] excluded in autonomous phonemics, is allowed in systematic, in fact is a quite com-

---

[4] Assuming a grammar containing systematic and phonetic representations, autonomous phonological structure is intermediate in the sense that it is more abstract than the phonetic level but much less so than the systematic one. Or, put differently, while a phonetic representation provides by definition all phonetic information directly, an autonomous phonemic representation provides much of it directly but a limited amount by its limited set of associated allophonic rules or statements. But systematic representation eliminates as much direct information as possible from phonological strings and indicates pronunciation very indirectly by means of a very long, highly structured, and complex chain of phonological rules.

[5] For a discussion of complete overlapping with insistence that it cannot occur in a correct autonomous phonemic description cf. Bloch (1941), and for criticism of the argument cf. Chomsky (1964b). For a discussion of the question of the empirical existence of complete overlapping cf. the latter part of Chapter 9.

mon occurrence). It follows that identity or nonidentity among systematic phonemic representations does not permit determination of whether their associated phonetic representations are free variants or not. A grammar containing only systematic and phonetic representations thus does not, the autonomous phonemicist claims in effect, indicate the crucial distinction between free variation and contrast among utterances. Hence the need for the intermediate autonomous phonemic structure.

Let us consider a hypothetical example[6] which will illustrate the above argument in favor of autonomous phonology. Imagine a language in which there are vowel systematic phonemes $\underline{i}$, $\underline{e}$, $\underline{a}$, $\underline{u}$; systematic word boundary $\#$; and morphophonemic rules that consonants palatalize before non-Grave (front) vowel systematic phonemes, i.e. before $\underline{i}$ and $\underline{e}$ but not before $\underline{a}$ and $\underline{u}$. Assume further that this is the only source for phonetic palatalization. Finally assume that there is a morphophonemic rule that $\underline{i}$ drops word finally and late phonetic rules yielding voiced consonants between vowels. Consider now the following representations of some utterances in this language:

Systematic Phonemic	Phonetic
(1.5a) #katu#	(1.5b) [kadu]
(1.6a) #kati#	(1.6b) [kat$_y$]
(1.7a) #kate#	(1.7b) [kad$_y$e]
(1.8a) #kat#	(1.8b) [kat]
(1.9a) #katui#	(1.9b) [kadu]

Further, assume that all of the utterances represented by (1.5b) through (1.9b) are contrastive except for (1.5b) and (1.9b), i.e. no other pair are free variants. Then it is clear, so the argument runs, that a grammar containing only representations like (a) and (b) is inadequate. From the phonetic representations alone we do not know which utterances are free variants. For example, one cannot determine that (1.6b) and (1.8b) do not represent

---

[6] I have picked a hypothetical example to avoid superfluous and irrelevant factual arguments. The situation described here is based to a certain limited extent on that existing in Papago, a Uto-Aztecan language of the American Southwest. In particular, the palatalization of consonants before vowels which then drop is formally similar to a situation in that language. Cf. Hale (1965).

repetitions. And we also cannot tell this from the representations (a). The latter follows, for example, because although (1.5b) and (1.6b) are distinct in systematic representation and also contrastive, (1.5b) and (1.9b) are distinct in systematic representation and yet not contrastive. Hence the systematic representation is not an adequate guide to free variation and the grammar must also include an intermediate level of representation of the autonomous phonological type in which these utterances are represented. For example:

Autonomous Phonemic

(1.5c) /katu/
(1.6c) /kat$_y$/
(1.7c) /kat$_y$e/
(1.8c) /kat/
(1.9c) /katu/

From this representation one can determine the facts of contrast exactly, i.e. one can immediately infer that the utterances associated with (1.5c) and (1.9c) are necessarily free variants, but that every other pair of utterances represented by (1.5b) through (1.9b) are in contrast, which is exactly right. Hence the need for autonomous phonological representation is simple and straightforward. And the advocate of autonomous phonology is justified in claiming that those apparently rather too-easily misled linguists who have wanted to throw out representations of type (c) must be willing to do so only because they have abandoned all interest in that fundamental class of facts which it is really the job of a phonological description to account for: namely, the difference between free variation and contrast. Q. E. D.

I have tried to put the above argument for autonomous phonology as clearly and persuasively as I can. It is clear to me that this kind of reasoning can be found in essence in many places in the literature. Usually, of course, it is found just as an absolute justification of autonomous phonemics or justification of it with respect to phonetic description alone, rather than as a direct argument against the sufficiency of descriptions containing only systematic phonemic and phonetic representations. It seems to me, as mentioned above, that reasoning like that above is much of the basis for so many linguists' continuing discomfort with the

elimination of autonomous phonological representation on which
those of us working in generative phonology continue to insist.
If this is so, linguists must face the fact that the grounds for
maintaining autonomous representation are illusory, for the above
argument is thoroughly unsound, as will be shown in the next part.

THE FALLACY

The heart of this argument showing the apparent need for
autonomous phonological representations in adequate linguistic
descriptions is the claim that a grammar containing only systematic phonemic and phonetic representations for utterances cannot
correctly represent the differences between free variation and
contrast. The argument is unsound because this claim is simply
false. The argument which was given obtains its veneer of plausibility because it involves, surreptitiously, an assumption which
many no doubt subscribe to but which is really without foundation.

We seem to have shown in the first part of this chapter that
a grammar containing only systematic phonemic and phonetic
representations cannot characterize repetition. But actually what
was shown is not this, but only that such a grammar does not
characterize this class of facts in one particular way. Namely, it
does not characterize them by providing some particular *single*
level of representation from which, given two utterances described
in the grammar, it is possible to 'read off' directly whether or not
they are free variants. Underlying the above argument is the
assumption, with which rightly there is universal agreement
today, that a grammar must:

(1.10) Predict free variation and contrast over the sentences of the
language it describes.

There is, however, the further surreptitious assumption that
not only must a grammar do this, i.e., indicate for any pair of
phonetic representations *possible* in the language[7] whether or
not they are contrastive, but must do so in a very definite and
limited way, namely, by:

---

[7] This must be taken literally. It is not enough for the grammar to
specify contrast over the sentences of the language since speakers have a

(1.11) Providing a single level of representation whose *markers*[8] (strings, sets of strings, etc) *directly indicate this relation.*

A grammar containing only representations of types (a) and (b) as in our hypothetical example above certainly predicts free variation and contrast. And it does this in a completely precise sense. Such a grammar makes such predictions by <u>generating</u> the class of <u>free variation sets,</u> where by 'free variation set' I refer to the maximal classes of phonetic representations which describe utterances in free variation.

---

knowledge of contrast for all phonetically possible utterances in that language. Thus, for example, English speakers know that possible, though nonexistent, forms like [mɛk] and [lɛk] are necessarily contrastive. Knowing this is a result of knowing that the rules of English phonology could not possibly assign both of these representations to any single input systematic structure. One should, along these lines, raise the question of how the theory of grammar should characterize the fact that certain phonetic differences are obviously too great for *any language* to have them in free variation. For an extreme example, it is obvious that two phonetic representations each fifteen segments long could not possibly be in free variation in any language if all fifteen segments were different. Building such restrictions into the theory of phonology will evidently involve very strict and as yet poorly understood constraints on the class of possible phonological rules. This class is obviously much narrower and smaller, in ways we do not yet know how to characterize fully, than previous statements of systematic phonological theory might imply.

[8] By the 'markers' of a linguistic level I refer to the formal structures which the rules of that level assign to sentences as part of their total structural description. Thus the markers on the phonetic level are strings of phonetic segments: on the level of Deep Syntactic Structure they are sets of strings of constituents and complexes of syntactic features defining highly structured phrase markers. It is apparently a by-no-means-obvious fact that natural languages have structures which are such that the markers on every level can be looked upon as sets (sometimes unary sets) of strings of elements. The overall structural description assigned by all three components of the grammar (syntactic, semantic, and phonological) as the total description of a sentence can thus be looked upon as a set of sets of strings in varying vocabularies, some of them, as those in phonology and phonetics, not atomic (i.e. with a componential structure). A formal account of linguistic theory in terms of this conception of structural description was stated by Chomsky (1955), its developer, at the very beginning of work in generative grammar. This view underlies all successive work in this framework, often of course only implicitly.

A systematic grammar accomplishes the above in the following way. Two distinct phonetic representations are in the same free variation set and hence descriptive of noncontrastive utterances just in case they are assigned by the rules of the phonology to the same single input systematic phonological representation and not otherwise.[9] Nondistinct (identical) phonetic representations are, of course, always in the same free variation set regardless of which systematic structures they are assigned to. Hence in our above hypothetical example, (1.5b) and (1.9b) are assigned to the same set trivially because of their identity. Every other pair of phonetic representations is contrastive because no two of them are assigned by rules of this language to the same input systematic structure. (This is, of course, not conclusively shown by the small set of examples invented. Assume that it is the case.) Suppose, however, that we specify the structure of our hypothetical language further by assuming it has in addition an optional rule which replaces word final t by [ḷ]. Then not only is (1.8a) #kat# mapped by the rules of the phonology onto (1.8b), it is also mapped onto [kaḷ] (1.12). But now the grammar claims that (1.8b) and (1.12) are free variants since both are assigned to the same input, (1.8a). It also claims that (1.12) is not a repetition of any other utterance represented by (1.5b) through (1.9b), assuming again that the facts of these few examples generalize to the language as a whole, i.e. assuming that there is no additional systematic structure which is mapped onto both (1.12) and any of (1.5b), (1.6b), (1.7b),(1.9b). There are then two different sources for free variation. Trivially it arises through the generation in any way whatever of identical phonetic representations. Nontrivially it arises through the operation of optional rules or their equivalent[10] which associate $\underline{n}$ ($n \geq 2$) phonetic repre-

---

[9] Of course, within systematic phonemic theory the input representation consists not just of a string of phonemic elements (including word, morpheme, and other boundaries) but also of the associated Surface Grammatical Structure which includes a labelled bracketing of the string (as well as a syntactic feature representation of the grammatical formatives). This does not affect our argument here in any way, however, so that for simplicity it can be assumed here that the input structure is simply a string of systematic phonemes.

[10] This remark is indicative of the fact that the way in which free variation is to be described within an explicit system of phonological rules is by no means settled. This turns out to be a rather complicated formal

sentations with a single systematic representation.

We see then that the claim that a grammar *without* autonomous phonological representation cannot correctly describe the facts of repetition is completely groundless. The putative justification for autonomous phonology rests not upon this claim, i.e. upon the unchallenged assumption (1.10), but rather rests only on the claim that phonological distinctness or contrast must be directly 'readable' from some single level of representation. It rests in other words completely upon assumption (1.11). For it is only this premise which excludes an account whereby free variation is characterized, as in generative phonology, without autonomous phonemic representation, in terms of pairs of markers drawn from two different levels.

However, no one has argued for (1.11) or given the slightest justification for imposing it as a condition on linguistic descriptions. And there are perfectly good grounds for this absence of justification since (1.11) is completely without linguistic significance or basis. For whether or not a grammar meets (1.11) has nothing whatever to do with the correct characterization of any linguistic facts. Assumption (1.11) has no more justification than would a similar condition on the grammar with respect to a property like structural ambiguity. In a grammar there is no single level of structure which necessarily permits one to tell whether a sentence is structurally ambiguous. A sentence (i.e. a phonetic representation) is characterized as structually ambiguous when it has two or more distinct origins in the set of Deep[11] Syntactic Structures, i.e. when the phonetic representation is a mapping from two or more Deep Syntactic Structures by virtue of the rules of the syntax and phonology combined. Thus the English form indicated by 'the troops stopped stealing' receives only a single Surface Syntactic Structure so that this superficial level predicts no ambiguity. Any adequate grammar of English must, however, assign the phonetic representation of such a sentence at least two distinct Deep Syntactic Structures which can be rather crudely indicated by this diagram.

---

problem, and it may be that rule optionality is only a first approximation. Fortunately, the exact nature of the formal devices which assign more than one phonetic representation to a single input structure is irrelevant to our present discussion.

[11] In some cases the difference in Deep Structures leads to two distinct Surface Structures for the same string of formatives, in other cases not.

(1.13a)

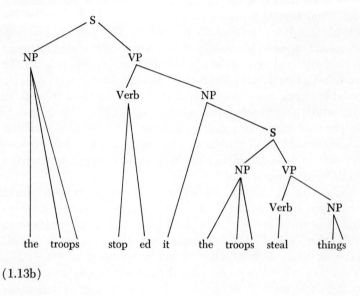

(1.13b)

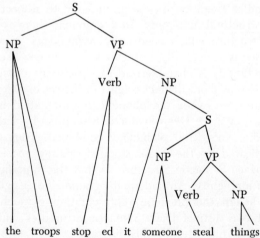

The rules of the grammar must map both of these onto the single Surface Structure of 'the troops stopped stealing,' thus indicating that the utterance tokens this represents may be interpreted in two different ways, and that the difference lies in whether the underlying subject of the embedded sentence is identical to the subject of the sentence as a whole (*the troops*) or whether the embedded subject is a maximally unspecified human Noun Phrase (*someone*).

Hence the way a grammar accounts for structural ambiguity is exactly parallel to the way it accounts for free variation. Namely, in each case the property is defined in terms of the assignment of two or more structures of one level to one structure of another level. The account of these properties is thus 'relational' in the sense that it involves considerations of the markers drawn from two different levels of the total grammar. Clearly it would be absurd to suggest that such a relational account of ambiguity be supplemented by requiring within linguistic theory that particular linguistic descriptions provide some single level of linguistic structure whose markers directly indicate whether the phonetic transcriptions they describe are ambiguous or not. But the basis of (1.11) is no stronger. In these cases, and with respect to other linguistic properties as well, the only requirements on grammars which make sense are those designed to guarantee that, with respect to the linguistic property in question, they specify which sentences possess it and in what respects, and that with respect to relational properties (like repetition) they specify which forms bear them to each other and in what ways, etc. Such necessary requirements on the correct description of linguistic facts in no way entail such arbitrary requirements as (1.11) or analogous assumptions.

But since only assumption (1.11) leads to the conclusion that a description of the free variation-contrast distinction requires autonomous phonological representation, and since (1.11) is without basis, it follows that the facts of repetition in no way support the claim that correct linguistic descriptions must contain autonomous phonemic structure. Hence the facts of contrast cannot justify the claim that phonological theory must be a version of the theory of autonomous phonemics.

In effect, the essence of the unsound argument we have been dealing with has been given briefly by C. F. Hockett in his recent study of sound change. Hockett defines a condition or assumption of phonology which he calls Audibility (1965:195):

The difference between any two distinct sentences of a language is audible to a native speaker in the absence of noise, even if there is no defining context.

He then goes on to remark that:

By forgetting about audibility, we arrive at a representation of the sentences of a language in terms of units that Chomsky and Halle call 'phonemes,' but that many others call 'morphophonemes.'

Hockett then argues that, in effect, there is a lower level of representation, a variant[12] of autonomous phonemic, which does not 'forget about audibility.' But here we see the same fallacy uncovered above. A grammar with systematic representation plus the phonological rules which map this into phonetic structure in no sense 'forgets about audibility.' For, as we have seen, such a grammar precisely characterizes the free variation-contrast distinction which is what Hockett's audibility principle is about. Hockett's conclusion is based only on the assumption, which he does not even state, to say nothing of justify, that a grammar which does not provide some *single* level of structure from which free variation may be inferred 'forgets about audibility.' Hockett's most recent discussion thus provides an excellent instance of the kind of reasoning which, we claim, has led many linguists to unsound conclusions similar to his, namely, that systematic representation must be supplemented with autonomous phonemic structure to account for free variation.

---

[12] The variation involves the assumption that a condition which Hockett calls 'Linearity,' typical of past autonomous phonemics, must be given up. We discuss this matter in Chapter 4.

2

FURTHER COMMENTARY ON CONTRAST AND AUTONOMOUS PHONEMICS

A VARIANT OF THE ARGUMENT

Having seen that a superficially plausible argument for autonomous phonology from facts of free variation and contrast is fallacious, it is worth considering a certain common variant of this argument which is equally fallacious, although again not without its temptations. Let us return to our hypothetical language and its phonetic strings, (1.6b) [kat$_y$] and (1.8b) [kat]. Recall that these are contrastive and have respectively the systematic representations (1.6a) #kati# and (1.8a) #kat#. The new version of the argument goes something like this: (1.6b) and (1.8b) are contrastive and the only phonetic difference between them is the presence or absence of palatalization in the final stop. Hence this palatalization is a 'distinctive feature' of this language in contrast, for example, to the feature which distinguishes (1.8b) from (1.12) [kal]. But the systematic representation does not indicate this fact, since in such terms the *structural* difference between phonetic (1.6b) and (1.8b) is given as the presence or absence of final i. Hence the linguistic description needs the intermediate autonomous representations (1.6c) of

19

(1.6b), and (1.8c) of (1.8b), and (1.12) to permit derivation of the fact that in this language palatalization but not lateralization is a distinctive feature, i.e. a feature which distinguishes contrasting utterances.

The fallacy in this new version of the argument is essentially that of the previous version. Once more, the justification for the autonomous phonological representation is the argument that without it 'contrasts are ignored.' But there is no single fact, for example, about (1.6b), (1.8b), and (1.12) which a grammar *without* the autonomous phonemic representations (1.6c) and (1.8c) fails to characterize. What are the facts? Clearly the following:

(2.1) (1.6b) and (1.8b) are contrastive
(2.2) (1.6b) and (1.12) are contrastive (assume this now)
(2.3) (1.8b) and (1.12) are free variants
(2.4) (1.6b) differs from (1.8b) in palatalization in the final stop
(2.5) (1.8b) differs from (1.12) in lateralization in the final stop

We have already seen how facts like (2.1) through (2.3) are characterized without autonomous phonemic representation. Facts like (2.4) and (2.5) are obviously trivially accounted for by virtue of the fact that the grammar generates just these phonetic representations. Notice that the only *facts* behind the assertion that palatalization but not lateralization is a 'distinctive feature' is that (1.6b) and (1.8b), which are contrastive, differ in just the former feature while no contrastive pair in the language differ by just the latter. But these facts are all given by the grammar without autonomous phonemic representation.

The version of the argument we are now discussing can be illustrated from the recent literature by the following statement of S. Lamb (1964a:75–76):

In this connection, one of the cardinal principles of phonemic analysis is that it be done so that there will be no neutralization between the phonemic and phonetic strata. In other words, (assuming an idealized phonetic representation which is free from noise) it must always be possible to convert uniquely from the phonetic to the phonemic stratum. . . . If in a provisional solution there are any cases of neutralization, it means that the level of the putative phonemic stratum has been set, as it were, too high, and that it must therefore be pushed down to the point at which the neutralization will have been eliminated; that is, the instances of neutralization must be treated instead as morphophonemic phenomena. *The level would also be set too high if there is a failure to recognize some contrast, i.e. a phonetic distinction that is correlated with a difference in content.* (Emphasis is mine: PMP.) On the other hand, the level would be set too low if there were still too many putative phonemes recognized in the system, some of them still in mutually noncontrastive distribution. This would mean that not enough grouping had been done, i.e. that distinctions lacking structural significance had been made. When the phonemic stratum is correctly established, then, there will be as much diversification between it and the phonetic stratum as possible (without ignoring contrast), but no neutralization.

Lamb illustrates his argument with the following example:

For illustration we may consider the analysis of stops in Russian, for which, as in some other languages, there is no voiced:voiceless contrast in final position. That is, many morphemes have final voiced stop alternating with final voiceless stop, depending on what follows, while others have voiceless stop everywhere. One might be temped to eliminate this alternation at the phonemic stratum by setting up phonemic voiced stops in the forms with alternation and a phonemic rule accounting for the voiceless phonetic representation in final position. But such an analysis would violate the principle that neutralization between the phonemic stratum and the phonetic is not allowable. This rule must therefore be made a morphophonemic rule. An attempt to group all occurrences of corresponding voiced and voiceless stops (including those which do not alternate) into single phonemes would be an example of failure to recognize a contrast, since the difference in voicing of stops correlates with meaning differences in intervocalic position.

Here Lamb objects to the adequacy of representations of Russian morphemes of the following sorts:

Systematic Phonemic	*Phonetic*
(2.6a) …od…	(2.6b) […ot…]
(2.7a) …ot…	(2.7b) […ot…]
(2.8a) …ada…	(2.8b) […ada…]
(2.9a) …ata…	(2.9b) […ata…]

He insists that the (a) representations must be supplemented with autonomous representations of the form:

Autonomous Phonemic

(2.6c) /...ot.../
(2.7c) /...ot.../
(2.8c) /...ada.../
(2.9)   /...ata.../

This follows because otherwise, Lamb claims, the grammar will 'fail to recognize a contrast.' But again one can immediately see that the argument is thoroughly unsound. Assuming the final devoicing rule which Lamb posits, all facts of contrast are completely described *without* the (c) representation. Items (2.6b) and (2.7b) are specified as free variants because of their phonetic identity, (2.8b) and (2.9b) as contrastive because there is no single systematic structure to which they are both assigned. Voice is predicted as a 'distinctive' or 'contrastive' feature in intervocalic but not final position in Lamb's rather superficial sense (cf. 'Some Implications of the Fallacy' later in this chapter) because the grammar will generate phonetic sequences differing by just this difference only in the former. As before, the only thing that can be said, both in our hypothetical example and in the Russian case discussed by Lamb, is that without the autonomous representation there is no *single* level of structure from which the facts about 'distinctive features' can be directly read off. That is, the analogue of (1.11) above is not met. But once again there is not the slightest reason why it should be. It is crucial that Lamb gives no justification for any principle of this sort either in this article of anywhere else as far as I know. We see then that this version of the argument is as fallacious as the former and also provides no grounds whatever for including autonomous phonemic representation in a linguistic description. Again there are no facts describable with such apparatus that are not described without it.[1]

Of course, those linguistis who have maintained that palatalization but not lateralization is a 'distinctive feature' in cases like the hypothetical one above have meant something more than simply

---

[1] In Chapter 9 our discussion of the question of the transitivity of contrast will show that the present apparent equivalence of autonomous and systematic representations with respect to the ability to predict contrast is only apparent.

the fact that (2.6b) and (2.8b) or, in general, pairs of contrasting utterances, differ or not phonetically by the features in question. They have no doubt meant also to claim that in some sense palatalization is the 'crucial perceptual feature,' what acts as a 'cue,' what is 'relevant perceptually for identity and difference,' etc. This kind of view is stated rather clearly in the following very explicit quote which exhibits much of the kind of argument for autonomous phonemics we have been criticizing (Lounsbury, 1963:568–569):

The method of phonemics is not one of psychological experimentation; rather, it involves the search for circumstantial evidence as to the distinctiveness or nondistinctiveness of phonetic features in naturally occurring speech data. The only 'psychological' test which the linguist performs is to ascertain whether two phonetically different forms are the same or different as linguistic stimuli to natives. The specific purpose of the same-or-different test is to determine whether a particular feature of phonetic difference is the result of *free variation* or of *contrast*. Beyond this, one studies the distributions of phonetic types.... In particular, one seeks to determine whether two phonetic types which are similar in some features but different in others are in *complementary distribution* or in *contrast*. If a rule can be formulated whereby the occurrence of one or another of two such phonetic types is shown always to be a function of the phonetic context, then they can be regarded as conditioned variants of one unit. The "phoneme" is generally regarded as a class of phone types which have a phonetic feature in common and whose differences are either in complementary distribution or in free variation in respect to their environments.

It is generally assumed that the allophones of a phoneme are in some sense equivalent stimuli. They are defined so that they share the same distinctive features (features that function as cues for differential responses in the given language) and differ from one another only by nondistinctive features (those which do not function as cues).

However, the fact that in cases like the one we have been dealing with the systematic representation does not represent the 'distinctive features' as in any sense the perceptually crucial cues is hardly relevant criticism because there is not the slightest evidence that this status (whatever it is exactly—the claims made are quite vague) is a real one. The systematic theory claims that the crucial perceptual fact in our hypothetical example is not the completely predictable (from systematic structure, not of course from phonetic)[2] palatalization but, rather, the underlying systematic i which determines the palatalization before it is deleted from the representation. Notice that this is a perfectly empirical claim about perception which cannot be refuted by mere logical arguments. Nonetheless, some linguists have sometimes argued as if the view of perception under which, in our hypothetical language, the palatalization is necessarily perceptually crucial, were somehow a logical truth. This is completely false, however, and it is not out of place to illustrate why.

Consider the example which has been much discussed (Chomsky, 1957b:238–239; 1962:156–157; 1964b:96, 99); (Harris, 1951:70) of those English dialects in which forms like 'writer' and 'rider' differ phonetically only in the length of the first vowel, the latter having a long vowel. Both are pronounced with the same voiced flap [D] as medial consonant. The present writer's dialect is such. In autonomous terms such a pair immediately shows that length is a 'distinctive feature,' with resultant extreme complication of the grammar discussed in the literature mentioned above. But in systematic terms, such forms are represented something like rvt+r and rvd+r,[3] and the length in the phonetic form of the latter is a function of the very general, independently motivated rule of English phonology which lengthens vowels before systematically voiced consonants. The rule which turns all dental stops to [D] before an unstressed syllable is also in-

---

[2] One very revealing way to characterize autonomous phonology is that it insists that the environments of all the rules which relate phonemic to phonetic representation must be phonetic in nature. Put differently, it is a view of phonology which allows the removal of features from the phonetic representation only provided that they may be predicted by regularities statable in terms of those phonetic features which have *not* been removed. These latter combinations of phonetic features are then the autonomous phonemes. Regularities in terms of morphophonemic elements, word boundaries, constituent structure, etc. are excluded. Cf. the emphasis in the quote from Lounsbury above on *phonetic* context. This characterization naturally relates synchronic autonomous phonemics to the Neogrammarian view of sound change. The latter insists that all of the statements which describe regular sound shifts have purely phonetic environments and hence in a natural sense is simply the historical analogue of autonomous phonemics. Cf. the discussion in Part II.

[3] I write v instead of some particular vowel to avoid irrelevant concern with the way English vowel nuclei are to be represented.

dependently required. In systematic phonemic terms, then, the crucial 'perceptual' fact here should be not the completely automatic length, but, rather, the underlying t̲-d̲ contrast. But now these conflicting perceptual views permit testing. The autonomous theory suggests, for example, that hypothetical forms like [la'yzər] and [la'y:zər] should be just as easy to hear and discriminate for speakers of such dialects as hypothetical pairs like [ma'yDər] and [ma'y:Dər]. Both have the same 'distinctive feature' difference. But the systematic theory suggests that pairs of the *latter* type should be easier to distinguish, since only in these is there a possibility of interpretation in terms of the underlying t-d contrast, with merging of stops to [D]. Evidence for one or the other of these claims would of course support one or another of the positions we have been discussing. I have no serious evidence bearing on this question, but it is perhaps not totally irrelevant to point out that speakers of such dialects, for example myself, have difficulty distinguishing long and short vowels in other languages even after some phonetic training. Regardless of the truth of the above claims, the fact that they are distinct shows that the view associated with autonomous phonology is an empirical one and follows from no a priori considerations.

The linguist who claims that perceptual facts support autonomous phonemics vis-à-vis systematic must actually give the evidence showing this. I know of none. And indeed there are many notorious counterexamples. For example, we can note the evident inability of English speakers to recognize and discriminate the four stress phonemes obviously minimally required by autonomous phonemics. This has been admitted even by the most ardent supporters of the four-stress system and of autonomous phonemics. The following extraordinary passage is indicative of the lengths to which such linguists have been forced to deal with such recalcitrant facts (Hill, 1958:17–18):

In this discussion a somewhat radical position has been implied throughout. Until a few years ago (sic!:PMP), it was an assumption almost universal among linguists that a speaker, even without special training, would infallibly and automatically hear the contrasts in his own speech and that the only things he would not hear would be sounds which are not contrastive. Consequently, it would at that time have been necessary to say that any speaker who had trouble in hearing four grades of stress would be one who had only three contrasts.

We have taken the position that there are speakers who have four contrasts but who still have difficulty in hearing all the distinctions they make. Such difficulties occur not only in the system of stresses, but with other sounds as well.

Hill then tries to explain such facts on the basis of 'variation':

In every instance where a speaker has difficulty in hearing a distinction which he actually makes, the reason can be found in the kind and frequency of variation. If most words have a form in secondary and another in tertiary and if a speaker has become habituated to hearing words with both varieties, he will be accustomed to disregard the difference.

But obviously the explanation fails for the majority of stress cases since it is my experience that for most speakers, as with myself, any distinctions beyond those of primary versus nonprimary are difficult to hear (even with some phonetic training), and even this distinction is not without its difficulties. And there are no conceivable facts of word variation which can explain this since most words are spoken with a quite determinate stress pattern which is simply resistant to perception.

We may note the following highly relevant remarks of W. S-Y. Wang on this topic (1964:69–70):

In the summer of 1957, a conference was held in Ann Arbor on the topic 'linguistics and the teaching of English as a foreign language.' In the session on phonological problems, two of the three papers presented were on English stress. Both of the speakers devoted great portions of their paper to argue that there are *four* stress phonemes in English. At the end of their papers, someone asked for 'a show of hands in the room from those people who find difficulty in distinguishing four stresses in English.' To this request, about half of the participants raised their hands. The results of this demonstration become all the more striking when one examines the list of the participants of the conference, which reads very much like a 'who's who' of experts on the English language. Had the participants planned beforehand to highlight this problematic area of English phonology, they could not have done better than to stage such a sequence of events. When so many language experts fail to hear *phonemic* distinctions in their own language, there is every reason to scrutinize the basis for calling these distinctions 'phonemic'—at least as this term is commonly used. Indeed, a most important observation about phonemic distinctions has long been that native speakers respond to them with effortless consistency. The system of English stress, if held to be phonemic, would constitute a contradiction to this very general principle. The considerations presented by Hill and Hockett in their papers to explain the difficulties in hearing four degrees of stress include (1) dialectal variation, (2) the low functional load of the English stress system, and (3) the 'phonetic closeness' between stresses in some major American dialects. These explanations are all unsatisfying. The difficulty in differentiating stresses is not substantially reduced when the speakers are from the same dialect area. Taking functional load to mean some measure of the relative frequence of contrastive environments, we can easily distinguish phonemes whose functional load must be near zero, e.g. ð/θ. Furthermore, the functional load of the stresses is probably quite high since they have high relative frequencies and occur only on syllabics.

It is thus evident that the inability of English speakers to hear the stress contrasts, which the view of autonomous phonemics unquestionably necessitates, is strong evidence against this approach.[4] Note, however, that contemporary systematic phonemics requires representations of English in which no stress distinctions are marked and hence correctly predicts that untutored speakers should have the actually observed difficulties with stress distinctions. Cf. Chomsky (1961b, 1962, to appear); Chomsky and Miller (1963); Chomsky, Halle, and Lukoff (1956); Halle and Chomsky (to appear). For further 'perceptual' evidence against autonomous phonology cf. the discussion of the important and neglected phenomenon of 'phonemic interchange' in Chapter 9.

SOME IMPLICATIONS OF THE FALLACY

We have considered two variants of an unsound argument that linguistic descriptions must contain autonomous phonemic

---

[4] Among the strongest counterevidence known to me against the perceptual reality of autonomous phonemic contrasts is that presented in Lieberman (1965). He shows experimentally that the most highly trained and expert linguists can, in the absence of grammatical information, consistently mark nothing more than the position of main stress in English. Similar negative evidence was accumulated for the various phonemic pitch levels which autonomous phonemics requires for English.

representations. One way of characterizing our result is to point out that it can be looked at as a somewhat more detailed exposition of a point made briefly by Chomsky in the course of his criticism of autonomous phonemics (1964b:97):

> In general, it should be observed that 'minimal pair' is not an elementary notion. It cannot be defined in phonetic terms but only in terms of a completed phonemic analysis. Consequently, the 'commutation test' is of only marginal interest if formulated, in the usual manner, as a procedure for phonemic analysis.

In short, what has been shown is that, contrary to almost every introductory exposition of autonomous phonemic theory or practice, the discovery of phonetically minimal pairs does *not necessarily* permit an immediate conclusion about underlying phonological contrast. As was seen in the previous hypothetical example, the existence of [kat$_y$] and [kat] as contrasting forms does not necessarily show the contrastiveness of palatalization. And indeed in this case palatalization was not distinctive, but rather predictable from an underlying i̱ which later dropped and hence had no direct phonetic realization as a vowel.

Autonomous phonemics has in general assumed that the inference from surface contrasts, minimal or otherwise, to underlying or phonemic contrasts is somehow automatic, almost a matter of logic. This is by no means the case. For obviously it is *logically possible* for the phonemic contrasts to be only indirectly related to phonetic ones, as in systematic phonemics. It is notable therefore that no one has ever given any empirical evidence for the view that a phonetic difference associated with a contrast necessarily entails a directly corresponding phonemic one. Of course this does follow if one assumes that phonemic structure is exactly like phonetic structure except that a subset of predictable (from exclusively phonetic contexts) phonetic features are removed. This is exactly what autonomous phonemics assumes, and the idea that phonemic structure must be a result of segmenting and classifying phonetic structure is the underlying philosophical or methodological basis for autonomous phonemics. But this assumption cannot be brought forward as a justification for the view that phonetic contrasts reveal all and only the phonemic contrasts, since it is exactly this logically contingent assumption about the relation between phonetic and phonemic structure which is in question. In showing that arguments from free variation do not justify the existence of autonomous phonological representations, we have shown that one common type of argument in favor of the existence of such a close relation cannot stand. Since there are an unchallenged number of arguments from almost every language ever considered showing the undesirable results autonomous phonemic structure has on the formulation of explicit sets of phonological rules,[5] this means that the burden of proof is, to say the least, strongly in the hands of those who would claim such a narrow relation. However, in later sections we shall review evidence which shows the exact opposite of the view assuming a direct correspondence between phonetic and phonological contrasts.

Hence in Part I (Section I) we claim to have cleared the ground for what follows. It has been shown in effect that the basic empirical (i.e., narrowly understood as independent of the formal properties of the rules, in particular independent of their simplicity) grounds which are brought forward in favor of autonomous phonemics are without substance. We are now in a position to consider more clearly the very substantial body of facts, internal and external to grammars, which are incompatible with the claims of the theory of autonomous phonemics. First, however, we comment on the basis of the fallacious argument we have considered.

ON THE BASIS OF THE FALLACY

One need not search far, I think, to find why linguists working within the framework of autonomous phonology have not seen that the linguistic data with which they deal, in particular the free variation-contrast distinction, do not require autonomous phonological representation. Within a systematic phonemic description, the notion of free variation is characterized in terms

---

[5] Cf. Chomsky (1957b, 1962, 1964b); Chomsky and Halle (1965); Foley (1965); Hale (1965); Halle (1959, 1960, 1962); Halle and Chomsky (to appear); Halle and Zeps (to appear); Keyser (1963); Keyser and Halle (to appear); Langendoen (1964a); Lees (1957, 1961); Lightner (1965); McCawley (1965); Postal (1964a, to appear b, to appear c); Schane (1965).

of a rich conception of grammar (in particular of phonology) as a set of precise rules which pair individual systematic phonemic representations with sets of phonetic representations. And it is only in such a context that free variation can be predicted without the appeal to an intermediate autonomous structure. The first basis for the fallacy is that linguists working within the framework of autonomous phonemics have generally ignored the notion <u>phonological rule</u>. For them the crucial elements have been phonemes: their internal structure, distribution, methods of determining them, etc. The rules which, for example, relate phonemes to allophones, the <u>allophonic statements</u> as they are sometimes called, have almost always been left inexplicit. Most often such facts are merely given by listing for each phoneme its allophones in each environment. No explicit theory of allophonic statements developed, although the assumptions about the relations between phonemic and phonetic representation which are generally accepted do entail a theory of such rules.[6]

But within a framework in which there is no explicit conception of phonology as a generative device which associates phonological and phonetic representations, it is easy to see how linguists could come to the erroneous conclusion that in order to indicate free variation it is necessary to have a special level of linguistic structure whose strings permit such facts to be directly ascertained. This false conclusion is thus one of many extremely deleterious effects on modern linguistic work arising from the failure to give the notion <u>linguistic rule</u> its proper central place.

Secondly, believers in autonomous phonemics have assumed that autonomous phonemic structure is necessary to predict free variation because they have not recognized the linguistic reality

---

[6] In particular, the class of possible rules excludes deletions, permutations (metatheses), reduplications, etc. Each rule would in effect have to be of the very elementary form: A ⟶ X in B___C, to be interpreted 'A has the allophone (variant) sequence X̲ in the context B___C' where A̲ is a single phoneme; X̲ is a finite, nonnull string of phonetic segments; and B̲ and C̲ are finite, possibly null strings of phonemes. Such rules are thus formally analogous to so-called phrase structure rules in syntax. This is no accident, for both of them are the formalization of the kind of relations which must hold if a linguistic level A-1 is related to level A exclusively by processes of segmentation and classification. For some discussion cf. Chomsky (1964b:53).

of phonetic representations. A systematic grammar is able to generate specifications of free variation without autonomous phonemic representation by associating phonetic representations with morphophonemic structures. Were it the case, however, that there was no level of linguistic structure between the systematic and actual articulation, it would indeed be impossible to characterize the free variation-contrast distinction without autonomous phonemic representations. Since the markers of the systematic level do not *by themselves* indicate these distinctions, and since actual physical facts of articulation do not indicate them, it is true that *some* level of linguistic structure lower than the systematic must exist. Denying the existence of a level of mentalistic phonetics, modern linguists were thus naturally led to a lower level which would directly indicate free variation-contrast, and this was just the level of autonomous phonemics.

But since the 'intermediate' level of autonomous phonemics has no independent motivation or justification (cf. below), and since a level of mentalistic phonetics is an absolute prerequisite of a coherent linguistic theory (to deny the existence of a mentalistic system of phonetic instructions is to deny that people know how to pronounce the sentences of their language; cf. Chapters 5, 13, and 14), this basis for assuming the necessity of autonomous phonemic structures on grounds of free variation-contrast is totally unfounded. The false conclusion that autonomous phonemic structure is required to predict contrast is thus also one of the many extremely serious negative effects of the modern linguistic confusion about the nature of phonetic representation.

3

FAILURE OF THE STRATIFICATIONAL DEFENSE OF AUTONOMOUS PHONEMICS

PRELIMINARIES

At the start let us stress certain features of the description of a sentence in systematic phonemic terms. Within such a theory, a sentence has two crucial types of phonological structure. One is the systematic phonemic, a labelled bracketing and syntactic feature analysis of the string of systematic phonemes with appropriaite boundaries. Such structures are at once both the final output of the transformational part of the syntax and the input to the phonological rules. The other crucial type of structure is a universal phonetic representation providing a theory of the instructions required by the speech apparatus to produce utterances which will be tokens of the sentence. The phonetic representations are the final output of the entire set of phonological rules. The rules which connect systematic phonemic and phonetic structure form a partially ordered series (cf. Chapter 7), each rule operating on the output generated by the previously applied rule. This means that, besides the two crucial structures, each sentence has a very large number of intermediate representations, roughly one for each operation of each rule of the phonology which must be applied in the derivation of its phonetic representation.[1]

Let us then emphasize that if, in some language, the so-called autonomous phonemic representation is identical with any of these subrepresentations of a systematic description, the theory of systematic phonemics does not of course deny its existence. However, this theory does claim that these representations are of no particular significance, i.e. that they are not to be considered a separate level which has, for example, its own independent principles of combination (phonotactics), nor one which has any grammar-external importance in language learning, perception, etc.

Let me give an example. In Mohawk, stress must be marked in autonomous phonemic representations (Lounsbury, 1960), and there is an essentially minimal pair: [thi':gade?] 'she is standing up' versus [thiga':de?] 'it is different.' But it is in fact predictable in systematic phonemic terms. Therefore the rules of a systematic description of Mohawk will derive for every Mohawk sentence some relatively low-level (i.e. very close to phonetic)

---

[1] One way to characterize autonomous phonemics is to point out that it allows no intermediate representations. Phonemic representation must be directly converted to phonetic representation by unordered rules (the lists of allophones). This fact is directly related to the assumption that phonetic features can be considered predictable only if their range of distribution can be predicted from those phonetic features which remain. Ordering is of significance only because the output of an earlier rule may determine a class of environments for a later rule distinct from those which existed before its application. But the assumption that only phonetic environments may appear in allophonic statements, which is fundamental to autonomous phonemics (cf. footnote 2 of Chapter 2) is in effect equivalent to requiring all the allophonic rules to operate on the original phonemic string (which is in this view simply a sequence of phonetic segments with some phonetic features not explicitly indicated).

representation in which stress is marked. And with respect to stress at least, this low-level set of strings would be formally equivalent to the autonomous representation suggested, for example, by Lounsbury. In such a case the systematic theory differs from the autonomous in claiming the insignificance of this level of representation since it is fully a function of automatic rules. For example, the systematic theory regards any talk of the phonotactics of stress phonemes, etc. in such cases as completely artificial and mistaken (cf. first part of Chapter 9). Similarly, the systematic theory would claim that Mohawk speakers should have difficulty in hearing stress distinctions in the absence of the nonphonetic information needed for stress prediction since, in systematic terms, stress is not 'distinctive' (i.e. not marked on the level of systematic phonemic structure).

AN OLDER TYPE OF ARGUMENT

A logically possible type of argument against autonomous phonemics would not be cases like the Mohawk stress example above, where the autonomous representation is essentially identical with some relatively late representation automatically provided by the systematic rules. Rather, the argument would involve instances where the independently motivated intermediate representations derived by the phonological rules include no representation which meets the conditions for autonomous phonemic structure, and where to include this *special morphophonemic rules must be added for just this purpose.* Most significantly, such a logically possible type of argument can in fact be given on the basis of a variety of empirical facts in many languages.

The original argument of this type was developed by Morris Halle on the basis of his work in Russian, and it was this discovery which was at first the chief motivating force for the rejection of the theory of autonomous phonemics by those interested in constructing explicit generative accounts of linguistic knowledge. Halle showed with examples that have been repeated many times in the literature (Halle, 1959:22–23 and Chomsky, 1962:133–134, 1964b:100–101) that there are intolerable consequences from a major condition on autonomous phonemic structures.

Autonomous phonemics assumes that, given a phonological description of a language $\underline{L}$ and an arbitrary phonetic representation of a sentence in $\underline{L}$, the description must provide a means for automatically determining the unique phonological representation of this phonetic form. Halle demonstrated that in Russian this condition means that the grammar must add otherwise unneeded rules, rules whose only function is to meet this condition. In Russian the very general rule of voicing assimilation must be broken into two rules, one morphophonemic and the other phonetic. In other words, one very general rule must be broken into two less general rules and therefore a special rule must be added to the grammar of Russian which plays no other role than to permit the phonological representation to meet the conditions of autonomous phonology. (Cf. the further discussion of this case in 'Initial Failure' later in this chapter.)

An analogous example from English was in effect discovered by Bloch (1941) many years ago, although its relevance for the point under discussion was first brought out by Chomsky (1964b). A rather similar case from Mohawk has also been described in the literature (Postal, 1964a). This example is so simple that I will briefly repeat it here. Systematic phonemic $\underline{t+y}$ and $\underline{k+y}$ fall together phonetically as [dž] by very general rules which make all consonants other than $\underline{w}$ non-Grave and non-Diffuse (Palatal) before $\underline{y}$, and then drop the $\underline{y}$. But the representations these rules generate provide no structure meeting the conditions of autonomous phonology since in some cases [dž] is represented as $\underline{k+y}$ and in others $\underline{t+y}$. Furthermore, this is full overlapping not partial since this may happen in identical phonetic contexts.[2] Hence, in order to meet the conditions of

---

[2] Autonomous phonemics of certain varieties can accept partial overlapping but never full overlapping, i.e. cases where the phonetic sequence does not uniquely indicate the phonemic representation. The assumption that full overlapping must be prohibited was often defended on some kind of perceptual grounds. For example, cf. R. Wells (1947:270–271):

"A purely phonemic transcription, by definition, records all and only the significant distinctions that can be heard. If two utterances or parts of utterances sound perfectly alike to native speakers of the language to which they belong, their purely phonemic transcription is identical, even if they differ in grammar or lexicon. The rationale of this stipulation is clear. Phonemics takes the point of view of the hearer."

But there can be no such direct perceptual argument for a view of

autonomous phonemics, it is necessary to add a completely use-less rule to the effect that morphophoneme k̲ goes to autonomous phoneme /t/ before y̲ (and of course that morphophoneme t̲ goes to /t/ here as well as in other environments).[3] This assumes that [dž] is given the autonomous representation /ty/. If given /ky/ then the opposite ad hoc rule must be given.[4]

---

phonological representation in which the relation to phonetics allows for no ambiguities. Even if one agrees that there is a level of phonemic structure which is unambiguously related to phonetics, ambiguities obviously still arise between the phonemic and morphophonemic levels. Hence the perceptual process must be such as to allow for the assignment of more than one analysis on some level A to a marker from level A–1. To give a perceptual argument for a phonemic level related without ambiguity to the phonetic level, it would therefore be necessary to show some lack of symmetry between the processing of phonetic structure to determine phonemes and the processing of phonemic structure to determine morphophonemes. No such argument for asymmetry was ever even attempted. To put it more concretely, what would need to be shown is why the Mohawk utterance type [džatga'hthos] with am-biguous systematic representations #ka+y+atkahtho+s# 'they two women look at it' (the first a in this form drops before the dual) and #t+y+atkahtho +s# 'you singular and I look at it' must be perceived by way of a process which first determines a unique phonemic structure, say /tyatkáhthos/, and then determines an ambiguous morphophonemic representation rather than by a process which directly determines the ambiguous systematic representation of the unique phonetic form without intervening autonomous structure. The lack of serious grounds for an assumption of such a preception process is apparent.

Incidentally, the step-by-step view of perception implied in these remarks should not be taken seriously. This was only a device of argument. It is well established that perception of speech involves a far more complex process in which lower level structures are at least in part perceived on the basis of already assumed higher or more abstract level analyses. For discussion of the rules which relate the ambiguous systematic representations of [džatga'hthos] to its phonetic form cf. Postal (1964a).

[3] This latter rule is required if it is assumed, contrary to systematic phonemics, that the elements of higher levels of linguistic structure and those of lower levels are totally distinct and that every member of a higher level must be mapped onto some (perhaps null) members of the next lowest level by special rule. For discussion of this incredibly complicating assumption which is, for example, basic to stratificational grammar, cf. the discussion later in Chapter 4.

[4] An important fact which contributes to showing the artificiality of the level of autonomous structure here is that the choice between /ty/ and /ky/ is perfectly arbitrary. However, /ty/ is no straw man, but is the rep-

We may say, then, that a most important grammar-internal argument against the theory of autonomous phonology is that there exist cases where the latter forces the addition of useless, linguistically unmotivated morphophonemic rules to grammars just to provide a representation meeting its criteria. Or, put differently, there are real cases where the independently motivated route between systematic and phonetic representation yields no intermediate representation with the properties required by autonomous phonemic theory. To my knowledge, this type of argument against autonomous phonemics has never been challenged in print.[5]

Such arguments have, however, been disputed by Sydney Lamb in several public lectures.[6] Lamb claims that it is possible to avoid the conclusions reached by Halle, i.e. that it is possible in all cases to maintain most of the conditions of autonomous phonemics and still avoid redundant morphophonemic rules of the type just illustrated. He has thus claimed in effect that there is a variant of autonomous phonemic theory, henceforth <u>stratificational phonemics,</u> which permits just this. These claims are so important that they warrant very detailed investigation, and for this reason we devote much of this and the next chapter to their

---

resentation used and suggested by the most experienced and knowledgeable Iroquoianist (Lounsbury, 1960).

Significantly, there is another similar example of unnecessary morphophonemic complications required by autonomous phonemic representation based on the same rules which merge <u>ty</u> and <u>ky.</u> These rules automatically turn <u>sy</u> to [š]. But then there is a rule which, except after <u>h,</u> turns this to a single dental affricate [dz]. The motivated autonomous representation for this sequence is /ts/, and this is actually the representation utilized by Lounsbury (1960). But with this representation the grammar requires a special and otherwise unneeded rule to turn <u>sy</u> to /ts/, and then special phonetic rules to turn this two-phoneme sequence into the single segment [dz]. In the systematic grammar it is possible to move directly from [š] to [dz], avoiding the former useless rule. The single segment character of [dz] is, it should be emphasized, quite indubitable. It is revealed clearly by the fact that these segments obey the voicing, tenseness, and aspiration rules of single segments, not those of clusters.

[5] Assuming that contentless remarks like those mentioned in footnote 1 of Chapter 1 are ignored.

[6] Particularly in a paper 'On Redefining the Phoneme' read to the Linguistic Society of America in Chicago, December 1963, and in a talk given at MIT in the spring of 1965.

analysis. In doing this, I would, of course, prefer to deal with written statements of Lamb's position in detail. However, although several years have passed since the first talk, no publications have been forthcoming, and attempts on my part to obtain a written version have failed. In the absence of such, I have been forced to deal with Lamb's argument as I recall it from the informal presentations (but see the appendix to this chapter).

INITIAL FAILURE

Lamb has challenged Halle's argument from Russian, but his approach is such that it is relevant to all of the examples which have been given. The term 'stratificational' in the title of this chapter is indicative of the fact that Lamb's challenge to Halle's argument and his general solution to the difficulties involved is not an isolated matter. Rather, it is part of a general approach to questions of phonology and language generally. Other apparent advocates of a phonological position similar to Lamb's today include C. F. Hockett, H. A. Gleason, and perhaps others who are convinced that there is a viable alternative to theories of language developed within the framework of generative grammar, an alternative referred to as 'stratificational grammar.'[7]

Halle had argued that the following kinds of representations of Russian forms show that autonomous representation necessarily requires otherwise unnecessary morphophonemic rules:

Systematic Phonemic		*Autonomous Phonemic*		*Phonetic*	
(3.1a)	da′t,l,i	(3.1b)	/da′t,l,i/	(3.1c)	[da′t,l,i]
(3.2a)	da′t,bi	(3.2b)	/da′d,bi/	(3.2c)	[da′d,bi]
(3.3a)	že′čl,i	(3.3b)	/že′čl,i/	(3.3c)	[že′čl,i]
(3.4a)	že′čbi	(3.4b)	/že′čbi/	(3.4c)	[že′ǰbi]

The forms in (c) may be derived from those in (a) by the general rule schematically stated: (3.5) voice all obstruents in

---

[7] The available literature is small. Most of the exposition of this view has, up to now, been in oral presentations or unpublished papers. Published works which are relevant include Lamb (1962, 1964a, 1964b, 1965); Gleason (1964); Hockett (1965).

the context-before voiced obstruent.[8] But the (a) representations
fail the usual conditions of autonomous phonology since, given a
phonetic representation with the sequence [voiced obstruent of
type X + voiced obstruent of type Y], one does not know without
consideration of the grammar whether the representation in
column (a) should be <u>voiced or voiceless obstruent of type X +</u>
<u>voiced obstruent of type Y</u>. The representations in (b), on the
other hand, have essentially this property and directly represent
the fact that, in terms of purely phonetic environments, [t,]-[d,]
contrast while [č]-[ǰ] do not. But as Halle pointed out, if a
grammar of Russian is to provide the (b) representations <u>it can-</u>
<u>not contain the above maximally general assimilation rule</u>. Rather,
it must have instead the pair of less general rules:

(3.6) Voice all obstruents except for c, č, x in the context before voiced
       obstruent

(3.7) Voice /c/, /č/, /x/ in the context before voiced obstruent

Now (3.6) is a <u>morphophonemic rule</u> connnecting morphophonemic and autonomous phonemic representations, but (3.7)
is a <u>phonetic rule</u> connecting autonomous phonemic and phonetic
structures. Hence the autonomous representation is incompatible
with the correct general description of Russian obstruent voicing
assimilation, and it forces the breaking of this rule into two more
complicated rules. In other words, it forces the grammar to treat
as exceptional facts which are actually perfectly regular and
general.

Lamb does not actually challenge the argument that, given
representations like (3.1) through (3.4a, b, and c), Halle's conclusions follow. Rather, he maintains that the (b) forms *do not
give the appropriate autonomous representation,* and that there
is another solution which both meets the conditions of autonomous phonology and avoids the redundancy and loss of generalization on which Halle's argument was based. Instead of
the representations in (b), Lamb suggests the recognition of a
'devoicing phoneme' /h/ and representations for the relevant
forms like:

---

[8] Formally this rule would be stated within systematic phonemics as:

$$\begin{bmatrix} +\text{Consonantal} \\ -\text{Vocalic} \end{bmatrix} \longrightarrow [+\text{Voiced}] \text{ in } \underline{\hspace{1cm}} \begin{bmatrix} +\text{Consonantal} \\ -\text{Vocalic} \\ +\text{Voiced} \end{bmatrix}$$

Stratificational Morphophonemic		Stratificational Phonemic	
(3.8a)	da′dh+l,i	(3.8b)	/da′dhl,i/
(3.9a)	da′dh+bi	(3.9b)	/da′dbi/
(3.10a)	ž,e′ȝh+l,i	(3.10b)	/ž,e′ȝhl,i/
(3.11a)	ž,e′ȝh+bi	(3.11b)	/ž,e′ȝbi/

Ignoring irrelevant differences in the representation of palatalization, etc., it is clear that Lamb has reinterpreted the /t/-/d/ contrast of ordinary autonomous phonemics (and also analogously the other voice contrasts) as the contrast /dh/-/d/, etc. He is then able to give a single rule for the voicing assimilation of, schematically, the form:

(3.12) h̲ drops in the environment before voiced obstruent[9]

which is, for him, a morphophonemic rule.

Lamb therefore claims to have avoided Halle's argument

---

[9] Actually our schematization suggests that the stratificational description can capture certain generalizations which in fact are quite incompatible with it. It must be emphasized (cf. Chapters 4 and 5) that stratificational grammar insists that the morphophonemes, or 'morphons' in their terms, are unanalyzable symbols, quite in contrast with systematic phonemics. Furthermore, each rule 'realizing' morphophonemic structures as phonemic ones must be defined exclusively on a domain consisting of strings of morphons. But this means that the rule we stated schematically in terms of the terminology 'voiced obstruent' can actually in stratificational phonemics only be given by listing all of the morphons before which the morphon h̲ drops. This theory thus totally fails to represent the fact that there is a real linguistic generalization involved for a language to contain environments which can be informally given as 'voiced obstruent' not present if the environment contains any arbitrary set of morphophonemes. On the contrary, within systematic phonemics environments like 'voiced obstruent' can be given with far fewer features than arbitrary sets of morphophonemes. This theory thus claims that environments sharing properties embody real linguistic generalizations. As if to emphasize its vacuity here, stratificational grammar permits the use of ad hoc cover symbols (cf. Lamb, 1964b:122) in such cases. But since a cover symbol can be defined ad hoc for *any* set of environments, those which are 'natural' as well as not, this simply serves to point out the failure of stratificational theory to differentiate true linguistic generalizations from arbitrary reductions in the number of symbols appearing in the rules. For further discussion of stratificational confusions about the nature and role of 'simplicity' and symbol reduction in linguistic descriptions cf. Chomsky and Halle (1965) and Chapter 7.

with these representations. He maintains that his phonemic representations, which I am calling 'stratificational phonemic' to distinguish them from older and, as we shall see presently, significantly different traditional autonomous phonemic structures, meet the fundamental autonomous condition of 'no neutralization' (cf. the quote from this article given in Chapter 2). That is, they do not involve complete overlapping. Therefore, given any phonetic sequence, its stratificational phonemic representation is uniquely determinable given the phonemic description. This claim of Lamb's is perfectly true. However, this still hardly counts as a defense of traditional autonomous phonemics for the following reasons. In giving this account of the Russian example discussed by Halle, Lamb has been forced to accept a treatment which is incompatible with principles he himself explicitly maintains are characteristic of the phonemic 'stratum.' Furthermore, although it might be argued that this inconsistency is due to a minor and correctable mistake, I shall show that, independently of this, Lamb's approach, with its elimination of the natural line between phonological feature and phonological segment, does not really avoid useless redundancies.

Let us requote a section from the article of Lamb's we discussed earlier (1964a:75–76):

On the other hand, the level would be set too low if there were still too many putative phonemes recognized in the system, some of them still in mutually noncontrastive distribution. This would mean that not enough grouping had been done, i.e. that distinctions lacking structural significance had been made. When the phonemic stratum is correctly established (emphasis mine: PMP) there will be as much diversification between it and the phonetic stratum as possible (without ignoring contrast) but no neutralization.

Neutralization is the situation where one phonetic (sub)string has two distinct phonological representations. Diversification refers to the number of phonetic properties which have been eliminated as nondistinctive and made predictable from phonetic context.

Taking this quote, consider what is being asserted. Lamb is claiming that for every language there is a significant (i.e. psychologically real) level of representation, stratificational phonemic, which meets at least the following conditions:

(3.13) Condition: There is no neutralization between this stratum and phonetic structure.

(3.14) Condition: Maximal Reduction or Diversification . . . every phonetic feature which can be predicted in terms of purely phonetic context is eliminated and not marked in the phonemic representation.

(3.15) Condition: There will be no redundant morphophonemic rules of the type Halle showed are required by representations like (3.1b) through (3.4b).

(3.16) Condition: There will be no other types of redundant rules.

But now note carefully that *these conditions are not met in Lamb's treatment of the example Halle discussed.*

Lamb's morphophonemic representation is evidently formally equivalent to Halle's, differing only in 'linearity' considerations and in the fact that Lamb regards morphophonemes as atomic, unanalyzable elements. That is, where Halle writes the morphophonemes t̲ and d̲ as bundles of features differing in [−Voice]-[+Voice], Lamb writes d̲h and d̲. Hence in effect he is simply writing the systematic feature [−Voice] as h̲ and not marking [+Voice] explicitly. (We will see presently that there is an enormous loss involved in such notational shifts.)

The really crucial step in Lamb's argument is his new 'phonemic' representation. And here one must distinguish two classes of contexts, voicing-assimilatory and not. In the assimilatory contexts Lamb writes the 'voiced' member of a phoneme pair, that is, just the single symbol. But consider a nonassimilatory position in Russian such as before vowels. The phonemes /t/ and /d/, etc. contrast in these contexts. Hence Lamb will have both stratificational /d/ and /dh/ here, etc. However, for the three old phonemes /c/, /č/, and /x/, not only is there no contrast in such a position but they in fact have *voiceless* variants in these contexts. Hence in such positions Lamb must in his notation write /d̂zh/, /ǯh/, /xh/. But the hole in the argument is now clearly visible. For these representations which are, crucially, exactly those which differ from the traditional phonemic representation in other than the 'linearity' shift of voicing, *do not meet Lamb's condition of maximal diversification* (cf. (3.14) above), i.e. they are not maximally reduced. Obviously so, since they indicate voicing in a so-called 'phonemic' transcription and yet (as everyone has long known) voicing in /c/, /č/, and /x/ is predictable in Russian *from purely phonetic contexts.* In fact, one can see this from Lamb's own examples (3.10b) and (3.11b) /že'ǰhl,i/ and /že'ǰbi/ which are the stratificational phonemicizations of phonetic [že'čli] and [že'ǰbi] respectively. One sees, that is, that [č] and [ǰ], which do not contrast, are nonetheless assigned contrasting stratificational phonemicizations, one with and one without an /h/. Hence to avoid Halle's objections, in the Russian assimilation case, Lamb has surreptitiously been forced to violate not only the expressed intention of previous phonemicists, but his own theoretical requirements as well. The representations of (3.1b) through (3.4b) meet the conditions of no neutralization and maximal reduction, but fail that of ad hoc and redundant morphophonemic rule elimination. The representations of (3.8b) through (3.11b) meet the first and third of these but *fail the second.*

There is a relatively clear and important set of claims made in traditional autonomous phonemics. These include the assertion that there is a significant level of linguistic structure which is that arrived at by removing from phonetic transcriptions all those features which are predictable in *purely phonetic terms.* The second of these claims is that the resultant level is supposed to play a role in perception, language learning, historical change, etc. and to provide an adequate basis for morphology and grammar. Much evidence against claims of the former types has been presented, some of it above. As for the latter claim, Halle's argument is counterevidence. Lamb's attempt to get around this argument fails simply because the representation which he proposes that avoids Halle's arguments fails to meet the conditions for autonomous phonemics, either of the older or newer stratificational varieties.

It is important to understand the general logic of Lamb's unsuccessful attempt to get around the unnecessary morphophonemic rule argument, for it will be equally applicable in other cases. It was shown that between the motivated systematic and phonetic representations, the rules of the grammar provide no level which can be called phonemic of type T. Lamb's argument is in part an attempt to take advantage of the fact that between T and the absolute phonetic representation there will always be some lower, less general, closer to phonetic representation, U, which is still not identical to the final most narrow phonetic structure. Therefore, in any case where it is shown that the path between the systematic phonemic and phonetic representations cannot go through an intermediate level T, it will always be possible to suggest some new lower representation U which avoids this consequence and is still not ultimately phonetic, and which can therefore be called 'phonemic.' It is crucial, however, that such can be done only by giving up the claim that a 'phonemic' representation is one which is maximally reduced, i.e. one which marks no phonetic features predictable in purely phonetic terms, which has been insisted on not only by traditional phonemicists (cf. the previous quote from Lounsbury) but by Lamb himself.

For example, similar logic can be applied to the Mohawk example described earlier. Instead of recognizing the phonemic representation /ty/, that of the traditional student of Iroquoian who accepts autonomous phonemics, the stratificational phonemicist is of course free to 'lower' the phonemic representation of [dž] to /dž/, i.e. to recognize a new single phoneme for such affricates. Now the rules which merge k+y and t+y can be accepted since they are rules which merge morphophonemic strings into phonemic ones. And no rule analogous to the useless k——>/t/ before y is needed. This still keeps /dž/ distinct from [dž] since the voicing of the phoneme is predictable. It should be evident that such a move is in a sense not really objected to by the student of systematic phonemics. For in such a case to talk of /dž/ simply amounts to *naming* one of the representations which the independently required rules automatically yield from the systematic representation, and it is not the kind of representation which would have been accepted as phonemic in the past.

As an argument that a 'level' (or *stratum* in Lamb's sense) containing /dž/ is wholly an artifact and of no independent significance, we may note that such a 'phonemicization' is incompatible with the view of the effects of sound change generally held by autonomous phonemicists. Sound change is supposed to be structurally significant only if it affects the set of superficial contrasts. We know, however, that Mohawk [dž] is the result of relatively recent sound changes from proto ty and ky. The very closely related language Oneida still has [dy] and [gy] as cognates of Mohawk [dž]. Notice then that the falling together of proto Mohawk-Oneida /ty/ and /ky/ as [dž] in Mohawk, which not only added no contrast *but actually eliminated one,* under Lamb's assumptions nonetheless still added a new phoneme to the language. This is straightforward evidence of the artificiality and lack of significance (cf. also first part of Chapter 9) of the 'phonemic' representations which stratificational phonemicists will be led to in cases where arguments are brought forward showing that normal autonomous phonemic representations cause unnecessary morphophonemic rule additions.

The key point of what has just been shown should be emphasized. Given the systematic representation of forms and the partially ordered rules which connect them to their phonetic manifestations, the derivation of each form includes a whole series of intermediate representations. The existence of a level of autonomous phonemic structure in human language is properly formulated as the question of whether there is some *unique* stage of intermediate representation which qualifies as an independent linguistic level. Halle's argument seemed to show that this was not the case, since the motivated intermediate route in fact contained no stage at all which met the conditions of autonomous phonemics. Lamb's reinterpretation of the facts in terms of /h/ seemed, however, to avoid this consequence. That is, under his reformulation it appears that there is an intermediate representation which is both distinct from the phonetic and in accord with such fundamental autonomous conditions as 'no neutralization.' However, while true, this in no sense counts as a defense of autonomous phonemics. Lamb's assumption that it does is based on a confusion of *necessary* conditions for autonomous phonemics with *sufficient* conditions. 'No neutralization' between phonetic and phonemic structures is certainly a necessary condition in autonomous phonemic theory. But it is not sufficient, and there is an equally fundamental necessary condition which Lamb's reinterpretation of the facts, even if adequate on all other grounds (cf. below), does not and cannot meet.

For it is quite crucial that in the Russian example any intermediate representation which is low enough to avoid the necessity of an ad hoc assimilation rule necessarily must contain features which are predictable in purely phonetic terms. But it is a necessary condition on autonomous phonemics that all such features must be removed, a condition which, furthermore, Lamb insists on (cf. (3.14) above). Additionally, and most crucially, there will always be *several* (often *many*) stages of representation between systematic and narrowest phonetic which avoid the need for redundant rules and still meet the 'no neutralization' condition. How is it possible to choose nonarbitrarily the one to call 'phonemic'?[10] And furthermore, not only nonarbitrarily, but in terms restricted to information about phonetics and free variation, i.e. terms independent or autonomous of the grammar as the theory intends. Observe that, without a basis for nonarbitrary choice, the claim of significant independent level collapses. For whatever such a claim means, it clearly involves an assertion of uniqueness of structure. However, no such basis for choice in purely autonomous terms exists. The one principled way to make such a choice independently of the grammar (including morphophonemic considerations) is to pick one of the several[11] representations which eliminate *all* phonetically pre-

---

[10] The availability of multiple stages meeting the 'no neutralization' condition and consequent arbitrariness which this involves is pointed out by Hale (1965:302–303) in terms of a detailed discussion of actual analyses of Papago, an American Indian Language of the Southwest.

[11] It is correct to look upon such traditional autonomous principles as phonetic similarity, minimization of the number of phonemes, etc. as attempts to give a nonarbitrary, non ad hoc basis for choosing a unique analysis from among the never unary set of distinct analyses which are available for any language, all meeting the condition of eliminating all features predictable in purely phonetic terms. Such principles were, of course, never anything like fully successful and a good deal of arbitrariness always remained in the choice of an autonomous analysis.

It should not be thought, incidentally, that the notion 'eliminating all features predictable in purely phonetic terms' is a completely clear one. There are many cases where, for example, one feature can only be predicted if another is not and vice versa so that some decision must be made about which is *really* predictable, and this involves other considerations. It is generally believed that the principle of complementary distribution (or, modified to take account of free variation, noncontrastive distribution) specifies those features which are phonetically predictable. But this is by no means the case. On the one hand, as Chomsky (1964b:102–103) has shown, elimination of features which are complementary can lead to nonunique analyses in cases of neighboring elements. That is, sequences of the form [XabY] and [XbaY] will receive identical phonemicizations even though contrastive. But more importantly, the notion of complementary distribution is not even clear. As discussed in detail in Postal (to appear b), there are two senses of the concept. In a *precise* sense, two phonetic segments are complementary unless there is a completely minimal pair for them. But in this sense the principle fails to distinguish systematic variation

dictable features. But any stage of representation meeting this condition requires loss of morphophonemic generalizations, as Halle showed. Neither Lamb nor anyone else has been able to dispute this point.

We then see that even on grounds considered so far, Lamb's recent discussions fail to bear on the fact, central to current assumptions within the theory of systematic phonemics, that the fundamental idea of autonomous phonemics is a mistake. The essential claim is and always was that there is a unique, significant level of representation which is determinable by the application of various principles to phonetic and free variation data alone, i.e. by eliminating from phonetic representations all those features predictable in purely phonetic terms. However, as Halle's argument, or rather argument type, shows, such a level not only does not play a basic role in an overall grammar but cannot even be looked upon as one of the automatic derivative intermediate representations.

---

from accidental gaps in the lexicon. This sense of the principle is largely useless in most languages since a vast array of segments will all be complementary. In another, and actually utilized, sense, elements are *not* complementary even if there is no totally minimal pair, if they occur in 'relevantly' identical environments. Hence in this distinct sense [p] and [b] might be said to contrast and not be complementary in the absence of a totally minimal pair if there existed froms like [api], [epu], [abu], and [ube]. Both would be said to occur in the abstract environment V_V. What is involved here is a notion that the environments which determine complementation cannot be too complex, i.e. cannot consist of some large and highly unsystematic list of contexts (including ultimately possibly all the words in which the segments appear). But this notion is not precise, and hence the notion of 'relevant' complementary distribution is vague since no principle can be given to pick out the right relevant environments. That is, why in the example above is V_V relevant for *contrast* rather than [a_u] and [u_a] for *complementation*? Clearly there is some real notion being hinted at here, but it cannot be formulated in terms of purely phonetic conditions. What is evidently involved is a notion of simplicity of the overall linguistic description and more importantly constraints on the class of environments which can occur in possible rules.

It follows, then, that complementary dstribution in no sense serves to precisely characterize the notion 'features predictable in purely phonetic terms.' As a consequence of this and other indeterminacies, this theory is vague to a very great extent. However, the intention with respect to phonetic predictability is clear and a majority of actual cases are probably clear one way or another. In any event the idea is clear enough to be disconfirmed in ways already discussed and in Chapter 9.

One should, of course, raise a somewhat different question. Granting that the fundamental idea of autonomous phonemics is mistaken, is it not still possible that there is a somewhat weakened position, much closer to autonomous phonemics than to systematic phonemics, which is right? Namely, is it not true that there is a significant unique level of structure which is much closer to phonetic than systematic phonemic representation, but which meets the 'no neutralization' condition? This level would have to be chosen, of course, on grounds which take partial account of the grammar. For example, a natural principle defining this level might be: pick the *highest* level (one eliminating the most phonetic features) which does not complicate the morphophonemics. Such a conception would then abandon what Lamb calls 'maximal diversification' (3.14) in favor of a principle of 'maximal diversification not in conflict with morphophonemic generalization.' In this new position, determination of the 'phonemic' level would depend upon all those factors which determine morphophonemic structure, and this includes important segments of the grammar.

Although this 'intermediate' theory as such has nothing to do logically with the correctness of the theory of autonomous phonemics, it of course, deserves consideration as a proposal about linguistic structure.

In Chapter 9 we give new *kinds* of arguments against true autonomous phonemics. Unlike the type of argument first given by Halle, these show the falsehood of the 'intermediate' position as well. In other words, these show that none of the intermediate representations between systematic and phonetic structures qualifies in any sense as a level of linguistic structure. Furthermore, in Part II it is shown in effect that no such stage of representation plays any role in sound change. We have already given one type of fact which shows this in the discussion of the historical artificiality of the 'intermediate phonemic' representation /dž/ for Mohawk [dž].

It was shown above that Lamb's attempt to maintain a version of the theory of autonomous phonemics in the face of Halle's argument from Russian failed because the stratificational phonemic representation of Russian presented by Lamb met neither the conditions of traditional autonomous phonemics nor his own. That is, in certain positions the use of a 'devoicing' phoneme

/h/ required the so-called phonemic level to include phonetic features which are predictable in phonetic terms. It might, however, be argued that this failure was due simply to a relatively minor mistake on Lamb's part, namely, the decision to represent such contrasts as /t/-/d/ as /dh/-/d/. It might be maintained that everything Lamb wishes to accomplish can be achieved instead by representing such contrasts as /t/-/tv/, i.e. by recognizing instead a 'voicing' phoneme /v/. I am far from sure this is true, i.e., that by using such representations it would be possible to meet all of Conditions (3.13) through (3.15). But in any event this is quite irrelevant, since all such proposed phonemicizations which involve giving up the natural line between feature and segment necessarily must fail Condition (3.16) which will be discussed in Chapter 4. And this fact is really the deepest objection to the kind of 'stratificational phonemics' now being advocated by linguists such as Lamb and Hockett.[12] In short, the kind of argument proposed by Halle is really only relevant to a brand of autonomous phonemics which maintains a kind of 'natural' relation between phonological and phonetic structures. To the kind of theory now advocated by supporters of stratificational grammar there are much more basic and fundamental objections.

APPENDIX: BRIEF COMMENTS ON LAMB'S 'PROLEGOMENA TO A THEORY OF PHONOLOGY'

At the beginning of this chapter, I pointed out that certain views of S. Lamb, conflicting with systematic phonemic criticisms of autonomous phonology of the type first proposed by M. Halle, had been given only orally. Although these arguments were given verbally by Lamb more than three years before the submission of this manuscript to the publisher (in May, 1966), no published version of them had appeared at that time. That is why the discussion at the beginning of Chapter 3 is based on a reconstruction of the informal presentation in lectures. However, between the

---

12 Hockett proposed a similar analysis for English in a paper read before the Linguistic Society of America in Chicago, December 1963. He discusses the theoretical basis for this briefly in Hockett (1965). Cf. the discussion in Part II.

time the manuscript was submitted to the publisher and the time the author received the copyedited version back, a more complete and extensive version of Lamb's ideas about phonology has appeared in the form of the article listed in the heading of this appendix [*Language, 42,* 536–573 (1966)].

This article includes those arguments referred to at the beginning of this chapter as having been given orally, but not being available in printed form. Except for irrelevant details, the published version (especially the section headed *The Biuniqueness of Phonemic Solutions of Phonetic Systems*) can be taken as the text criticized in Chapters 3 and 4, since it does not differ substantially from the position I reconstructed on the basis of the oral remarks.

Ideally, it would be desirable to present an analysis of the overall contents of this recent article. But the timing of its appearance prevents that here. However, the bulk of the points made in this new work are in fact already dealt with somewhere in the present monograph. Most crucially, perhaps, Lamb states quite clearly as justification of the Biuniqueness Principle, which he still holds is a cornerstone of phonological theory, the fallacious argument documented and analyzed in Chapters 1 and 2. That is, he argues fallaciously that a biunique phonemic level (called 'C-phonemics') is necessary to distinguish those phonetic features which are distinctive from those which are not. To quote (1966: 542)·

But speech, even of a single language, exhibits innumerably many different sound features, and only some of these differences are distinctive, i.e. are able to distinguish different meanings. It is of fundamental importance to identify these distinctive features of difference and to distinguish them from those which are not distinctive. This is the reason for separating the C-phonemic level from the phonetic in describing spoken languages. It allows the description to distinguish those features of the diversity in the medium of expression which have communicative significance from those which do not.

The unsound argument is thus given quite directly and falls immediately under the discussion of Chapters 1 and 2. Notice, for example, how it surreptitiously requires the baseless assumption (1.11) which is neither stated nor justified.

Other aspects of Lamb's recent discussion are also subsumable under statements made above and below. Certain claims and arguments are new, however, and these are not unrelated to positions taken in this work. Unfortunately, a discussion here is precluded.

Overall, although this most recent statement of stratificational phonology involves the presentation of a new and complex diagrammatic notational system, I do not see that it in any substantive way necessitates modification of the fundamental criticisms of earlier statements of stratificational phonemics found in this book above and below.

4

PHONETIC-PHONOLOGICAL RELATIONS AND THE DEEPER FAILURE OF STRATIFICATIONAL PHONEMICS

THE NATURALNESS CONDITION

The phonetic representation of an utterance consists of a string of <u>phonetic segments,</u> each of which is a complex of independent multivalue features describing some aspect of the ideal behavior of the speech apparatus. Let us assume somewhat oversimply that the phonological representation of an utterance consists exhaustively of a string of symbols of some kind. Then the task of the phonological rules is to map phonological strings into phonetic ones. Stratificational phonemicists recognize that there is some relatively traditional assumption about the relation between phonetic and phonological representation which they are giving up. Rather misleadingly, however, they refer to this assumption as a condition of <u>Linearity.</u> Thus Hockett defines a number of conditions which have played a part, he claims, in phonological theory. One of these is (1965:195):

<u>Linearity</u>. The arrangements in which units occur in sentences is exclusively linear (that is, one after another, with no simultaneity or overlapping).

He then remarks:

Of these five, the superfluous one is the assumption of linearity—inspired of course by the essentially linear nature of most writing systems.

However, in a serious sense, this kind of condition is not at all what is being rejected when Lamb represents the traditional /t/-/d/ contrast in Russian as /dh/-/d/, or when both Lamb and Hockett represent the traditional /t/-/d/ contrast in English as /hd/-/d/. For obviously in the traditional autonomous phonemic system, in the stratificational phonemic system, and in a systematic phonemic system, units at both the phonological and phonetic levels are combined by the linear operation of concatenation. And the fact that some linguists, in particular those developing the theory of systematic phonemics, regard the elements at both the phonetic and phonological levels as composed of features (i.e. neither phonetic segments nor systematic phonemes are without an internal componential structure) is not really what is at issue with respect to the new kind of phonemicizations proposed for voicing contrasts by stratificational linguists.

What is involved is not anything indicated by Hockett's formulation of the linearity condition, but, rather, issues raised by the statement of a condition with the same name given by Chomsky. Chomsky pointed out in 1962[1] that the following sort of condition follows from various widely accepted versions of autonomous phonemic theory:

The linearity condition (32i) requires that each occurrence of a phoneme in the phonemic representation of an utterance be associated with a particular succession of (one or more) consecutive phones in its representing matrix as its 'member' or 'realization'; and, furthermore, that if A precedes B in the phonemic representation, then the phone sequence associated with A precedes (is to the left of) that associated with B in the phonetic matrix. This condition follows from definitions of the phoneme as a class of phone sequences (as in post-Bloomfieldian

---

[1] In his paper prepared for the Ninth International Congress of Linguists. The published versions appeared several years later. For the quote cf. 1964b:93.

American linguistics, typically) or as a bundle of distinctive features (Bloomfield, Jakobson) or a minimal term in a phonological opposition (Prague circle).

Chomsky went on to argue as part of his general critique of taxonomic (autonomous) phonemics that no level of phonological structure meeting such a Linearity Condition is part of natural language. Systematic phonemic representation and phonetic structure are, of course, connected by no such condition. Notice, however, that Chomsky's condition differs from that defined by Hockett in, among other things, the fact that it refers not to the structure of markers of individual 'levels' separately, but rather is *relational* in the sense that it specifies interconnections between phonetic markers and their possible phonemic representations. And it is such relational conditions between phonetic and phonological representations which are at issue in the new phonemicizations proposed by linguists such as Lamb and Hockett.

Although systematic and phonetic structures are not connected by the Linearity Condition as defined by Chomsky, they are related by what is in a real sense a far weaker version of both this condition and the Invariance Condition,[2] a version I shall refer to as the Naturalness Condition. The Naturalness Condition is not easy to define simply, and I shall approach its specification discursively. I shall argue that what is involved in the type of phonemicizations proposed recently by Lamb and Hockett is an implicit rejection of the Naturalness Condition, and that this rejection necessarily involves the addition of useless rules to individual grammars (violations of (3.16) above) and

---

[2] It should be noted that most of those who accept the Linearity condition in Chomsky's sense also accept what he called the Invariance Condition. This requires that each phoneme have associated with it a set of defining phonetic properties. Whenever the phoneme occurs in a phonemic representation, a phonetic segment with the associated properties must occur in the corresponding position in the phonetic representation, and each instance of a phonetic segment containing the defining features of a phoneme P must be assigned the phonemicization P. What is called in the text the Naturalness Condition is the systematic phonemic alternative to both the Invariance and Linearity conditions which are too strong in the sense that they exclude the optimal analysis in many cases. Cf. Chomsky (1964b) for many examples. If phonological representation meets both the Invariance and Linearity conditions, then it in effect meets the Naturalness Condition to be discussed, but not conversely.

the concomitant loss of the possibility of stating an enormous mass of true phonological universals.

The Naturalness Condition is concerned with a fundamental fact about human language—the emphasizing of which fact is among Roman Jakobson's most important contributions. Namely, the relation between phonological and phonetic structures is a *natural* one. We can today interpret this insight as claiming that the categorization of lexical items given by phonological structure, i.e. required to represent morphemes in the dictionary, required to state morphophonemic and phonological rules, needed to state constraints on sequences of phonological elements, needed to state phonological universals, etc., is not, from the point of view of phonetic structure, an arbitrary code. Rather, this representation is *closely related* to the representations needed to state the phonetic properties of the various sequences which represent individual lexical items. If this claim is true, much, although by no means all, of the mapping between phonological and phonetic structures *can be given universally.* That is, much of the differences between these two levels in all languages is statable within the general theory of language and need not be specified again and again in each linguistic description. Putting the same point somewhat differently in terms of language learning, when a child has determined the phonetic representation of a form, he has thereby determined a great part of its phonological structure.[3] Unfortunately, this contribution of Jakobson's has tended to be obscured by his involvement with the artificial view of autonomous phonology . . . so that he has looked upon this claim of a natural relation as having to do with the relations between that kind of structure and phonetic form . . . and by a failure to keep clear the distinction between

---

[3] It is thus proper to look upon the theory of systematic phonemics as intermediate between autonomous phonemics, which assumes in effect that phonological structure is mechanically determinable from phonetic information plus contrast, and a theory, like that in part approximated by stratificational grammar, in which phonological structure would be an arbitrary code. Systematic phonemics is intermediate in the sense that it recognizes phonetic structure as providing a substantial, but far from complete, portion of the information relevant for the determination of phonological structure, the rest being provided by grammatical information, i.e. information about word boundaries, morpheme boundaries, syntactic and morphological categorizations, morphophonemic alternations, etc.

phonological and phonetic representations (cf. the discussion in Chapter 5).

Before considering how systematic phonemic theory attempts to reconstruct this idea of a *natural* relation and how stratificational grammar fails to do so, let us consider in slightly greater detail what it means. We can perhaps reveal this most clearly by imagining a situation *in which no such relation obtained.* What would this mean? This would be a situation in which morphophonemic representation was a perfectly arbitrary code. In view of the fact that phonetic structure consists of a sequence of segments, each of which is a specification of values for a large set of phonetic features, arbitrariness on the level of dictionary representation would include absence of componential structure. All of the elements would be atomic and structures on this level would simply be strings of arbitrary symbols without internal structure. The most natural notation for them would be arbitrary integers. Furthermore, arbitrariness of relation to phonetic properties would mean such things as the following. Classes of these symbols which were relevant for various types of morphophonemic rules would not have phonetic realizations which shared any phonetic properties beyond those due to chance. That is, if for example there is a rule which deletes certain morphophonemes, say, 1, 14, 16, 19, 23, before another morphophoneme (i.e. which says that in this position these morphemes have null phonetic representations), one will find that the phonetic properties of the phonetic representatives of 1, 14, 16, 19, 23, share no properties in excess of those determined by chance. Hence, 1 for example might be represented phonetically by glottalized velar fricatives, 14; by high front rounded vowels, 16 by [m]; 19 by rounded apicodental plain stops; 23 by a palatal lateral.

Similarly, classes which are relevant for stating sequential constraints would have only randomly related phonetic mappings. For example, suppose that there is a certain class of morphophonemes which cannot appear at the end of morphemes. Absence of a natural relation between phonetic and phonological structure would again mean that the phonetic realizations of this class of systematic elements would share properties only at random. And in general throughout the grammar, nonexistence of a natural relation would mean that all of the classes relevant for phonological rules and restrictions would have such 'nonnatural' pho-

netic classes as realizations. Stated in this way, it is immediately
evident that in some strong, though far from completely clear
sense, a natural relation between phonetic and systematic struc-
ure does obtain in all known human languages since situations
like that described in the early part of this paragraph are clearly
impossible in real languages.

In general, the situation is exactly the opposite. Morphophonemic elements which fall into classes from the point of
view of rules of the grammar, from the point of view of restrictions on combinations, from the point of view of historical changes,
dialect variations, indeed from every known linguistic point of
view, have phonetic realizations with a high degree of similarity.
A few illustrations from Mohawk are perhaps in order. In Mohawk
the basic stress rule marks stress on the second of a class of
elements from the end of a word. These elements all have
phonetic vowels as ultimate mappings. There is a rule which
drops members of this same class of elements before other members. Within morphemes certain classes of elements cannot
occur in sequence. These include the class with vowels as
realizations and also another class with phonetically highly
similar [h] and [ʔ] as members. There is a rule which inserts
epenthetic [e] between sequences composed of class 1 elements
and class 2 elements. But the members of class 2 are in general
phonetically represented by resonant nonvowels ([n], [r], [w],
[y]), those of class 1 by phonetic consonants; etc., etc. It is obvious that these facts are perfectly typical and simply one of the
defining features of human languages.

The theory of systematic phonemics attempts to reconstruct
precisely, and hence explicate, this idea of a natural relation between phonological and phonetic structures and therefore to embody the Naturalness Condition in roughly the following way.
Phonetic representation is properly looked upon as a two dimensional matrix which graphs phonetic segments against a set of
(it now appears on the order of thirty or forty[4]) universal pho-

---

[4] This number is intended to include features for describing prosodic
properties like tones, stress, etc. Even so, this number is substantially
larger than that implied in previous work on generative phonology which
has, it is claimed here, stuck much too closely to various not fully acceptable formulations of Jakobson. These formulations have illegitimately reduced the number of features by combinations of distinct features, and by

netic features. A phonetic segment is then formally an unordered set[5] of specifications for the values, 1-n, of each of these features.[6] The basis for the two dimensional structure of phonetic representations is clear. Such linguistic equipment is descriptive of the ideal behavior of the vocal apparatus with respect to its production of speech. The 'vertical' dimension in the phonetic matrix is then descriptive of the fact that the human vocal system is composed of a number of at least partially independent subparts capable of independent action and of different types of action. Therefore to specify the behavior of the whole system for a period of time, it is necessary to specify the proper activity of each of these linguistically relevant aspects of this physical system. This is the function of the set of phonetic features and of the 'vertical' dimension in phonetic representations which they provide.

The 'horizontal' dimension is of course based on the fact that utterances which represent the sentences of human languages in general require a succession of distinct states of the whole vocal apparatus for their production. Hence phonetic representations which describe ideal pronunciation must consist of sequences of phonetic segments, each segment descriptive of the articulation instructions determining one of the succession of total states of the system during the production of a sentence-representing utterance.

---

ignoring certain kinds of facts (such as the existence of non-Strident affricates). The class of features underlying the numbers 'thirty to forty' is a result of important reformulations in the theory of phonetic features which has resulted from thus far unpublished work, mostly due to M. Halle. For some discussion cf. Halle and Chomsky (to appear); Postal (to appear c). Certain aspects of the inadequacy of some Jakobsonian formulations are discussed briefly in Chapter 5.

[5] The assumption of no order is the weakest one possible and that which has in a sense been traditionally made. Recent work, as yet unpublished, by M. Halle on various types of clicks may suggest that a certain amount of ordering is necessary. And independently of this, the fact that both phonetic and systematic features seem to fall into a poorly understood kind of hierarchy also indicates that the assumption of no ordering is only a first step. It is this latter hierarchy which, for example, presumably makes it unnecessary to say that all consonants are maximally un-Stressed, or that all vowels are non-Strident etc.

[6] Different features will, no doubt, turn out to have different ranges of values. Some phonetic features may be binary, others ternary, etc. Some (say Stress) may require as many as five or six phonetic values.

Systematic phonemics then assumes that dictionary representation, or abstract base forms, the equivalents of the morphophonemic representation of older approaches, also consists of a two dimensional matrix which graphs features against segments. Furthermore, and fundamentally, it is required that, with a few specific exceptions (to take care of universal kinds of boundaries[7]), the features utilized in the systematic or categorial matrix are exactly those countenanced by the *correct*[8] universal phonetic theory. However, it is claimed that while in phonetics the values of features may be n-ary, the values in the phonology are binary. Hence the dictionary representation consists of a matrix which graphs the j features against segments marked either + or −.[9] In this way the theory of systematic phonemics embodies Jakobson's claim that phonological representation involves only binary feature values, but in a way radically different than Jakobson would ever have interpreted it.[10]

---

[7] That is, word boundaries, morpheme boundaries, possibly phrase boundaries. By insisting that the boundaries be of universal types, and by insisting that they occur only in grammatically defined positions, the theory excludes the possibility of arbitrary junctures which would otherwise be allowed in the absence of autonomous conditions like Biuniqueness, Invariance, etc.

[8] I emphasize the term 'correct' to indicate that any changes in the theory of phonetic representation, i.e. uncovering of errors, discovery of new features, etc., necessarily imply, given the Naturalness Condition, corresponding changes in the class of features available for the construction of systematic phonemes. In particular, those changes hinted at in footnote 4 have had important ramifications on the class of systematic features.

[9] This is actually a simplification. In the earlier versions of the theory of systematic phonemics, predictable features were, of course, not marked either + or − but were indicated in the dictionary by a 'no information' notation, namely, 0. Hence only unpredictable or 'distinctive' features were given by + and − markings. In the most recent version of the theory these assumptions have been significantly modified. Cf. Chapter 8.

[10] If the binary hypothesis is interpreted, as Jakobson has insisted, as a remark about autonomous phonemic structure, it is, if formulated in a significant way, quite obviously false. The theory would then claim that there are no significant phonetic dimensions in which more than two contrasts can be found . . . i.e. no cases where all values except two along a diminsion cannot be predicted in terms of allophonic statements *with purely phonetic environments*. This claim is clearly refuted by such phenomena as the four (at least) stress contrasts in English which are unpredictable without the utilization of nonphonetic environments. This is just the basis for the recognition of four stress phonemes by American autonomous

It is important to emphasize that in claiming that the class of phonetic features determines the features which define the possible systematic phonemic matrices, one is not committed to the view that all possible combinations of both binary feature values for all features may actually occur. In other words, one is not committed to the obviously false claim that, assuming j systematic features, the number of possible systematic phonemic segments is 2^j. It is evident that the features fall into a poorly understood kind of hierarchy, and that there exists a set of universal restrictions which define the class of possible combinations of feature values. Hence the class of possible systematic phonemes is nothing like the class determined by the intersection of all possible values of the full set of features. New insights into this notion of hierarchy among features seem to be provided by investigation of the notions of Marked and Unmarked for feature values. For some discussion cf. Chapter 8.

One of the crucial aspects of this attempt to reconstruct the idea of a natural relation between phonetic and dictionary representations is that the dictionary or systematic representation has phonetic consequences *independently of any particular rules of an individual grammar*. This is just the basis for insisting that the features which form systematic phonemes be specified by the required set of phonetic features. That is, given some dictionary

---

phonemicists. Jakobson has often sought to preserve the binary claim in such cases by recognition of new features. However, if this practice is not constrained in some way it renders the theory impervious to disconfirmation. It is therefore important to require that all features posited both serve a multitude of functions in a wide variety of languages and have clear homogeneous articulatory characterizations. It is obvious that such conditions cannot yield any bifurcation of the feature Stress into several subfeatures. Hence the multiple contrasts along this dimension in languages like English which are inexplicable without nonphonetic contexts (including Surface Constituent Structure categories such as Noun, Verb, Noun phrase, etc.) definitely falsify a binary version of *autonomous phonemic theory*. This fact is of limited interest, however, against the background of the deeper inadequacy of the whole conception of autonomous phonemics. And it is crucial that the insightful assumption of binarity can be captured within systematic theory utilizing more abstract environments in phonological rules. The point is that all cases where binarity is violated from the point of view of purely phonetic contexts are predictable from independently assigned structural properties such as the Surface Syntactic categories which are crucial for the prediction of English stress. Cf. Halle and Chomsky (to appear) for further discussion.

representation (systematic base form), this will automatically be mapped onto some phonetic representation (in general of course not a fully correct one), even *without the application of any particular rules of the grammar*, by virtue of universal principles (rules) for interpreting the binary phonological values as n-ary phonetic values. This means that, all other things being equal, one always wishes to represent forms phonologically in ways which will yield the derivation of their phonetic forms by way of the maximal utilization of the universal interpretive principles. This will reduce to a minimum the number of special, language-particular rules which must be set up. Thus one can represent a phonetic vowel as a phonological glide, a phonetic velar consonant as a phonological labial one, a phonetic high vowel as a phonological mid one,[11] etc., but always at the cost of adding special language particular rules. Therefore one only posits such 'nonnatural' representations when these have simplifying effects on the overall grammar *which outweigh the required special rules*. So what is involved here is not the Linearity and Invariance conditions in Chomsky's sense, but only the claim that whenever these are violated there is the cost of special rules.

Consider an example. There is a very large class of words in Mohawk, of which [onû':daʔ] 'milk' can serve as an illustration, that have phonological representations which begin in a way that can be abbreviated wa+o. The full representation for 'milk' is #wa+o+nuʔt+aʔ#. (That is, full as far as purely phonological features go. Constituent structure and syntactic and morphological features relevant for the phonology are, for expository purposes, artificially not represented). Such a phonological representation does not and obviously could not assert that the word represented begins with the universal phonetic reflex of the set of systematic features abbreviated by w, say the set of phonetic

---

[11] It should be emphasized that it is just because of the assumption of the Naturalness Condition and universal principles for mapping all phonological structures onto phonetic ones that it makes sense to talk about representing phonetic vowels as phonological glides, phonetic velars as phonological labials, etc. In short, it makes sense to use a large class of phonetic terms for phonological entities. A phonological labial consonant is, for example, a set of systematic features which is converted into *a phonetic labial consonant*, independently of special rules of any language, by the universal phonetic interpretation of phonological structures.

features normally abbreviated [w]. What the representation #wa+o . . . asserts is only that the word will begin with this *unless there are special Mohawk rules which say otherwise.* In this case there are, since there is a general rule of Mohawk that word initial w and y drop in nouns, and [onǔ':daʔ] is a noun. Similarly, the presence of the systematic sequence a+o does not assert that the phonetic representation of the form in question will contain a sequence of vowels, even in conjunction with a universal rule for representing systematic morpheme boundaries as phonetically null (i.e. deleting them). Again the claim is only that such will result if no special Mohawk rules determine otherwise. And again in this case they do, for there is a general rule that one systematic vowel element drops if immediately before another.[12]

It is of course extremely pertinent and important to inquire why the phonological representation of a form like [onǔ':daʔ] contains the systematic elements w and a which have no phonetic consequences in this case. The reason is the way that this form fits into the overall system of syntactic and phonological rules. The wa in this case is the N(euter) formative. The o is representative of the objective element, and this is added by syntactic rules after certain person morphemes including N and Z(oic) which happen to share a base form wa (Postal, 1962). Most crucially, in other forms the sequence of elements N + objective, and each element separately, have phonetic consequences which justify the base forms wa+o. So, for example, the presence of an initial glide is revealed by a verbal form like [yosta'thʌʔ] 'it is dry' where N + objective appears phonetically as [yo] before a stem

---

[12] Chomsky, in thus far unpublished work, has pointed out that there is apparently an important principle governing the application of phonological rules with respect to the occurrence of morpheme boundaries (for the moment represented by '@'). This principle asserts that a rule of the form (schematically):

$$A \longrightarrow B \text{ in } X\underline{\qquad}Y \text{ (where X and Y contain no @)}$$

applies not only to sequences of the form XAY but also to all other sequences differing from XAY only in the *presence* of one or more instances of @. Significantly enough, the opposite principle does not hold. That is, rules which have environments *which actually mention* @ do *not* apply to sequences differing from the given environment only in the *absence* of the stated occurrences of @.

beginning with s̲. The justification for a vowel a̲ in the base form
of Z and N is revealed in such verbal forms as [yawehyarâ':ʔuʰ]
'she has remembered it.' This form shows Z+objective before
a stem beginning with e and the objective realized as a phonetic
[w]. Nominal forms like [awerya'hsaʔ] 'heart' also reveal the
basis for the a̲ since they have the Surface Structure N+objec-
tive+stem beginning with e. The fundamental point is that assignment of the basic form w̲a̲ to N and Z and o̲ to the objective[13]
yields the varied phonetic forms of prefixes of the form N and Z,
including [w], [y], and [null], and of prefixes of the form N and
Z+objective, including [yo], [yaw], [o], [aw], [ya], [y] by
means of independently justified and required general rules.
These include the rule to drop initial glides in nouns, the rule
to drop one vowel before another, a rule to dissimilate w̲ to y̲
before (vowel)+rounded vowel (i.e. o̲ or u̲), and a rule to turn
o̲ to [w] before another vowel. Each of these rules (which must
be properly ordered) is required quite independently of how
the set of prefixes involving N, Z and objective is described, and
they can only determine the proper phonetic consequences from
a single base form if one assumes the systematic structures w̲a̲
and o̲ for the varied phonetic sequences just discussed.

It is claimed that, despite the abstract relation between the
systematic sequence w̲a̲+o̲ and the varied phonetic representatives just touched upon, in each case this representation is a
natural one. That is, were it not for the special Mohawk rules
just discussed, the universal interpretation would predict uniform
phonetic prefixes [wao]. No actual prefix has this form but, disregarding deletions, the differences are quite small: they involve
that between phonetically very similar [w] and [y] and very
similar [w] and [o]. Hence, even in this case where many highly
structured rules are relevant, the realizations of particular systematic elements are phonetically similar to an extent far beyond
chance. And this is just what the Naturalness Condition claims
will be the case.

In general then, systematic phonological representation

---

[13] w̲a̲ is only one of the basic forms of N and Z, in fact the basic form
before vowels (other than i̲). Before i̲ and nonvowel systematic elements
the base form is k̲a̲. This naturally generates a further class of phonetic
sequences as representatives of the formatives N and Z.

makes a set of *indirect* phonetic claims, claims that the phonetic form of a particular systematic representation must be such and such unless there are special phonological rules which determine otherwise. What the Mohawk illustration just given, and the evidence which Chomsky, Halle, and others have brought forward against the traditional assumptions of autonomous phonemics shows, is that rules which 'say otherwise' are far from uncommon and not at all of the simple classificatory, unordered nature required by autonomous conditions. Hence the Naturalness Condition cannot be strengthened to the Linearity and Invariance Conditions without excluding optimal (i.e. correct) grammars in a wide variety of cases.

The correct way to state the relation between the binary phonological values of features and their often more than binary phonetic values is by no means completely determined. In particular, it is not clear to what extent these relations are universally statable and to what extent language-particular limitations must be accepted. Limited knowledge here is an almost necessary consequence of the tenuous character of present understanding of universal phonetic theory. A priori, there are two fundamentally different types of relation which could obtain for a particular binary phonological feature F_i and its $\underline{n}$-ary $(n>2)$ phonetic correspondent. It is conceivable that among the set of $\underline{n}$ possible phonetic values, two (in each context) are 'natural' and are the universal reflexes of the two binary values. Suppose that the phonetic feature is $\underline{3}$-ary and that such a relation obtains. Suppose further that it $\overline{is}$ the two extreme values which are 'natural' in all contexts. This would mean that there are universal rules that $[+F_i]$ becomes $[1F_i]$, $[-F_i]$ becomes $[3F_i]$. To derive these respective phonetic reflexes for $+$ and $-$ values of F_i is without cost. But for a language to derive the $\underline{2}$ value, it is necessary to incorporate a special language-particular rule. If such an approach involving 'natural' values were correct, one might expect to find that the 'unnatural' values were significantly rarer in the phonetic representations of the languages of the world than the 'natural' values. Similarly, one would expect that, within a particular language which contained both, the 'natural' values would occur in a wide variety of contexts while the 'unnatural' ones would be rare and highly restricted.

While there is no basis to reject outright an approach to phonological-phonetic value relations like that sketched in the previous paragraph, it evidently involves claims which go beyond those that are at present justifiable. At the moment there is no real evidence for choosing which values to pick as 'natural.' For example, it is evident that strong stress in Russian is in general louder than strong stress in English, and one aspect of a Russian accent is the pronunciation of stressed vowels with excess stress. Assumption of a 'natural' value approach therefore commits one to determining which degree of loud stress, that of Russian or English, is the 'natural' mapping from [+Stress] and which requires a language-particular rule and, similarly, for all other features for which a 'natural'-'unnatural' status is claimed. Without ruling out such an approach, at least for many features, it should be emphasized that it is *not* a necessary consequence of the overall theory embodying the Naturalness Condition and the notion that phonological features are binary reflexes of the set of universal n-ary phonetic features.

There are a number of alternatives of varying degrees of weakness, that is, of varying degrees of universality, which do not assume any differential status among phonetic feature values with respect to their relation to the binary values. We shall describe one of these and assume it without justification in what follows. Assume that for each feature (some specified subset of features?) there exists a set of universal Detail Rules of the form:

$$\left\{\begin{array}{ccc} +F_i & \longrightarrow & 1F_i \\ \cdot & & \cdot \\ \cdot & \longrightarrow & \cdot \\ \cdot & & \cdot \\ -F_i & \longrightarrow & nF_i \end{array}\right\} \text{ in } X\underline{\quad}Y$$

X_____Y is a schema for environments. To fully specify the shift from binary to n-ary values it is only necessary for a particular language to indicate the proper subset of Detail Rules and to fill in the environment schemata for actual environments in each. Although as here stated the degree of universality of phonological-phonetic relation statement is limited in contrast to the 'natural'-'unnatural' alternative, it is not at all negligible. That is, all that must be learned in a particular case is which of the a priori possible Detail Rules is applicable in which environments. And the overwhelming mass of facts relevant to this decision is given by the phonetic forms which are the input data for one learning the language, since these forms will contain phonetic feature value specifications identical to the right hand sides of the appropriate Detail Rules.[14]

Furthermore, it is quite conceivable that the phonetic value of the features in phonetic forms not only determine the right hand sides of the appropriate Detail Rules, but the left hand sides as well. That is, it may well be that in some or even all cases a particular phonetic value can only be a mapping from one particular binary value. This would mean that, even though the phonetic and phonological values cannot be one-to-one related, the extra differentiation of phonetic features is systematically related to phonological structure in an extremely restricted way. Thus the relation could be represented something like:

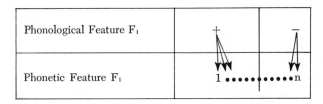

Phonological Feature F_i	+	−
Phonetic Feature F_i	1 •••••••••••n	

(4.1)

In other words, there may be no overlapping, i.e. no n-ary phonetic value which is a possible mapping of both + and − values.[15] Determination of the phonetic value of F_i in a segment

---

[14] It should be obvious that in those cases where a feature is *phonetically* binary the Detail Rules involve no choice whatever, but are simply the completely universal notational shifts from $[+F_i]$ to $[1F_i]$ and from $[-F_i]$ to $[2F_i]$.

[15] Both here and later we describe the Naturalness Condition as requiring that every phonological structure convert to *some* phonetic structure by virtue of purely universal principles. In cases where there are actually a set of alternative Detail Rules associated with a particular binary phonological feature value, this statement requires a minor amendment. That is, we must say that the theory requires that such phonological structures convert by universal principles to a small set of alternative phonetic structures differing only along those dimensions permitted within the relevant sets of universal Detail Rules. Only if an assumption analogous to the 'natural'-

would fully predict the phonological value of F_i at the lowest point of the derivation where $+$ and $-$ values of F_i are still found. At earlier stages, and especially in the dictionary, the value might be different, but this would be a function of phonological rules operating on $+$ and $-$ values.[16] If such a relation obtained, the particular Detail Rule required in the grammar to convert $[+F_i]$ or $[-F_i]$ to the relevant numerical phonetic values of F_i would be fully determined (except for the proper environment specification) by the input phonetic forms available as data to the language learner. And with such low level rules, there might even be principles to determine the environment specifications mechanically from the phonetic forms.

The implication is that, if a phonological-phonetic relationship like that represented in (4.1) holds, the extra differentiation of n-ary $(n>2)$ phonetic features with respect to their two valued phonological correspondents imposes almost no burden on the learner of the grammar. For, although given a particular binary value of a feature, there is a choice of Detail Rule apparently not statable universally, the right rule would in fact be almost (possibly completely) determined by the phonetic forms which are given. Under these assumptions, therefore, Detail Rules have a status which is between that of truly universal principles and completely language-limited rules. Detail Rules can be stated within linguistic theory *as a set* for each feature, but the choice of

---

'unnatural' status of phonetic values is correct will each phonological structure convert to a unique phonetic structure by virtue of the universal phonological-phonetic interpretation principles.

[16] In other words, if the situation represented in (4.1) actually exists, the phonetic value of a feature predicts a binary value or, put differently, fully determines the character of the rule converting the binary value to an integral phonetic value (fully determines, that is, ignoring questions of the context in which the particular conversion is relevant). But the binary value so determined is not necessarily that present in the dictionary correspondent of the phonetic segment. To assume this would be to assume in effect the binary version of autonomous phonemic theory mentioned above. So, in the case discussed directly below in the text, the [s] of 'piracy' would uniquely determine a Natural Categorical Segment identical to that determined by the [s] of 'soup.' But although the latter gives, in effect, all the information required for the dictionary representation, the former does not, since in the dictionary the [s] of 'piracy' is represented with a systematic t̲ identical to that in 'pirate.' And this fact is of course unpredictable from the phonetic specification of 'piracy' alone.

which member of the set is applicable to a particular binary value in a particular context in a particular language is evidently not universally representable. However, this choice is almost entirely determined mechanically by the phonetic form which is to be the output of the particular derivation. Therefore, if the kind of approach we have outlined can be maintained, the mapping between binary features and more than binary phonetic features does not really add to the complexity of particular grammars. That is, it imposes almost no task on the language learner beyond those which would exist if phonetic features were binary or phonological features n-ary.

It should be emphasized that the above discussion is not intended to preclude the possibility that, at least for some features, languages may contain their own particular systems of rules which assign a whole set of n-ary values. That is, our account is not intended to imply that all mappings from + and − values to n-ary values are a function of Detail Rules. In fact this is certainly not the case. For example, the rules of stress assignment in English (Halle and Chomsky, to appear) impose an n-ary representation on vowel segments. Our intention is that Detail Rules come into play only when the independently motivated rules of a particular phonology terminate with + and − values for particular features. For example, in Mohawk the stress rules will not in any motivated way assign any structure beyond [+Stress] or [−Stress] to particular vowels. Detail Rules are thus relevant to assign the proper value of this phonetically perhaps 5-ary feature. The suggestion is that because the structure of (4.1) obtains the two values of stress which actually exist in Mohawk phonetic representations automatically determine which of the universal Detail Rules for the feature Stress must be regarded as part of Mohawk phonology.

Another aspect of the Naturalness Condition should be emphasized. A phonetic segment is a set of value specifications for a large number of phonetic features, possibly between twenty and forty. The former figure is more reasonable assuming many features are not relevant, that is, not marked, in some segments; for example, that Stress is not marked for true consonants, Stridency not marked for vowels, etc. If we assume the kind of systematic relation between phonetic values and binary phonological values discussed in the previous paragraph and diagrammed in (4.1), one can define for each phonetic segment a corresponding type of phonological segment which can be called its <u>Natural Categorial Segment</u>. This will simply consist of the same set of features with only the appropriate + and − values. Some Natural Categorial Segments will of course be associated with more than one phonetic segment as a consequence of, among other things, the one-many relation between phonological and phonetic values for some features represented in (4.1). One could then define a binary, or Jakobson-like, version of autonomous phonemics as one which insisted that the phonemicization of a string of phonetic segments must necessarily always be the corresponding string of Natural Categorial Segments with phonetically redundant binary values not given and predicted by allophonic statements. To really characterize actual theories, this would have to be modified a bit to allow for *phonetically* predictable epenthesis, etc., but the main outlines are certainly right.

Systematic phonemic theory, on the other hand, does not claim that the systematic representation will consist of the appropriate sequence of underspecified Natural Categorial Segments since the class of rules relating systematic and phonetic levels is much larger and richer in structure than such an assumption would allow. However, the Naturalness Condition does imply that in general the categorial segment underlying a particular phonetic segment [p_i] is much, much closer to the Natural Categorial Segment of [p_i] than to some arbitrary Natural Categorial Segment. If this were not the case, the idea of relating systematic and phonetic representations by a set of partially universal rules would have no point.

Consider an example. In systematic description (Chomsky, 1964b:89) the phonetic [s] of English words like 'opacity,' 'democracy,' 'piracy,' would be represented with systematic $\underline{k}$ or $\underline{t}$ because of related forms like 'opaque,' 'democrat,' 'pirate,' etc. The [s] is then the result of rules which (within the Romance Vocabulary[17]) soften these stop elements before certain vocalic sequences.

---

[17] The condition about subclass of the vocabulary is needed because of such forms as 'keen,' 'team,' etc. in which $\underline{t}$ and $\underline{k}$ do not soften. This is only one of many facts showing the need for subdivisions of the vocabulary, which in part define the domain of phonological rules, and is simply further

However, although the [s] elements in these cases have categorical segments which are different in several features from the Natural Categorial Segment of [s], the overwhelming majority of specifications in the Natural Categorial Segment of [s] are right *even for the t̲ and k̲ representations.* Those features which would be present in the Natural Categorial Segment of [s] but still correct for both t̲ and k̲ include:

(4.2)

$$
\begin{bmatrix}
+\text{Consonantal} \\
-\text{Vocalic} \\
-\text{Sonorant} \\
-\text{Nasal} \\
-\text{Long} \\
+\text{Tense} \\
-\text{Aspirated} \\
-\text{Voiced} \\
-\text{Pharyngealized} \\
-\text{Rounded} \\
-\text{Palatalized} \\
-\text{Velarized} \\
-\text{Glottalized} \\
-\text{Lateralized}
\end{bmatrix}
$$

The only features in the Natural Categorial Segment of [s] which would be different from those required in the systematic t̲ and k̲ would be Grave, Diffuse, Apical, Abrupt Onset, Abrupt Offset[18] and Strident. And of these the first three would be correctly marked in the t̲ cases.[19] Hence the systematic representation of

---

evidence of the relevance of grammatical information for the phonology. It is generally the case, of course, that such vocabulary divisions mirror in large part, though seldom completely, the historical origin of the vocabulary. Thus in English the gross divisions seem to correspond to the Germanic, Romance, and Greek provenience of forms (Halle and Chomsky, to appear). For further discussion cf. Chapter 6.

[18]Many of the features mentioned in this example are new to discussions of generative phonology, although not completely nontraditional. Abrupt Onset is new in terminology, but simply represents the older feature of Interrupted. Abrupt Offset is, however, an entirely new feature suggested by Halle to distinguish plain stops from affricates.

[19] Probably the particular English rules which shift the stop elements to the dental continuant need not mention the features Strident, Abrupt Offset, Apical, and others. This follows, since the principles of Marked and Unmarked must be constructed in such a way that, for example, the

the phonetic [s] of forms like 'piracy,' and 'opacity' is at least seventy percent determined by the phonetic structure of the forms. The differences between the actual representations and

---

Unmarked dental continuant is of the [+Strident] type; that the Unmarked value of Abrupt Offset is [+Abrupt Offset] when the segment is [+Abrupt Onset] and [−Abrupt Offset] otherwise; and that the Unmarked value of Apical is [+Apical] in the dental region but [−Apical] in all other regions. Therefore, the theory of phonological rules can be constructed in such a way that when a feature value is changed (from + to − or vice versa) all features which are, in a sense to be made precise, 'subordinate' to the features shifted, take on their Unmarked values automatically. Hence, for example, in shifting a dental stop, which would have feature specifications including

$$
\begin{bmatrix}
-\text{Grave} \\
+\text{Diffuse} \\
+\text{Apical} \\
\vdots
\end{bmatrix},
$$

to a labial stop, which would have feature specifications including

$$
\begin{bmatrix}
+\text{Grave} \\
+\text{Diffuse} \\
-\text{Apical} \\
\vdots
\end{bmatrix},
$$

it is necessary for the rule to change only the value of Grave since the [−Apical] specification in the labial stop is a function of the universal fact that the Unmarked value of Apical is [−Apical] in nondental regions. There must, of course, be rules which do not have consequences of this type, i.e. rules which would, for example, shift the dental stop to a labial stop which was [+Apical]. Such rules must be allowed but made more expensive. A natural way to distinguish them is by use of Unmarked feature values in rules, together with the assumption that such markings in rules, unlike + and − values, have zero cost. Hence a rule of the form:

$$
\begin{bmatrix}
+\text{Consonantal} \\
+\text{Diffuse} \\
+\text{Abrupt Onset}
\end{bmatrix} \longrightarrow [+\text{Gravel}] \text{ in } X\underline{\quad}Y
$$

which shifts an Apical dental stop to a non-Apical labial stop is, under the assumptions just discussed, to be regarded as an abbreviation for a rule which specifies all those features 'subordinate' to Grave as U on the right hand side. Since Apical is 'subordinate' to Grave, this rule then determines that the resulting segment is [−Apical] even though the − value of this feature is not explicitly mentioned in the rule. If, however, a [+Apical] output were correct, this would require the more expensive rule identical to that above except for an additional specification [+Apical] on the right of the arrow. The ideas of this footnote, which are due basically to M. Halle and N. Chomsky, are discussed further in Chapter 8.

the Natural Categorial Segment are then the minimal necessary to take into account regularities of the language, most crucially in this case alternations of [t] and [k] with [s].

Consequently, although systematic phonemic theory does not and cannot claim that the phonetic properties of a form *fully* determine its phonemic structure given knowledge of free variation, it does claim that the phonetic properties directly determine a substantial percentage of the phonological properties. In fact these latter properties differ from the sequence of Natural Categorial Segments only to the minimum extent necessary to state the general rules required by alternations, predictable distributions, phonological constraints, etc.; in short, only to the extent required by the existing regularities of the language and of language generally. It is in this sense that systematic phonemic theory strongly differs from past and certain current views of morphophonemic structure by insisting that this is formed, not of ad hoc, arbitrary symbols, but on the contrary of elements with systematic relations to phonetic structure stated within linguistic theory and hence in large part universal. In brief, it is a theory which, while denying that there is any level of linguistic structure which is mechanically determinable *in full* from phonetic structure, as so much modern linguistics has assumed, insists that the level of systematic phonemic structure is related to phonetics by the Naturalness Condition.

The discussion of the Naturalness Condition can largely be rephrased in terms of the notion <u>natural class</u>, as defined by Halle (1961:90):

We shall say that a set of speech sounds forms a *natural class* if fewer features are required to designate the class than to designate any individual sound in the class.

Furthermore, this rephrasing can serve to contribute to the precision with which it is possible to specify this fundamental constraint on the relations between phonetic and systematic systems of representation. In terms of a theory which sharply segregates n-ary *phonetic* features from binary *systematic* (categorial, phonological, structural, morphophonemic) features, we can reformulate the basic point as follows. If one considers those classes of systematic segments (morphophonemes) which must be referred

to in the rules of natural languages, one will find that in general
these have phonetic realizations which form natural classes in
terms of phonetic features, and that the variant phonetic mappings
of a single systematic segement will form a natural class. Even
more significantly, it will be found that the Natural Categorial
Segments defined by the phonetic representations of forms meet
an important set of conditions with respect to systematic structure and natural classes. Let us elaborate this point.

Just as we defined for any particular phonetic <u>segment</u> its
Natural Categorial Segment containing only binary values, we
can more generally define for any phonetic <u>representation</u>, that
is, sequence of phonetic segments, its <u>Natural Categorial Sequence,</u> which consists of the sequence of Natural Categorial
Segments of the phonetic segments in the corresponding order.
Very often a particular morpheme will have several variant
phonetic representations in different contexts. One aspect of the
Naturalness Condition is the claim that the systematic base form
representation for the vast majority of morphemes is either one
of the Natural Categorial Sequences[20] of its phonetic variants or
a structure which deviates from one of these only in a very small
number of ways predicted either by general regularities of the
language, or by universal phonological rules and conditions, or
both.[21] Thus, for example, the morpheme 'opaque' in English

---

[20] Actually, this is of course an oversimplification. The Natural Categorial Segments of such sequences contain a + or − specification for many
features which are fully a function of general rules. For example, in English
every Natural Categorial Segment will contain the specification [−Glot-
talized]. Obviously there is no sense in taking such specifications to be
part of the systematic representation, since they are specified by rule. In
terms of + and − representations, it is natural therefore to view the systematic
representation as a submatrix of the Natural Categorial Sequence in which
such specifictions are not given. This accounts for the 0 or 'no information'
symbols of the early version of systematic phonemic theory. In current
versions utilizing the notions of Marked and Unmarked this is handled
rather differently. Cf. Chapter 8.

[21] The universal phonological rules in question here include those
which, for example, specify that two Natural Categorial Segments are associated with the same phonetic segment. A real example is, I believe, that
which asserts that a Sonorant, labial, non-Nasal consonant is realized
phonetically as the non-Consonantal [w]. In other words, the phonetic [w]
is the natural representative of *both* a labial glide and a labial non-Nasal
liquid consonant. What the rule claims then is both (1) that no longuage

has phonetic variants which include (ignoring stress, etc.) [opeyk] and [opæs] which have Natural Categorial Sequences that can be respectively abbreviated <u>opeyk</u> and <u>opæs</u>. In fact the base form here is <u>opæk</u> (with a tense vowel) which deviates from a submatrix of the Natural Categorial Sequence <u>opeyk</u> only in ways fully predicted by general rules of vowel shift and dipthongization in English (cf. Halle and Chomsky, to appear). The crucial point is that the general claim that Natural Categorial Sequences essentially provide correct base forms is subject to verification *in terms of natural classes*. That is, it is an important constraint on the systematic representation of forms that those classes of morphophonemes which must actually be referred to in the rules are in general natural classes in the technical sense. Therefore, the claim that Natural Categorial Sequences provide the basis for systematic representation entails that the elements referred to in rules will actually be natural classes in terms of systematic representations which deviate from submatrices of Natural Categorial Sequences only in ways predicted by general rules, either universal or language particular.

The structural identities among elements predicted by those elements which form classes in the rules of a particular language and predicted by the Natural Categorial Sequences defined over the phonetic representations of that language by a universal phonetic system and the principle of binarization are *logically* distinct. But the Naturalness Condition claims that in general they are empirically identical, i.e. that the classes required for the rules of all languages will be technically natural classes in terms of systematic phonemic representations which differ from Natural Categorial Sequences only to the extent defined by linguistic regularities. Although weaker than conditions like the autonomous Linearity and Invariance, this is nonetheless a tremendously strong and nontrivial claim. The fact that it is true is a fundamental characteristic of human languages.

Once it is recognized that a relation like that discussed in the previous paragraphs obtains in natural languages between phonetic and systematic representations, such knowledge may in

---

has actual phonetic labial non-Nasal liquid consonants and (2) that in many languages non-Consonantal [w] functions as a phonological labial non-Nasal liquid consonant. Mohawk is a good instance of a language of the latter type. (cf. Part II, Chapter 11).

turn be brought to bear in a noncircular way on the choice of a universal phonetic system. That is, besides those constraints on this system which can be inferred from articulatory, perceptual, and acoustic facts as such, the phonetic system and its individual features must meet the condition that the Natural Categorial Segments it defines do in fact provide the basis for adequate systematic representation in the languages of the world. Or, more generally, once we see that the Naturalness Condition is *in general* true, we may use it as one of the relevant factors in determining the description of *particular* phonetic facts. Recognition of the existence of the Naturalness Condition means that all of the facts of phonology, morphophonemics, etc. are as relevant to the choice of a universal phonetic system as phonetic facts are to the choice of language-individual phonological systems. The relations are largely symmetrical, though not entirely so. This is noncircular because there are constraints on phonetic structure which are indepedent of phonological representation and of linguistic rules, and because a significant portion of the structure of any phonetic system is therefore necessarily given in advance of any considerations of systematic phonological structure. Most crucially, circularity is avoided by insisting on the universality of the phonetic system, so that features posited for any one language must play a role in others as well, and by insisting on the universality of aspects of phonological representation such as, for example, the conditions which define Natural Categorial Sequences. Given these universality assumptions, each assertion about every feature of the phonetic system has consequences for both the phonetic and systematic descriptions of every language and is thus testable far beyond the facts of any small group of languages which might have motivated it.

Let us finally emphasize the meaning of the Naturalness Condition with respect to formal conditions between phonological and phonetic structure and the linguistic rules which express these conditions. It is logically possible to imagine a theory of language which assumes that phonological and phonetic structure are totally distinct, i.e. based on totally distinct sets of elements. Under this assumption it would be necessary to have in every language rules particular to that language only which relate *every* aspect of phonological structure to its particular phonetic realization. In fact, as we shall see, stratificational phonology is just such a theory. In contrast, systematic phonemics incorporating the Naturalness Condition claims almost the exact opposite. It claims that phonological and phonetic structure are essentially similar and require special language-limited rules to relate them only with respect to a very limited number and kind of properties. Much of the work of generating phonetic representations from input systematic phonological structures is a function of universal rules and conditions. This is possible just because the vocabularies upon which systematic structure is based are in significant part given by the phonetic vocabulary. Hence, except in the irreducible cases of completely special language-limited facts, systematic structures automatically pass into phonetic structures without the need of setting up ad hoc rules.

STRATIFICATIONAL PHONEMICS AS A VIOLATION OF THE NATURALNESS CONDITION

Against this background discussion of the meaning and justification of the Naturalness Condition, we are in a position to consider what is involved in such descriptions as the Lamb-Hockett reformulations of voicing contrasts and the 'deeper inadequacy' of stratificational phonemics which was referred to at the beginning of this chapter and which is revealed by such phonemicizations. This can actually be stated quite simply. The Naturalness Condition is a property of human language, and stratificational phonology denies it. However, in view of the extraordinarily strong claims which have been and are being made for this approach (Gleason, 1964; Lamb, 1964a, 1964b), it is necessary to show in some detail the way this denial is manifested in this view. The examples treated by Lamb and Hockett involve a voice contrast, so we shall base our discussion on such a situation. If a voice contrast is represented naturally within a system incorporating the Naturalness Condition, the contrasting phonological entities at one level of dictionary representation[22] will be

---

[22] At the deepest level of dictionary representation these will, in the current theory, be given as

$$\begin{bmatrix} \text{MVoice} \\ \text{D} \end{bmatrix} \text{ versus } \begin{bmatrix} \text{UVoice} \\ \text{D} \end{bmatrix}$$

$$\begin{bmatrix} +\text{Voice} \\ \text{D} \end{bmatrix} \begin{bmatrix} -\text{Voice} \\ \text{D} \end{bmatrix}$$

where D is an abbreviation for the set of feature specifications common to both terms and not predictable by rule. Consider what must be added to the grammar in order to map these phonological structures into the correct phonetic representations. There are several possibilities. If Voice is actually *phonetically* binary, then the grammar requires absolutely nothing at all. [+Voice] will convert to [1Voice] and [−Voice] will convert to [2Voice] by virtue of completely universal principles. On the other hand, Voice may be phonetically n̠-ary (n>2) although evidently the maximum differentiation here would require it to be at most 3-ary (because of so-called 'half voiced' segments[23]). Under these conditions, it is necessary for a particular grammar to indicate which of the set of Detail Rules relating the two binary values to the three phonetic values is correct for each phonological value in each relevant context. At the worst, this represents very little addition to the grammar, simply the choice among a universally stated set of alternatives. If the assumption of a 'natural'-'unnatural' status for phonetic values as discussed above is correct, such a choice actually only need be made for a subset (n minus 2) of values for an n̠-ary phonetic feature. Or, assuming that the condition of nonoverlapping assignment of phonetic values to phonological binary ones as represented in (4.1) is correct, these rules are essentially fully determined by the phonetic representations. Notice incidentally that the 'natural'-'unnatural' assumption and the structures represented in (4.1) are not necessarily exclusive. Thus the information which a particular description based on systematic phonemic theory must provide with respect

---

with the level of M and U values related to that of + and − values by universal rules. Cf. Chapter 8.

[23] Recent unpublished work by Halle strongly suggests that Voice is only phonetically binary and that so-called 'half voiced' stops are actually a function of the feature Tense. That is:

ordinary [t] = Tense, Voiceless
ordinary [d] = Lax, Voiced
half-voiced [d] = Tense, Voiced

Articulatorily it seems that the tension of the stop delays the onset of voicing, giving the half-voiced effect.

to phonological-phonetic relations in a situation like the Voice contrast we are discussing is either: (a) absolutely null if Voice is phonetically binary; or: (b) at worst limited to the extremely restricted domain of specifying the phonetic degree of a known property, that is, of specifying which of several universally stated alternative rules is to be applied. Furthermore, much of this choice may in fact be determined if certain conditions we have discussed actually hold.

But in a system like the stratificational one, where a voice contrast can be represented as /dh/ versus /d/ or the like, the amount of information which must be provided by the rules of particular linguistic descriptions is simply enormous. That is, particular descriptions must bear the burden of incorporating a variety of special ad hoc rules of several different sorts. On the one hand, a special set of rules is needed to indicate that when <u>h</u> is not 'associated with' a sequence of elements these elements then have *voiced* phonetic realizations. It cannot be emphasized too strongly that this is necessary. Just because the stratificational approach contains no universal principles relating phonological and phonetic structure, principles which are largely excluded by the segment-feature confusion, the presence or absence of a following /h/ or any other symbol provides as such no information whatever about Voice or any other phonetic property. In other words, without ad hoc rules particular to the language in question, phonological entities are related to no phonetic properties whatever. Thus, given a phonemic representation of a word like 'tiger' with a form which can, for now, be abbreviated ^P/hdaygǝr/[24], there is no way of predicting in linguistic theory that /d/ has a voiceless phonetic realization, and /a/, /y/, /g/, /ǝ/, and /r/ have voiced phonetic realizations. It goes without saying that there is no general way of predicting that /h/ has no segmental realization at all. All of this information must then be provided ad hoc by the rules of the particular language, in this case English. And this is true not only for the feature Voice, but for every phonetic feature of every phonetic segment in the

---

[24] The nature of the stratificational structures which are being abbreviated here is discussed in Chapter 5. It will be seen there that nothing crucial for present arguments is obscured by the abbreviation.

language. Besides the obvious redundancy and pointlessness of this set of rules, which correspond to no linguistic regularities, it would be difficult to exaggerate the range of rich and crucial generalizations about human language whose statement the required existence of such ad hoc rules necessarily prevents.

It is a fact, for example, that in the languages of the world, liquids and vowels are generally voiced, that voicing is never contrastive (unpredictable) for such segments (if abstract morphophonemic environments are used in the rules of prediction), and that voiceless vowels and liquids are therefore always rare and contextually determined. This kind of fact, revealing the asymmetrical status of feature values, is captured in systematic phonemics with the Naturalness Condition by positing a number of universal conditions on phonlogical representation. First, it is assumed in this case, for example, that no dictionary segments which are [+Sonorant] (this characterizes vowels and liquids, including nasals) can have contrastive values for Voice. Second, it is assumed that there is a universal rule specifying the dominance of the [+Voice] member in all such segments. This universal rule will say in effect that, unless a language contains a special rule to the contrary, [+Sonorant] segments are always [+Voice]. Stating such conditions and rules as this requires a level of dictionary representation more abstract than that in which systematic features have values as either + or −. In fact, such conditions as the impossibility of a Voice contrast for liquids and vowels, and rules specifying the dominance of [+Voice] in [+Sonorant] segments, are among the grounds leading to the recognition of an ever deeper level in which features have values in terms of M(arked) and U(nmarked). This level is then related to that of + and − values by universal rules. One of these is just that discussed above, which says in other words that:

(4.3) [UVoice] $\longrightarrow$ [+Voice] in $\begin{bmatrix} +\text{Sonorant} \\ \underline{\hspace{1.5cm}} \end{bmatrix}$.

The condition that Voice is noncontrastive in liquids and vowels is then the condition that there is no possible M-U contrast for Voice in [+Sonorant] segments. These must be [UVoice]. These notions of Marked and Unmarked are discussed in somewhat greater detail in Chapter 8. Assuming such an approach, however, an approach which requires all that the Naturalness Condition represents, only the rare and universally unpredictable devoicing of liquids and vowels in special contexts in various languages must be stated ad hoc in particular grammars. That is, only ad hoc facts must be stated ad hoc.

But in the stratificational system, the fact that the phonetic reflexes of phonological liquids and vowels are, in the overwhelming majority of cases, realized as voiced segments must be stated for each such segment type in each language by special rules. In other words, a stratificational grammar is no simpler when faced with a normal language in which liquids and/or vowels are voiced than it would be when dealing with an impossible language in which all liquids and vowels were voiceless. In fact, all other things being equal, the two stratificational grammars would be of identical complexity. The stratificational theory thus completely fails to distinguish impossible from normal cases of this sort. This approach thus cannot provide an explanation for facts such as that there are no languages with only voiceless vowels, only voiceless liquids, etc., and claims that such impossible situations are no different from that of actually existing languages in which voiced sonorants dominate. Regularities of this sort, which stratificational grammar cannot in principle represent because of its denial of the Naturalness Condition, are not at all rare or special. There are in fact an enormous mass of such generalizations of which the following ten are only a very few examples:

(4.4)   Segments are normally non-Implosive. Hence there are no languages with only Implosive segments, although languages with only non-Implosive segments are found everywhere.

(4.5)   Vowels are normally non-Nasal. Hence there are no languages with only Nasal vowels, although languages with only oral vowel are common.

(4.6)   Non-Grave (front) vowels are normally non-Rounded; non-Compact (not low); Grave (back) vowels are normally Rounded. Hence there are no languages with vowel patterns like: ü ï   although those like   i u   are found everywhere
          ö ë   e o

(4.7)   Consonants are normally non-Glottalized. Hence there are no languages with only Glottalized consonants, although languages with only non-Glottalized consonants are common.

(4.8)   Consonants are normally non-Pharyngealized. Hence there are no languages with only Pharyngealized consonants, although languages with only non-Pharyngealized consonants are found everywhere.

(4.9) Consonants are normally non-Lateralized. Hence there are no languages with only Lateralized consonants, although languages with no Lateralized consonants are not uncommon.

(4.10) Consonants are normally followed by vowels, vowels by consonants. Hence although there are many languages without vowel sequences or without consonant clusters or without either, there is no language without consonant vowel sequences, etc.

(4.11) Dental fricatives are normally of the Strident ([s]-type) rather than of the non-Strident ([θ]-type). Hence there are relatively few languages with [θ], but almost every language has an [s]-type segment.

(4.12) Dental consonants are normally Apical, Palatal consonants normally non-Apical (i.e. articulated with the blade of the tongue and not the tip. Hence there are few languages with lamino-dental consonants, and apico-palatal (i.e. retroflex or domal) consonants are also relatively uncommon. But apico-dental and lamino-palatal segments are found almost everywhere.

(4.13) Labial consonants are normally non-Apical (i.e. are formed with the lower lip as moving articulator). Hence there are no languages with only apico-labial (i.e. formed with the tip of the tongue against the upper lip) consonants,[25] although languages with no Apical labial consonants are found everywhere.

Since all of these generalizations, as well as the mass of others which also exist, are quite unstatable within stratificational phonemics, the inadequacy of this theory in this regard is difficult to overemphasize. For further discussion of how such generalizations may be represented within systematic phonemic theory by

---

[25] In fact there is only one language, Bororo, a South American Indian Language, which is known to have Apical-labial segments at all. In view of the extreme ease with which these can be made, the distinctive acoustic result, etc. it is difficult to see general phonetic grounds for the rarity of such segments. That is, on grounds of Markedness, one would not expect the Marked Apico-labials to be relatively any rarer with respect to Unmarked labio-labials, labio-dentals, etc. than Marked lamino-dentals are with respect to Unmarked apico-dentals. But this is overwhelmingly not the case. It is possible, therefore, that this is a real case where the class of languages thus far examined or, more likely, the class actually existing today is, in at least one respect, highly skewed with respect to the class of all possible languages.

use of the notions of Marked and Unmarked feature values cf. Chapter 8.

We have seen how stratificational assumptions require ad hoc rules to specify such facts as that all those elements *not* 'associated' with 'devoicer' /h/ have voiced phonetic realizations, and that this means the impossibility of representing an extremely large number of rich phonological universals concerning the asymmetry of phonetic types. On the other hand, given the possibility of using 'phonemes' like the 'devoicer' /h/, there must be rules to interpret not only the *degree of voicing* which /h/ represents, but also the very fact that a following /h/ represents the phonetic feature of Voice in the preceding (or following) sequence of consonant segments rather than Glottalization in the following segment, or Pharyngealization in the vowel six segments to the left, or Rounding in the consonant twelve to the right, or Nasal in the liquid nineteen to the right, etc.

One sees, then, that by representing as a <u>segment</u> on the phonological level what natural phonological representation will represent as a <u>feature</u>, stratificational phonological theory necessarily burdens the description of individual languages with three kinds of ad hoc, and otherwise almost completely unnecessary rules. Assuming a binary phonetic <u>feature</u> F which is stratificationally represented by a <u>segment</u> P, there must be rules to indicate that: (1) sequences not 'associated with' P have phonetic manifestations in which feature F *is not* present. Furthermore, the notion 'associated with' must be defined ad hoc for each segment like P in each rule. For example, sometimes 'associated with' will mean that the segment immediately precedes, sometimes precedes with certain intervening elements, sometimes follows at such and such a distance, etc., etc. (2) Sequences 'associated with' P have phonetic manifestations in which feature F *is* present. (3) The segment P has no segmental phonetic manfestation at all. The price of allowing phonological features to be treated as segments is thus that the entire set of phonetic consequences of every aspect of all phonological structures must be stated ad hoc for each language. Hence the mistake is that an enormous range of information about phonological-phonetic relations in particular languages, which can be stated once and for all within linguistic theory if properly formulated, must, within the stratificational approach, be repeated again and again in particular linguistic descriptions. This theory necessarily misses the generalizations that can be achieved by assuming the Naturalness Condition, and each time the descriptions which it permits make use of 'unnatural' solutions like the 'devoicer' /h/ they necessarily violate Condition (3.16). Actually, even this is not strong enough. Since the very possibility of such solutions eliminates universal rules mediating between phonological and phonetic structures, this condition is in fact violated in all stratificational descriptions even if the possibilties are not used.

I remarked earlier several times that phonemicizations like /dh/-/d/ for phonetic [t]-[d] contrasts give up the natural line between segment and feature. It should now be clearer what was meant. What is involved in this kind of representation is the possibility of recognizing segments on the phonological level which correspond to no *kinds of* phonetic segments, and which are related to certain features of phonetic segments by special rules. That is, given forms which contrast and are phonetically something like:

$$\begin{bmatrix} \ldots \text{1Voice} \ldots \\ \text{D} \end{bmatrix} \begin{bmatrix} \ldots \text{2Voice} \ldots \\ \text{D} \end{bmatrix}$$

the natural representations are as given earlier. Use of a representation involving /h/ means that in the segments on the phonological level no feature representative of Voice is present, and voicing differences are indicated by a new segment. It should be stressed that much more is involved here than simply a lack of direct correspondence between particular individual phonological representations and the particular phonetic structures they represent. For such an abstract relation is also allowed in a system like current systematic phonemics which incorporates the Naturalness Condition. For example, we saw earlier that it was perfectly possible in systematic terms to represent a form like Mohawk [onû':daʔ] as a matrix of phonological features which can be abbreviated wa+o+nuʔt+aʔ. Is this any different than what Lamb and Hockett are doing with their /h/? The answer is that it is very different indeed.

Each of the elements of the systematic representation is a complex of features determined by a phonetic theory, and each segment in this representation will, by virtue of universal rules of interpretation, determine a possible phonetic segment. Furthermore, in *some* contexts the relevant morphemes will be manifested phonetically with phonetic segments identical to, or very close to, those determined by the universal interpretations. However, for the Lamb-Hockett type representations, no analogous remark can be made. It is not just that /h/ is indirectly related to its phonetic consequences, a common property of systematic phonological structures. What is crucial is, first, that /h/, a segment on the phonological level, is, *without ad hoc rule*, related to no segment on the phonetic level. Actually, it makes no sense to speak of a direct phonetic reflex of /h/ without ad hoc rule. On the other hand, as has been repeatedly emphasized above, every phonological segment in a systematic description is mapped onto some possible phonetic segment *independently of any language-particular apparatus*.[26] In other words, the Lamb-Hockett 'devoicer' phonemes are ad hoc, arbitrary symbols; but systematic w, a, o etc. in Mohawk are members of a class of elements defined in linguistic theory. Second, and equally importantly, the Lamb-Hockett proposals for abstract representation differ from those allowed in systematic phonemics in that the deviations from a representation which corresponds directly to the segmental structure of phonetics is without justification in terms of structural regularities of the language. That is, as was briefly shown earlier, the representation wa+o for the phonetic prefix [o] in words like Mohawk [onû':da?] is required to embed the description of these words in a system of independently motivated syntactic and phonological rules, rules which, for example, account for alternations between prefix sequences which include phonetic [ya], [yo], [yaw], [o], [aw], etc. To put it differently, one is driven to represent the [o] prefix as wa+o by consideration of other phonetic manifestations of the same morphemes in other environments, manifestations which justify the postulation of initial glide,

---

[26] It does not follow that each distinct systematic phonological segment is mapped onto a *distinct phonetic segment*. Thus, for example, although there are apparently Sonorant glides only in the labial and palatal positions phonetically ([w], [y]), there is good reason to think that possible phonological segments along this dimension include a dental and velar as well, both of which are, however, mapped onto phonetic [y]. Cf. footnote 18 of Chapter 8. There is no basis for thinking that this case is unique. Another case has already been suggested in footnote 21 above.

following vowel, etc. But no such considerations force one to extract Voice and treat it as a segment in languages like Russian or English. Such a proposal does not fit into any system of regularities, does not yield unique base forms for morphemes which would otherwise have suppletive alternants, does not reduce to generalization any facts which would otherwise have to be given in a list, etc. In short, this move has no motivation at all of the kind that leads to systematic representations which deviate sharply from direct correspondences with the phonetic forms.

To restate this, one can say that the Naturalness Condition insists that phonological segments are the same kind of things as phonetic segments, complexes of the same sets of features. The chief difference is that while on the phonetic level the values may be n-ary, in phonology they are binary. This amounts to the claim that phonetic detail along one feature dimension in excess of a two-valued choice is always predictable by rule and hence never has to be listed in the phonological part of dictionary representations. This is a clear empirical claim given a strong set of constraints on the class of possible phonological rules, on the way these may be interrelated, etc. It claims, for example, that one will never find a language in which there are thousands of forms differing in three degrees of length with no grammatical or phonological properties permitting the prediction of one degree. However, the Naturalness Condition, in the widest sense, is independent of the claim that the abstract representation is binary.

Of course there are certain precedents for the Lamb-Hockett phonemicizations which violate Naturalness. These date back at least to Chao's (1934: section IIb) famous discussion of 'two symbols for one sound,' and include many treatments of the problem of binary versus singulary interpretation of single segments such as (most often) affricates, dipthongs, etc. Lamb is also able to point out that quite frequently 'prosodic' features have been so treated and hence, for example, a contrast between two single phonetic segments [a] and [a:] would often have been given as /a/ versus /a:/ where /:/ is a single phoneme. The four English autonomous stress phonemes were abstracted in this way. However, although there are these traditional precedents, it must be noted that in the past such moves were always regarded with some suspicion and a feeling that something not well understood was going on. A treatment of the type given by Lamb's discussion of voicing would generally never have been countenanced. Stratificational phonemics has apparently taken one direction toward eliminating the inconsistency of older practice, which permitted some features to be extracted as phonemes but not others, while still attempting to maintain the Linearity Condition. Stratificational phonemics will permit the phonemicization of phonetic sequences to be perfectly arbitrary with respect to the linear relation of phonemic and phonetic structures (by perfectly arbitrary I mean governed by no universal constraints). The traditional autonomous phonemicist in general required an order-preserving relation, which he ignored in special cases with some misgivings.

However, there is another road which also eliminates this inconsistency. This has been taken by systematic phonemics, which gives up the untenable Linearity Condition but still maintains a universal set of conditions on phonological-phonetic relations by way of the Naturalness Condition. In systematic terms, it is regarded as just as much a mistake to permit length, stress, tone, etc. to be treated phonologically as segments as to permit voicing to be so treated.

It should be noted that the stratificational phonemicist faces an important difficulty beyond the mass of ad hoc rules of interpretation which his Naturalness violations require and the loss of universal generalizations which these entail. It is, after all, possible to eliminate the feature-segment line to a much greater extent than Lamb and Hockett have thus far done. Thus in English they have abstracted as a new segment only the feature of Voice. But why cannot other properties also be extracted, say Nasal, Stop, Front, Back, Medial, etc. What excludes stratificational phonemic representations like: /Front Stop h/ = traditional autonomous /p/, /Front Stop/ = /b/, /Front Medial Stop h/ = /t/,/ Front Medial Stop / = /d/, /Back Stop h/ = /fl/, /Back Stop/ = /g/, /Front Nasal/ = /m/. /Front Medial Nasal/ = /n/, /Back Nasal/ = /ŋ/, etc. The answer is that nothing does.

These are perfectly possible stratificational phonemic representations of English permitted by exactly the same absence of constraint between phonetic and phonemic representation which permits the segmentalization of Voice. The claim has been made that there is some simplicity metric which will exclude the choice of extreme representations like these. But on the one hand this claim is empty, since no such metric has ever been suggested (notice that these representations reduce the number of phonemes), i.e. there is no known metric which picks out a solution which segmentalizes Voice but not Nasal, etc. And on the other hand, since such representations as these are clearly not possible for any language, linguistic theory should exclude them in principle.[27] Systematic phonemic theory does so. Observe also the incredible arbitrariness which such representations involve. Why, for example, should one give traditional /d/ as /Front Medial Stop/ and not /Stop Front Medial/ or /Medial Front Stop/, etc. Obviously there is no reason for choice of any one order. And this necessary arbitrariness is simply a reflection of the mistake involved in a theory which allows what should actually only be components of segments to be treated as segments themselves.

The possibility of representations like those above (which should in fact be carried to the ultimate extreme whereby *every* feature is treated as a segment therefore further necessitating boundary markers to indicate the grouping given automatically by the Naturalness Condition) reveals that to a great extent the segmentalization of features allowed in stratificational phonemics is simply a notational device. That is, it is a misleading way of writing complexes of features. But it is a bad device since it cannot be made general, and there is no principle which indicates when to stop. Therefore choice of feature segmentalization is arbitrary and choice of order of such pseudosegments is almost entirely arbitrary. Most crucially, as we have seen, it necessarily involves the elimination of the possibility of stating much of the difference between phonological and phonetic representation universally, and therefore forces individual grammars to contain useless and redundant specifications of these relations.

There are a number of senses in which stratificational

---

[27] It is important to keep clear the role of a simplicity metric within linguistic theory. Independently of such a metric, a right theory will define the notion possible human language. With the addition of a metric the theory will in addition define the stronger notion possible language underlying data set X. Hence a linguistic theory is quite wrongly formulated if it allows impossible languages to be candidates for the right language for a specific data set and can only exclude these by some simplicity grounds.

phonemics is closer to traditional autonomous phonemics than the latter is to systematic phonemics. In particular, stratificational phonemics maintains the autonomous character of phonological representation, its independence of grammatical information and the view that each set of free variant phonetic representations has a unique phonemicization. In this sense, stratificational phonemics is reasonably looked upon as a variant of past autonomous phonemics. But there are other senses in which stratificational phonemics is a deviation from common features of previous autonomous phonemics and contemporary systematic phonemics. Recall that the chief methodological motivation for autonomous phonemics originally was the belief that certain taxonomic procedures of segmentation and classification could determine the phonemic structure of sentences from their known phonetic properties (and facts of contrast). The Linearity Condition (in Chomsky's sense) is a natural consequence of such a belief. By abandoning any vestige of a natural relation between phonetic and phonemic representations, stratificational phonemics has completely lost contact with these early motivations. But more importantly, in so doing stratificational phonemics has given up what was right in the Linearity and other early phonemic conditions, namely, their implicit recognition of a natural relation between phonetic and phonemic organization. It is worth saying a little more about how previous autonomous phonemics maintained such a relation in view of the fact that it was clearly not concerned with, nor would it in general have countenanced, universal rules mediating phonological and phonetic systems.[28] There is no real paradox here. Traditional autonomous phonemics was able to maintain a natural relation between phonetic and phonemic organization in the absence of any universal rules of the type required by systematic phonemics

---

[28] There is, to my knowledge, at least one serious instance of discussion of universal phonological rules within the framework of autonomous phonemics. It is probably not at all insignificant that it is found in one of the earliest writings on this topic, namely Chao (1934):

"Now the automaticity of variation within a phoneme has two senses. (1) The variation of [h] of shades [hₑ], [hₐ], [hₑ], [hₒ], etc., according to the following vowel is automatic practically in all languages which have these sounds. So is the variation of the [t] in [ts] and [tʃ] in all languages which have these affricates . . ."

It is quite characteristic that autonomous phonemicists never attempted to develop such ideas.

simply because its phonemic and phonetic systems were so close. It is natural to view autonomous phonemic representations as being exactly like phonetic representations except that certain 'redundant,' 'predictable,' 'noncontrastive,' etc., features of the phonetic representation have been eliminated. Therefore, if one looks upon phonetic representation as a sequence of complexes of phonetic features, autonomous phonemic representation consisted of sequences of complexes of features with, however, just those features removed which would be predicted using purely *phonetic* environments. In such an approach the gap between phonetic and phonemic organization is so narrow, and the substance of phonemic structures so largely given directly by phonetic structure, that the question of universal rules would hardly arise and in fact hardly did. All the attention could then be focused, as indeed it was, on the language-particular facts involving the differences between phonemic and phonetic structures, i.e. it could be focused on the facts of allophonic variation. The natural relation between phonetic and phonemic structure was then guaranteed implicitly by the fact that rules operating on purely phonetic environments can predict so few features that autonomous phonemic and phonetic organization can only differ by a few properties.

Therefore, with respect to the acceptance of the principle of a natural relation between phonetic and phonemic organization, one must group the three theories, traditional autonomous phonemics, stratificational phonemics, and systematic phonemics as follows. Both traditional autonomous phonemics and systematic phonemics recognize a natural relation between phonetic and phonemic structure, i.e. recognize that the former imposes very strong constraints on the latter. But the claims made by autonomous phonemics about this relation are too strong, and the much weaker Naturalness Condition assumed by contemporary systematic phonemics seems to be the strongest condition possible along this dimension. Stratificational phonemics, on the other hand, has largely given up the idea of a natural relation, and its phonemic structures may in principle be almost totally arbitrary with respect to their organization of the phonetic facts (as long as 'contrasts' are not ignored and some vague phonetic similarity conditions are met). Since this means giving up any possibility of a classificatory methodology for phonemicization, and since it has no basis in linguistic universals, internal simplicity of grammars, prediction of particular linguistic properties (like free variation, possible morpheme, etc.), its motivations remain totally obscure, at least to the present writer.

It is interesting that besides the substantive criticisms which can be made of the current proposals of Lamb, Hockett, and others to abandon a natural relation between the segmental structure of phonetics and phonology, such proposals are hardly new or original. I refer here not to the general practice of segmentalizing prosodic features, etc. discussed above, but rather to the fact that such solutions were allowed according to general principles suggested by Z. S. Harris in his well known study *Methods in Structural Linguistics* (1951). In fact, in this work dating from the late 1940's, Harris proposed in different places at least *two different devices* which are equivalent to allowing phonemes like the Lamb-Hockett 'devoicing' /h/. Most obviously equivalent was Harris's view that junctures could be posited as phonemes without direct segmental representation on the phonetic level in order to yield 'more compact' statements. This claim of Harris's about more compact descriptions was almost as vague and unsupported as is Lamb's about having a simplicity metric which indicates when to stop segmentalizing features. That is, in both cases what needs to be shown is why it is wrong (or right) to represent English 'pin' and 'bin' as /−bin/ versus /bin/, rather than as /pin/ versus /−pin/, and why /−bin/ is right and not /b−in/, or why either is better than /pin/ versus /bin/, etc. The important point, however, is that phonemes like the Lamb-Hockett 'devoicers' are essentially equivalent to Harris's arbitrary, 'nonphonetic' junctures. It is interesting in this regard that in the earliest post-autonomous work on systematic phonemics, Chomsky, Halle, and Lukoff (1956:67) were forced to exclude such junctures a priori:

Similarly, the number of segmental phonemes could be reduced. For example, one might say that English possesses only a single nasal consonant /N/ since the phonetic facts can be represented n as /N/; m as /-N/; ŋ as /N-/. Simplifications of this sort can be pushed even farther, to the extreme of a transcription with a single phoneme symbol preceded and/or followed by one, two, three, etc. junctures. Needless to say such solutions are entirely unacceptable and must be ruled out a priori.

Such solutions were excluded by Chomsky, Halle and Lukoff in 1956 by restricting the occurrence of junctures to morpheme boundaries, and by limiting different junctures to different grammatical processes. Today, systematic phonemics excludes them by insisting that the phonological structure of a sentence consists of its superficial syntactic structure with morphemes represented in a system which meets the Naturalness Condition, i.e. in which every phonological segment has a phonetic reflex by virtue of universal principles. It is more than a little curious that Lamb and Hockett should suggest in the mid-1960's solutions which essentially involve the use of arbitrary junctures, and claim that all that is being given up is a false constraint due to the misleading influence of linear writing (Hockett, 1965:195).

Above I claimed that Harris's nonphonetic junctures were 'essentially equivalent' to elements like the Lamb-Hockett 'devoicer' phonemes. The qualification 'essentially' is motivated by the fact that Harris's junctures deviate from ordinary autonomous phonemes in two ways. First, they give up the natural segmental relation with phonetic structure. But second, they also involve no condition of 'phonetic similarity.' While the Lamb-Hockett 'devoicers' involve the first deviation, it is not so clear that they also involve the second. That is, it appears that these linguists still wish to assume some kind of condition of 'phonetic similarity' for stratificational phonemes. For example, they would probably not allow a stratificational phoneme which represented glottalization in one environment, nasalization in another, voicing in a third, etc., which is not excluded for Harris-type junctures. At the same time, no formulation of a 'phonetic similarity' condition in stratificational terms is known to me. And since advocates of this approach deny the existence of a universal, discrete phonetic system (cf. Chapter 5), it is difficult to see how such a condition can be stated significantly within such terms. Furthermore, as Chomsky (1964b) has argued, the coherent version of a phonetic similarity constraint, the condition of Invariance, excludes correct solutions in a variety of cases. In Chapter 9 it is shown in effect that such a condition is even incompatible with the correct specification of free variants. This follows since there are cases where a phonetic sequence A is in free variation with a phonetic sequence B, although A and B share no phonetic properties not occurring in other sequences which are not in free variation with A or B.

Besides allowing arbitrary <u>junctures</u>, Harris also allowed violations of Naturalness by countenancing arbitrary <u>long components,</u> where by arbitrary I again mean governed by no universal substantive constraints. The aim of Harris's components, which were a more or less unique feature of his approach,[29] was to provide a method of stating more elegantly distributional constraints on phonemes. The general program was as follows. Suppose there are four phonemes A, B, X, Y and that AX occurs and BY occurs but not the other two combinations in this order (*AY and *BX). One then extracts a component from AX and says that BY and AX differ only in the presence or absence of this component. The component is defined as having a length of two phonemes so that it now represents the two phoneme restrictions. To put it more concretely:

(4.14)   If: AX occurs,   sp
                AY does not,   *sb
                BY occurs,   zb
                BX does not,   *zp
         Then: AX=$\overline{BY}$ sp=$\overline{zb}$

If one then takes zb and $\overline{zb}$ as the phonemic representations, and it is not clear that this was Harris's full intention, one has in fact got the equivalents of arbitrary junctures in a new non-linear notation. This typical example of Harris's is quite misleading since in this case the component extracted has direct phonetic meaning, namely, voicelessness. In other words, it appears from this example that the components generated by Harris's techniques may be candidates for a universal set of elements relevant to the description of all languages. But this is not at all guaranteed by the approach which in fact allows

---

[29] It is proper to look upon systematic phonological features as embodying the goals of both Jakobsonian distinctive features and Harris-type long components. This is one of the senses in which the theory of systematic phonemics can be looked upon as a joint development of ideas of Harris and Jakobson, adding to them the conceptions of generative grammar and the insight that phonological structure is morphoponemic in character, an idea which comes from such traditional sources as Boas and Sapir.

perfectly arbitrary components whose phonetic realizations can only be given by ad hoc, language particular rules. Thus for English nothing prevents:

(4.15)   sm
                  ° sr
                  ° gm
                    gr

                    $\widetilde{\text{sm}}$=gr

And it is components like the phonetically meaningless ≈ which will actually predominate if the proposed methods are applied generally. Hence the set of components which Harris's methods extract are in general arbitrary with respect to their phonetic consequences and require ad hoc specification. They thus fail to define properties which could qualify as systematic phonemic features meeting the Naturalness Condition in essentially the same, although probably a more extreme, way as the contemporary Lamb-Hockett 'devoicers' and similar spurious segmentalizations of phonetic features fail to qualify as possible systematic phonemes.[30] Because most of Harris's long components require ad hoc specification of their phonetic consequences, any contribution they make to increasing the simplicity of linguistic descriptions is largely illusory since whatever they add to the compactness of stating sequential constraints on phonemes is outweighed by the cost of the ad hoc statements needed to relate them to the phonetic facts. It is for this reason that the theory of systematic phonemics insists that sequential constraints be specified in terms of systematic phonemic features whose relation to phonetic features is in large part given universally within the theory of language.

SUMMARY

I hope to have shown that the question raised at the end of Chapter 3 concerning whether the difficulties involving Lamb's

---

[30] It should be pointed out that the theory of Prosodic phonology which has developed in Great Britain (cf. Langendoen, 1964a, 1964b for critical discussion) can be looked upon as a variant of the long component approach. It must thus be rejected as a theory which denies the Naturalness Condition. Cf. also latter part of Chapter 8.

postulated /h/ for Russian can be overcome by revision of the analysis in terms of a 'voicing' phoneme instead of a 'devoicing' phoneme is really irrelevant. The difficulties were that with /h/ Lamb's condition of maximum diversification (3.14) was not met. The irrelevance arises from the fact that all such 'unnatural' phonemicizations necessarily involve redundant and useless specifications in particular grammars of facts which can be stated universally. That is, such phonemicizations violate Condition (3.16) and this shows that, independently of the violations of Condition (3.14) discussed in Chapter 3, the stratificational attempt to get around Halle's antiautonomous phonemics argument by giving up any requirement of phonetic-phonemic naturalness is a failure. Halle's argument conclusively refutes brands of autonomous phonemics which meet such traditional conditions as Linearity, etc. Stratificational phonemic representations can, in certain cases, evidently avoid the redundant morphophonemic rules required by 'natural' autonomous phonemics in situations similar to that described by Halle. But this can be done only at the cost of a simply gigantic mass of ad hoc and useless rules specifying all of the phonetic consequences of every phonological entity in every language.

More importantly, in developing this negative discussion of the intolerable consequences which must ensue from a failure to require a natural relation between phonetic and phonological structure, I hope to have made some positive contribution: clarifying the a priori vague notion of 'naturalness' by specifying in some detail (though it is far from sufficient) how the present theory of systematic phonemics assumes this relation should be reconstructed even while denying such excessively strong traditional assumptions as Linearity and Invariance. To the extent that this is the case, the mistake of recent stratificational phonemics will have served to clarify the actual nature of phonetic-phonemic relations by providing a striking contrast between the actual situation and the empirically deviant conception of a theory which denies the Naturalness Condition.

It is obvious that in no sense is stratificational phonemics an approach which can lead to salvaging the fundamental assumptions of autonomous phonemics. Even on the grounds thus far considered, those interested in a theory of language which embodies all the generalizations possible about the phonological structure of human language, and which countenances individual descriptions capable of incorporating all existing phonological generalizations, must take as their point of departure the ideas of current systematic phonemics.[31] The claims of stratificational phonemics to provide a modern interpretation of autonomous phonemics which avoids the criticisms of generative writers while preserving the fundamental, autonomous character of the phonemic level are totally unfounded. This conclusion will be greatly strengthened by the discussion of the next chapter, which reveals further inadequacies and incoherence in stratificational ideas of phonology, and by new arguments against autonomous phonemics presented in Chapter 9, arguments which, most significantly, apply to the stratificational and nonstratificational variants alike.

---

[31] This remark about 'point of departure' must be taken seriously. No one working within the framework of systematic phonemics believes that the last word has been said on any point of theory. The number of open questions, areas of limited knowledge, and hence theoretical vagueness is quite enormous. What can be insisted on is only that the framework of current systematic phonemics is the *most* adequate known, and that this framework does not fail in innumerable ways which disconfirm other existing possibiliites. That is, the limitations of present systematic phonemics are not avoided in any other linguistic theory. They are, therefore, properly looked upon as limitations in our general knowledge of phonological structure.

5

INCOHERENCE IN STRATIFI-CATIONAL PHONEMICS

In discussing stratificational phonemics in the previous two chapters, we tacitly assumed for purposes of clarity of discussion certain things about this approach which cannot in fact be maintained. It is worth going into these assumptions to reveal by contrast the character of a correct theory of phonology and to clarify further the intention of the theory of systematic phonemics.

Most crucially, it was implicitly assumed that stratificational phonemics incorporates a level of mentalistic phonetic representation serving as the instructional system for the vocal apparatus, and that phonemic structures are mapped into phonetic structures by rule. Since this is a minimal condition for any rational theory of phonology, certainly no false criticisms were obtained from this assumption. In fact the opposite result really ensued. For on this particular point stratificational phonemics involves the fundamental, if now all too traditional, equivocation briefly discussed earlier in Chapter 1. That is, within this approach, phonetics is officially considered to be only the description of articulation and acoustic shape so that no discrete linguistic level is thought to intervene between the discrete stratificational phonemic stratum and the continuous, unsegmented, and infinitely varying realm of articulation. Thus Gleason claims (1964:77) that:

The problem of phonetic segmentation is in principle insoluble, and all that can be done is to set up a convenient ad-hoc organization of the data without theoretical justification of any kind.

Similarly, Lamb says (1964a:58–59):

In this paper I use the terms *phonemic, morphemic, lexemic,* and *sememic* for the four strata which apparently need to be recognized within linguistic structure. (In addition there are two peripheral strata which relate to the structure but are outside it: the *phonetic* and the *semantic.*)

One aspect of the equivocation and incoherence involved in such views is immediately apparent with respect to Lamb's version, since throughout this publication and others Lamb constantly makes use of a system of discrete phonetic representation involving such notions as dental, tense, voiceless, post-alveolar, etc. (1964a:59, 76). If phonetics were really the description of physical reality as such, these concepts would have no referents.

Even more fundamentally, however, the incoherence caused by a failure to recognize explicitly the existence of a discrete system of phonetic representation, distinct from both phonemic structure and physical reality, as the ultimate level of linguistic structure, shows up in the stratificational account of the lowest type of segmental phonological entities which are officially recognized, namely stratificational phonemes. This is best discussed in terms of certain features of the larger framework of phonology advocated within current stratificational writings. And it is worthwhile to partially place this framework in historical perspective.

We are now concerned with certain crucial dimensions along which linguistic theories differ, namely, the number and kind of significant distinct levels of phonologically relevant representation which they recognize as existing in language. It is possible to discern grossly at least the following different views:

(5.1) One level only, that of phonetics. This position is often attributed to Franz Boas, obviously mistakenly (Postal, 1964a). Perhaps it was never really fully maintained by anyone.

(5.2) Two levels only, that of phonetics and 'morphophonemics.' This is the position of Sapir in his famous 'Psychological Reality' and

'Sound Pattern' articles (1933, 1925) and of contemporary systematic phonemics.

(5.3) <u>Two levels only, that of autonomous phonemics and phonetics.</u> This is the *rational* interpretation of modern 'item and arrangement' American linguistics of the post-1940 type which eliminated morphophonemic representation and stated all morphophonemic facts by means of lists of alternates, that is, which assimilated all alternations to wholly irregular suppletions. A good example of this approach in practice is given by Lounsbury (1953). For discussion of this approach cf. first part of Chapter 8. For discussion of the weird elimination of morphophonemic representation from modern American linguistics cf. Postal (to appear b).

(5.4) <u>One level only, that of autonomous phonemics.</u> This is the apparently *intended* interpretation of modern 'item and arrangement' American linguistics which claimed that phonetics was only the description of physical phenomena and therefore not properly a level of discrete linguistic structure. This is the position of the theoretical sections of Bloomfield (1933; especially Chapter 5 and page 85).

(5.5) <u>Three levels, morphophonemic, autonomous phonemic, and phonetic.</u> This is Trubetzkoy's position (1939) and that of some American linguistics which utilized morphophonemic elements in the late 1930's and early 1940's if this may properly be interpreted as recognizing a discrete phonetic level. Cf. Swadesh and Voegelin (1939).

(5.6) <u>Two levels, morphophonemics and autonomous phonemics.</u> This is Bloomfield's position in his 'Menomini Morphophonemics' (1939), Harris's in those sections of *Methods* (1951) where he talks about morphophonemes (i.e. Chapter 14), and the current stratificational position. It is, in other words, the three level position of (5.5) modified by the impossible assumption of no discrete phonetics.

Stratificational phonemics maintains this two level or two strata view in roughly the following form. There is a level of morphophonemic representation in which the elements are unanalyzable, atomic elements, morphophonemes, (<u>morphons</u> in their special terminology) which are combined linearly into strings. The morphophonemic representation of any linguistic form consists exclusively of a string of morphons. That is, grammatical information, including IC structure, syntactic features, etc., is excluded, and all rules mapping morphophonemic structures into phonemic ones must be defined exclusively over strings of morphons (Lamb, 1964:111–122). This exclusion of Surface Syntactic Structure from phonological relevance involves its own blunders and loss of insights which were actually traditional in premodern linguistics. Cf. Chapter 6.

Most important here is the fact that each morphon in each language is an arbitrary symbol, which could be represented by an integer but is in practice given by some alphabetical symbol. By arbitrary I mean, of course, that its consequences (realizations) on the stratum one below are completely unpredicted by any universal principles. As a consequence there must be special morphons *even fo. those stratificational phonemes which take part in no alternations.* And, fantastically, there must be special rules mapping these morphons onto the invariant phonemes. This assumption, which runs directly counter to what is assumed by systematic phonemics (as well as by much traditional morphophonemic practice with its mixed phonemic-morphophonemic writing), is not, strangely enough, an oversight or accident, but actually, for some completely mysterious reason, a point of pride. Thus Gleason says in his enthusiastic praise of stratificational grammar (1964:87):

Finally, we come to the *morphophonic* rules which state the recoding relations between morphemic strings and phonemic matrices. These seem familiar, but there is a significant difference from the usual view of 'morphophonemic rules.' The latter are based on the assumption that morphemes are composed of phonemes. Morphophonemic rules are, therefore, required only for those morphemes which have allomorphs, and indeed only for those parts of morphemes that vary from allomorph to allomorph. The rules can conveniently be stated in terms of 'morphophonemes,' a strange sort of variable phoneme. However, morphemes are composed of morphons, and these are units in the morphemic stratum not the phonemic, nor are they any sort of bridge between the two strata. Morphons are realized, in general, by phonemes. This is true whether a given morphon has one consistent realization or some very complex pattern of realizations varying from context to context. A morphophonic rule is needed in either case.

The need for these useless morphophonemic rules in cases of no alternation is simply a special instance of the extraordinary extent to which stratificational phonological theory embodies a failure to meet Condition (3.16). These rules which Gleason insists upon are absolutely independent of linguistic fact. There are no properties which a phoneme could have which would render such rules unnecessary. To see this, imagine a language in which there is only a single morphophonemic alternation. Assume the language has thirty phonemes, but that only two alternate while twenty-eight do not. In spite of this, a stratificational description would have to set up a whole level of representation for this language distinct from its phonemic structure, and on this morphophonemic level there would have to be at least twenty-nine morphons completely distinct from the phonemes and twenty-eight special ad hoc rules mapping each of these morphons onto its invariant phonemic realization.[1] This mass of utterly useless and linguistically meaningless rules is a direct consequence of the failure of stratificational theory to contain any analogue of the Naturalness Condition. We see that these necessary statements are not rules to describe linguistic facts, but rather devices needed to maintain an a priori and mistaken theoretical framework.[2]

Another claim made by Gleason in the quote above is wrong. He assumes that the sole motivation for the view that morphophonemic rules are needed only for alternations is the assumption that morphemes are composed of phonemes. This is only one possible basis for such a correct assumption. Another

---

[1] I have assumed that there is one alternation rather than none because in a case like the latter the stratificational advocate might be willing to weaken the theory and allow a language with no morphophonemic level. But this is impossible if there is at least one alternation.

[2] Compare this palpable need in stratificational grammar for masses of useless statements with the following remarks by Gleason in his praiseful ode on stratificational grammar (1964:92–93):

"However, transformational-generative grammars have so much excess ad hoc complexity that it is meaningless to speak simply of adding apparatus."

"However, much of the difficulty with transformational-generative grammars seems to be in their form, rather than in the facts they describe."

Nowhere in this article nor in any other does Gleason even attempt to show any real defect in transformational grammars or any actual case in which they contain excess complexity or require complexities by virtue of mistaken assumptions about the form of rules. It goes without saying, therefore, that nowhere does he show how any such defects are overcome by stratificational grammar, although he claims this several times.

basis, that which is actually operative in systematic phonemics, is the idea that the level of dictionary representation of morphemes is connected to lower levels of representation by universal principles, as discussed above. In short, another basis is the Naturalness Condition. Given this, it of course follows that only those aspects of morphophonemic (i.e. systematic phonemic) structure which have language particular (i.e. from the point of view of linguistic theory arbitrary) phonetic realizations require special language restricted rules. Gleason's comments reveal, in the purest form possible, the extent to which the theory of stratificational phonology has been constructed as to require descriptions which exclude real generalizations and necessitate masses of unnecessary ad hoc statements.

Along roughly the same lines, other completely untenable consequences result from the assumption Gleason emphasizes, not only in cases where phonemes enter into no alterations. Consider a case where one morphon is represented by three phonemes, /a/ in context X, /b/ in context Y, and /c/ in context Z. The stratificational description is no simpler if phonemes /a/, /b/, and /c/ share phonetic properties than if they do not. Since a morphon is an arbitrary symbol, and since a rule is needed to say how each is realized on the phonemic stratum in every context (this is another crucial stratificational axiom, corollary of the general need to say ad hoc for each aspect of structure on stratum A how it is realized on stratum A–1),[3] it makes no difference what the different realizing phonemes are. This is a theory which makes the false claim that the set of phonetic realizations of a morphophoneme will, in general, not have greater phonetic similarity (more properties in common) than an arbitrarily chosen set of phonetic segments. On the contrary, sys-

------

[3] It should again be emphasized that this is no accident or oversight but an explicit and basic matter of principle. It is one of the most important defining features of the whole approach. Thus Lamb (1964b:116) insists:

"In the mutation rule it is not necessary that the subrules collectively cover all possible contexts in which the element can occur. If none of the subrules applies, then the element is not rewritten at all. The corresponding situation is not possible for realization rules because the set of upper stratum elements and that of lower stratum elements are disjoint sets. Therefore there must always be a realization, even for elements which have the same realization in all environments."

tematic phonemics, whose dictionary entries are complexes of features with indirect phonetic meaning by virtue of universal principles, requires language limited rules only where there are alternations or where the phonetic consequences of a systematic segment are not the universally predicted ones. In other words, to just the extent that the phonetic realizations of a systematic phoneme are not similar, the systematic grammar requires language particular rules. Therefore systematic grammars are much simpler, to the extent that the realizations of morphophonemic entities are phonetically similar; and this theory correctly claims that in general the degree of phonetic similarity among the segments which are mappings from a particular type of dictionary segment is far greater than that among arbitrary sets of segments.[4]

In working through some of the assumptions which are, for some reason, being brought forward today by advocates of stratificational grammar, we have not yet reached the central incoherence mentioned at the outset of this chapter. For this concerns, as already mentioned, the structure and interpretation of the phonemic entities postulated by this view.

Unlike the elements on the morphemic (i.e. morphophonemic) stratum which are atomic and unanalyzable segments, stratificational theory claims that the phonemes have a componential structure. This is why it was pointed out in Chapter 4 that stratificational representations like ^{P}/hdaygər/ were abbreviations. Each stratificational phoneme is a complex of one or more properties called phonons. Very little has been given in the way of illustration of these phonons, which evidently are intended as analogous to some kind of distinctive feature. We therefore cannot do better than to give as illustration one of the few examples which have ever been presented in such terms. I present the morphonic and phonemic representations given by Lamb (1946a:62) for the English sentence 'the man caught the tiger' (which ignores prosodic properties):

---

[4] In other words, the traditional use of phonetic-like symbols for morphophonemes is not at all merely mnemonic. It is representative of the truth that an element on this level has indirect phonetic meaning independently of language particular rules and is not simply an arbitrary symbol, as in stratificational ideas.

(5.7)

Morphemic (i.e.   ðə   m æ n   h g ɔ h d   ðə   h d a y g ə ɹ
string of
morphons)

Phonemic (i.e.
string of
bundles of
phonons)

Sp Vo Cl Lo Cl Uv Cl Lb Uv Cl Sp Vo Uv Cl Lo Hi Cl Vo Hi
Ap   Lb Fr Ap   Vo   Ap Ap   Ap Vo Fr
       Ns Vo Ns   Ac   Ac
          Ac

No explanation of these terms for features was given, but it is
no doubt safe to assume that they are abbreviations for the
following English terms:

Sp=Spirant   Lb=Labial   Ac=Accented??
Ap=Apical   Ns=Nasal   Uv=Unvoiced
Vo=Vowel   Lo=Low   Hi=High
Cl=Closed   Fr=Front

An enormous range of questions about the kind of representation involved in these componential notations has never been
answered, and almost nothing has been said explicitly about the
conditions they must meet, the primitive elements involved, etc.[5]
And this lack of explicit discussion is no doubt one important
cause of the basic equivocation we shall now examine. One can
see, however, that the phonons have as names terms which are
drawn from the stock of ordinary discrete (i.e. mentalistic)
phonetic properties. This fact is one aspect of the basic incoherence involved in the stratificational interpretation of the entities
of the phonemic stratum, an incoherence which is in one sense

---

[5] For exmple, are the phonons in a particular language drawn from a
universal set, as implied by the phonetic terms, or is each an ad hoc symbol
(this seems most likely)? It is evident that in the componential representation only the presence of a property is marked, i.e. /d/ is given as Closed
but /ð/ is not given as not Closed or Open. Is there some claim of asymmetry here (of the type made, for example, by current systematic phonemics
with its notions of Markedness)? (Cf. Chapter 8.) That is, what is the
justification for marking /d/ as Closed and leaving /ð/ unmarked rather
than marking /ð/ as Open and leaving /d/ unmarked for this, etc.?

similar to that involved in R. Jakobson's notions of distinctive feature. (See below.) For on the one hand, phonemes are being thought of as abstract complex symbols which are part of a discrete linguistic structure, and furthermore as symbols which are related to phonetic reality only by ad hoc language particular rules (as most notably with the Lamb-Hockett 'devoicers' above). In these terms it is not at all clear what functions the componential analysis of phonemes has. For the analysis into elements with phonetic-like names would appear to serve a function only if the phonemes were connected to phonetic reality by universal rules, and this is explicitly not allowed. In short, if a stratificational phoneme like English

$$\begin{bmatrix} \text{Cl} \\ \text{Ap} \\ \text{Ns} \end{bmatrix}$$

(traditional /n/) is an arbitrary entity related to phonetics only by special ad hoc rules of English, then the phonetic names of the components involve no linguistic claims and are completely mnemonic or notational. In other words, the phoneme might just as well be given as

$$\begin{bmatrix} 11 \\ 30 \\ 66 \end{bmatrix}$$

The use of phonetic names for the phonons tends to conceal the intended fact that, since there is no analogue of the Naturalness Condition between phonemic and phonetic structure, every phonon in every language must be specified ad hoc as being related to some phonetic property. In short the use of phonetic names tends to cover up the need for rules like (schematically):

(5.8)   Ns $\longrightarrow$ Nasalized.

However, rules like this latter make no sense for stratificational phonemics, and this is the second aspect of the incoherence. This is related to the fact that nowhere within stratificational writings is anything said explicitly about the relation between phonemic structure and allophonics. And this is the most crucial point. For obviously, as all modern linguists have agreed, it is necessary to specify the phonetic representatives or allophones of phonemic entities. But stratificational phonemics, again, rather like Jakobson's theory of distinctive features, is not really interested in this because it has confused the componential structure of phonemes with the distinct componential structure of phonetic entities, which officially the theory does not countenance ('outside of linguistic structure'). The confusion or equivocation consists at times of thinking of the sequences of bundles of phonons as the ultimate output of the grammar and as actual instructions to the vocal apparatus (i.e. as a discrete mentalistic phonetic system analogous to that which is the intended output of a systematic phonemic descrpition) and at times thinking of such sequences as a higher linguistic level than the phonetic with some detail of pronunciation removed and somehow 'predicted.' The former term of the equivocation is shown clearly by Gleason's remark (1964:78–79) that:

In one, the language apparatus has somehow generated a sequence of phonon bundles accordant with the phonotactics of the language. By some neurophysiological process the user produces a span of vocal sound which corresponds in some significant way to this phonemic structure. Considering this operation, the phonons can be thought of as 'commands' to the articulatory apparatus.

Another version of it is Hockett's claim (1965:200–201):

Another component of a generative grammar, called by Chomsky the 'phonology,' by Lamb the 'morphophonemics,' maps strings of morphons into successions of bundles of distinctive features (Lamb's phonons: PMP). Such arrays of distinctive features are the 'terminal strings' of the whole generative grammar.

To say, as Hockett does, that strings of phonemes are the terminal output of the whole grammar is just to say that allophonic description is not part of language and that the instructions to the vocal apparatus must be given by the strings of phonemes themselves. This is essentially what Gleason's comment asserts. But this view that the lowest level of language as a discrete combinatorial system is that of 'phonemes' with phonetics descriptive of only physical properties of one sort or another obviously makes no sense. Between the phonemic representation and actual

articulation there *must* stand some level of linguistic structure
just because the phonemic representation by definition does not
represent the phonetic variation or allophony which exists. Hence
it is impossible to transmit instructions to the speech apparatus
to 'pronounce' particular <u>phonemes</u> since these have diverse
realizations in distinct environments. This can be illustrated from
Lamb's example above. Both the [t$^\gamma$] of 'caught' and the phonetically quite different [t^h] of 'tiger' are given the phonemic representation

$$\text{/hd/} \left(\text{i.e.} \; \middle| \; \text{Uv} \; \middle| \; \begin{array}{c} \text{Cl} \\ \text{Ap} \end{array} \; \middle| \; \right)$$

by Lamb. Yet the instructions to pronounce here must be very
different, so that self-evidently the phonemic representation does
not provide enough information to serve as the instructional system for the speech apparatus. This is, in effect, to say nothing
more than that phonemic representations are not identical to
the most narrow phonetic representations. It follows that the
instructions to produce a certain sequence of articulatory gestures
must be given by some representation 'below' the 'phonemic'
and consisting exactly of the ideal articulatory 'intentions' which
mentalistic phonetic representation is intended to describe. In
other words, it is just exactly the function of the phonological
rules to derive from phonological representations, which are not
themselves directly descriptive of the ideally proper sequence of
articulatory movements, a representation which is. Incidentally,
it cannot be claimed here in defense of a position like Gleason's
above that the allophonic variation of a phoneme is uniquely
represented by a sufficiently long phonemic sequence. For this
still leaves totally unexplained how the speech apparatus is to
determine that in one language a phonemic sequence /ab/ is
to be pronounced say [ka] while in another language a phonemic
sequence /de/ is to be pronounced [ka]. In short, phonemic
sequences define allophonic variation *only in conjunction with
the set of phonological rules.* But these rules are unformulatable
unless they can have a discrete output. And the specification of
the set of such outputs is just the job of a theory of discrete,
mentalistic phonetic representation. It follows that the information
about how to pronounce phonemic sequences can only be provided by mapping the relatively abstract phonological repres-

sentations into phonetic transcriptions with direct, language-independent, articulatory meaning.

One can see an explicit contradiction between the incoherent view that the terminal representations of the grammar are strings of phonemes and other remarks when Lamb (1964b:108) says:

> By contrast, in the stratificational approach the phonetic distinctive features are not introduced in a generative description until the conversion from the phonemic stratum to the phonetic.

In fact we see several contradictions here. For on the one hand, contradicting other remarks that phonetics is a realm of physical continuity only, here Lamb asserts that phonetics is part of a (discrete) generative description and not simply a specification of the activity (and the resultant air disturbances) of the speech apparatus. And on the other hand, we are here told, contrary to other remarks such as those of Gleason and Hockett above, that the generative description ends not with the phonemic stratum but with the phonetic. In fact this is the only place I know where stratificational writings mention the term 'phonetic (distinctive) features,' and because of this one cannot even be sure that what is meant here is not the phonons. These contradictions cannot be passed off as simple disagreement between Lamb on the one side and Hockett and Gleason on the other, since Lamb's other remarks about phonetics being outside of linguistic structure and being a realm without the discrete properties of language proper agree precisely with the implications of Gleason's and Hockett's assertions.

We pointed out above that one aspect of the use of phonetic names for the nonphonetic phonons was the fact that this practice covered up the need, caused by the absence of an analogue of the Naturalness Condition which conflicts with fundamental stratificational doctrine, to map each phonon in each language onto some phonetic property. At this point, we can see another basis for the use of phonetic names for phonons, in the absence of any variant of the Naturalness Condition which would give this linguistic significance (of the kind which systematic phonemics obtains by utilizing features with the same names on both systematic and phonetic levels). The basis is simply the fundamental, pervasive, and unrecognized vacillation over whether the output of the grammar consists of discrete phonemic structures or discrete phonetic structures. In the latter case, the phonetic names seem to make sense except that the complexes of phonons actually given do not, even with their phonetic names, provide anything like enough detail to actually specify pronunciation instructions. In the former case, the phonetic names tend to partially conceal the fact that it is completely senseless to think of phonemic structures as providing pronunciation instructions, conceal it by making what are in fact phonetically arbitrary structures appear to have at least some direct phonetic meaning.

It was remarked above that the phonetic-phonemic incoherence in stratificational phonology is essentially similar to that found in Jakobson's approach to distinctive features. The basic confusion in the Jakobsonian version shows up most clearly in comparing the claims that, on the one hand, the distinctive features are all binary and, on the other, that these features have articulatory and acoustic characterizations and are just those relevant for phonetic description. Only a brief glance at the very small set of features countenanced by Jakobson is sufficient to show that these two claims are quite incompatible. For example, Jakobson recognizes only two features as relevant for describing front-back position in consonants, namely Grave and Compact (with Strident doing some limited work such as distinguishing the positions of $[\beta]$-$[f]$ and $[\theta]$-$[s]$, etc.) Maintenance of both the phonetic relevance and binary value views means that this theory embodies the claim that only four (or, including the minor Strident differences, eight) *phonetically* distinct positions of consonants exist in the languages of the world. But no one, certainly not a sophisticated and extremely widely experienced phonetician like Jakobson, is unaware of the fact that the number of actually distinct consonant positions is on the order of fourteen to sixteen. This shows that when making the claim of binarity Jakobson is not really thinking of the features as relevant for the description of phonetic detail, i.e. not thinking of them as the primitives of the narrowest phonetic representation required to give pronunciation instructions. The phonetic interpretation of the features only emerges when claims of physical definition are discussed.

These conclusions are strengthened by Jakobson's typical practice of grouping separate articulatory processes into one

feature in cases of complementation, i.e. his description of rounding, retroflexion, and pharyngealization with a single feature
Flat.[6] But this means that the level of Jakobsonian features is so
<u>gross</u> that it fails to distinguish for a segment *which one of these
distinct phonetic processes is involved*. It is thus self-evident that
a level of such features is quite incapable of serving as the system
of instructional phonetics. Jakobson's system is best interpreted
as involving a confusion between two sorts of features: phonetic
features whose values are not exclusively binary, which are the
primitives of a system for describing ideal pronunciation; and
systematic features, the binary projections of the right set of
phonetic features, which are relevant for the description of phonological structure. Put differently, Jakobson's theory can be looked
upon as embodying the Naturalness Condition in a very strong
but in part incoherent version, a version in which phonetic and
systematic features with their different functions are not kept
distinct. The difficulties are of course further compounded by
Jakobson's assumption that the binary features define autonomous
phonemes rather than systematic phonemes. This shows up very
badly in cases where, in order to maintain the binary claim plus
the assumption of autonomous conditions, he must posit new
features ad hoc (Sivertsen, 1958:491), although the contrasts
could be predicted if the richer environmental possibilities and
more abstract conception of systematic structure were substituted.

Although formally Jakobson's system involves a phonetic-
phonemic confusion of a type similar to that of stratificational
grammar, it should not be lost sight of that Jakobson's work with
respect to phonetic and phonemic structure has nonetheless made
an enormous and fundamental contribution to phonology of
exactly the sort which stratificational writings have failed to
make. In particular, it is Jakobson's work, rightly interpreted,
which of course provides the basis for the present systematic
formulation of the Naturalness Condition with its crucial assumption that systematic phonemes are bundles of features, with the
allowed features drawn from the binarizations of the class of

---

6 I would like to emphasize my own rejection of this practice and contrary assumption that each process requires a separate phonetic and phonological feature. The redundancy which Jakobson rightly noted can be handled
in quite different ways, namely, by universal rules for interpreting U markings as discussed in Chapter 8. For discussion cf. Postal (to appear c).

phonetic features required for pronunciation description. In addition, Jakobson's work has uncovered certain vital and hitherto ignored phonetic-phonemic features, such as most crucially Grave, Compact, Strident, Consonantal, which permit insightful and regular descriptions of a wide range of facts of an otherwise irregular and exceptional nature. This is not to say that some of his features which deviate from traditional phonetic practice (such as, in my opinion, those like Flat above, which group obviously distinct articulatory processes) are not mistaken.

The real and important flaws in Jakobson's phonological conception with its phonetic-phonemic confusion and assumption of autonomous structure should not lead one to overlook the crucial contributions it contains in addition. In comparing the Jakobsonian phonetic-phonemic confusion with that of current stratificational grammar, it is important to note the differing emphases. Basically, Jakobson thinks of the phonemic features as phonetic features, never grappling with the problems that his binarity assumption causes for phonetic description as such. Basically, stratificational grammar thinks of the phonemic features (phonons) as abstract entities with no direct phonetic meaning, only occasionally slipping into the assumption that they are phonetic. In short, basically Jakobson assumes that some version of a universal analogue to the Naturalness Condition is met and that phonetic structure narrowly constrains phonemic structure. Stratificational grammar, on the other hand, basically assumes that the phonetic-phonemic relation must be stated ad hoc for each language separately and that no such universal set of constraints given by phonetic structure exists. Therefore even though they embody a similar confusion with respect to phonetic-phonemic relations, the central emphasis of the two positions is very far apart. And obviously the older Jakobsonian position is much closer to linguistic reality. It is no accident then that it has led to an enormous range of highly productive studies and has finally served as part of the foundation for a theory which embodies its insights without many of its flaws.

The ultimate inadequacy of the stratificational view, sometimes maintained, that strings of phonemes are themselves the output of the generative description and the input to the speech apparatus (in a model of speech production) is that this is completely inconsistent both with the arbitrary, Naturalness

Condition violating analyses involving devoicing 'phonemes' like the /h/ proposed by Lamb for Russian, and by Lamb and Hockett for English, and with the 'linearity' ignoring principles of phonemicization which underlie them. For the whole point about these analyses, as we saw above, was that their phonetic consequences can in principle *only be determined by complex ad hoc rules*. But if, as on one term of the equivocation, the strings of phonemes are the output of the whole grammar, *then no such rules are possible*. Thus it would be completely impossible for a stratificational linguistic description to specify how representations like ᴾ/hydaygər/ are to be pronounced.

It is evident that the conceptual foundations of stratificational phonemics with respect to the relations between phonetic and phonemic structure are completely chaotic and inconsistent, and that the proponents of this view have involved themselves in a massive and undetected confusion between phonetic and phonemic structure. Underlying it all, I believe, is their attempt to maintain the typical modern American view that no level of discrete mentalistic phonetics exists as part of language structure. In Part II Chapter 14 we study in some detail the basis for such a view with respect to Hockett's attempt to construct a theory of sound change in conjunction with a rejection of mentalistic phonetics. The conceptual havoc which this official, though not consistently maintained, assumption of stratificational grammar causes is one further minor piece of evidence of its fundamentally mistaken character.

One can conclude from this discussion that the only consistent, coherent interpretation of stratificational phonology along the dimensions we have been discussing[7] is as follows. It recognizes three strata of phonologically relevant structure, morphonic, phonemic, and phonetic, each of which is a mentalistic system of discrete representations. The first consists of strings of unanalyzable morphons; the second of strings of phonemes, each of which is a complex of properties with no universal relations to phonetic properties; the third of strings of phonetic segments which are complexes with universal articulatory meaning, i.e.

---

[7] These are in fact quite limited in number. As further dimensions of phonological theory are investigated, the inadequacies of stratificational grammar expand far beyond those indicated thus far. For discussion cf. Chapters 6–9.

which serve as the instructional system for the speech apparatus. Furthermore, and as a matter of fundamental principle, there are no universal relations between morphonic strings and phonemic strings or between phonemic strings and phonetic ones. Every aspect of the two sets of interstratum mappings which are required must be stated ad hoc for particular languages. In other words, the arguments about unnecessary redundancies, etc., in Chapters 3 and 4 were not really sufficiently strong. In each argument it was assumed that there was only one set of arbitrary mappings while in fact there must be two. Hence, for example, given a phonetic segment in some language which enters into no allophonic or morphophonemic variation, it is nonetheless necessary to set up for it both a special morphon and a special phoneme and to give at least two rules, one to map the morphon onto the phoneme and another to map the phoneme onto the phonetic segment. Actually the latter would really be a set of rules for the different phonons of the phoneme, many of which would serve for other phonemes as well. Stated in this way, aspects of the theory are coherent. But the descriptions which such a theory requires are so burdened with redundant and linguistically useless and meaningless statements, so unable to take advantage of existing linguistic universals as discussed above, that the enthusiastic proposal of this view at this time cannot fail to strike one as especially peculiar.

Further inadequacies of stratificational phonology will be discussed in Chapter 6 where we deal with nonphonetic properties, in Chapter 7 where we deal with rule ordering, in Chapter 8 where we consider dictionary entries and the notions of markedness, and especially in Chapter 9. In the first part of this latter chapter we shall discuss another important feature of stratificational phonology, namely, its insistence that each stratum has its own tactical rules, showing that this assumption serves further to falsify this view. Finally, in the latter part of Chapter 9, it will be argued that the phenomenon of 'phonemic interchange,' which concerns the nontransitivity of contrast, further falsifies stratificational phonemics as it does other variants of autonomous phonemics which claim the existence of an intermediate level of structure between the morphophonemic and the phonetic.

6
NONPHONETIC PROPERTIES IN PHONOLOGY

BACKGROUND

In Chapter 4 we sketched certain aspects of systematic phonemic structure, aspects relating to representations in terms of a matrix which graphs systematic features against segments. It was insisted that the features were, with few exceptions, just those contained in the correct universal phonetic theory. In this framework, morphophonemes are, therefore, complexes of features, each feature the binary reflex of some phonetic property or else characteristic of a universal type of boundary. In the present chapter I should like to elaborate somewhat on the point, earlier made only in passing, that such a phonological matrix structure only *partially* specifies the total systematic phonemic representation. That is, in accordance with much traditional writing on phonology (such as that of Boas, cf. below), and in contrast with most modern ideas of morphophonemics, including especially current stratificational grammar, systematic phonemics insists that morphophonemic structure is by no means exhausted by the strings of morphophonemes.

The systematic phonemic representation involves not only the phonological matrix specifying properties determined by phonetics (hence in this chapter 'phonetic' properties) but also

114

properties provided by the output of the syntactic part of the grammar, that is, by the Surface Syntactic Structure. These properties include a categorization of the sentence into morphemes, words, phrases, etc., categorization of vocabulary items into various more or less ad hoc classes, and specifications of certain totally exceptional features of lexical items. Stratificational grammar explicitly denies such a claim and insists that morphophonemic structure is exhausted by strings of morphophonemes and that every morphophonemic rule has an environment defined exclusively over strings of morphophonemes. The complete untenability of this view is one of the points to be made briefly in the present chapter.

CATEGORIAL PROPERTIES

The 'nonphonetic' properties which are relevant for the phonology are of more than one type. The most widely discussed of these thus far are the <u>grammatical categories or branching constituents</u> present in the Surface Structures, i.e. elements like Noun, Verb, Noun Phrase, etc. For instance, the phonological structure of an English word like 'bookcover' is only partly given by a matrix of phonological features, even including those features which specify the word and morpheme boundaries. In addition, the Surface category information is relevant so that the structure is more nearly given by a representation like

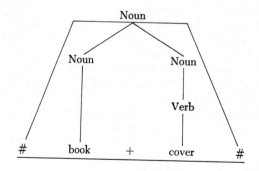

(6.1)

where the last or bottom line is an abbreviation for the appropriate feature matrix.

The reason for insisting on incorporating categorial properties in phonological structure is quite simple. There are some phonological rules whose environments are partly defined by such properties. In English, for example, the rules of stress assignment are largely of this character (Halle and Chomsky, to appear). The relevance of grammatical category to phonological rules is not a new discovery, but was something of a commonplace in pre-modern linguistics. For some discussion of examples of category reference in the phonological approach of Boas and his associates, cf. Postal (1964a). This is something which modern pre-generative or taxonomic linguistics has largely forgotten.

It will be worth illustrating here some very simple examples of the kind which cannot be handled without rules which take account of categorial structure, i.e. examples of the kind stratificational phonology in effect claims cannot exist. We shall consider two from Mohawk.

In this language no <u>Verb</u> may have less than two vowels in its phonetic representation. If at a certain, not very late) point in derivations a sequence which is a Verb has only one vowel in its representation, a segment identical to systematic <u>i</u> is added initially. Thus consider the following partial paradigms based on stems <u>k/ek</u> 'to eat' and <u>kʌ</u> 'to see':

(6.2)	[i'deneks]	'you 1 and I eat it'	t+ni+ek+s
(6.3)	[i'dewaks]	'you ≧ 2 and I eat it'	t+wa+k+s
(6.4)	[i':zeks]	'you 1 eat it'	s+ek+s
(6.5)	[i'zeneks]	'you 2 eat it'	s+ni+ek+s
(6.6)	[i'zewaks]	'you ≧ 3 eat it'	s+wa+k+s
(6.7)	[i':geks]	'I eat it'	k+ek+s
(6.8)	[ya'geneks]	'someone and I eat it'	ya+k+ni+ek+s
(6.9)	[ya'gwaks]	'they and I eat it'	ya+k+wa+k+s
(6.10)	[deni':gʌs]	'you 1 and I see her'	t+ni+kʌ+s
(6.11)	[dewa':gʌs]	'you ≧ 2 and I see her'	t+wa+kʌ+s
(6.12)	[i'sgʌs]	'you 1 see her'	s+kʌ+s
(6.13)	[zeni':gʌs]	'you 2 see her'	s+ni+kʌ+s
(6.14)	[zewa':gʌs]	'you ≧ 3 see her'	s+wa+kʌ+s
(6.15)	[i'kgʌs]	'I see her'	k+kʌ+s
(6.16)	[yageni':gʌs]	'someone and I see her'	ya+k+ni+kʌ+s
(6.17)	[yagwa':gʌs]	'they and I see her'	ya+k+wa+kʌ+s

In each case where the systematic representation contains only one vowel, an [i] is added in the phonetic representation. Such a vowel is also added in (6.2) and (6.5) because at the point where the [i] insertion rule is applied only one vowel is present. That is, in these cases the systematic representation has one vowel in front of another, but the first is dropped by the vowel dropping rule. This rule must precede the [i] insertion rule, a fact which guarantees the phonetic regularity that each verb has at least two vowels. It should also be noted that those [e] which occur between true consonants and sonorant nonvowels are epenthetic, and the rule for this epenthesis also follows the [i] insertion rule. Hence these epenthetic vowels do not count when determining if a verb contains more than one vowel. These rule orderings are discussed in Chapter 7.

It is quite crucial, however, that the rule of [i] insertion can only be stated in terms of the category Verb, since many Mohawk words which are not verbs contain only one vowel, for example [ya'h] 'not,' [nok] 'and, but,' etc. In a system like the stratificational, such a rule is therefore impossible. It is not at all clear how such a view would handle even this maximally simple case of category reference. Perhaps special allomorphs of the prefix morphemes would be set up. That is, the morphophonemic representation of a form like [i'zewaks] would be given as is+wa+k+s, where 'is' is now a new allomorph of the second person morpheme. There is obvious redundancy and loss of generalization involved in giving in a list facts which can be predicted by rule. Such multiple base forms with i would be required for several morphemes including second person, first person, inclusive person, masculine, feminine, and zoic. The linguistic inadequacy of this allomorphic listing approach to alternations is discussed at some length in the first part of Chapter 8. But the deeper point *here* is that choice of allomorphs must still be given in terms of vowel count and the category Verb since the various person and gender elements also occur in nouns. Therefore, even setting up new allomorphs like 'is,' etc. does not avoid the consequence that the morphophonemic rules must appeal to categorial properties. In fact, even in this most simple case, I do not see any way whatever to avoid this without adding a number of ad hoc rules and elements.

For example, a stratificational phonologist might posit a

special morphophoneme and associate this with the beginning of the representation of every verb, but not other forms. Since morphophonemes are ad hoc symbols in this system, this is possible. Then the rule of [i] insertion could be stated in terms of strings of morphophonemes alone. However, both the rule to add this special morphophoneme and the rule to delete it are otherwise completely useless and redundant. This structure is completely unjustifiable and serves only to avoid categorial reference. On the other hand, the rule stated in systematic phonemics appeals only to structure which the overall grammar must assign in any event, namely, the appropriate systematic matrices and categorial properties like Verb.

A similar case in this language arises from the fact that there are morphemes zoic, feminine, and objective with respective base shapes which include wa, yaka, and wa. These can occur initially in both nouns and verbs. But in nouns the phonetic representations are without the initial glides which are present in verb realizations. The natural way to handle this is with a rule referring to the constituent characterization which is independently assigned by the syntax. In short: word initial glides drop in nouns. But the transformational[1] rule schematically stated here is impossible in the stratificational system. Again, the stratificational approach would be forced to some ad hoc and complex alternative involving special allomorphs, ad hoc morphophonemes, and special rules.

Quite clearly, the stratificational rejection of phonological or morphophonemic rules which refer to Surface constituents is, even on the basis of these trivially *simple* cases, among the clearest evidence of the extent to which this theory fails to be descriptive of human language. When complex cases involving grammatical category such as those involved in the large set of cyclically ordered rules which assign English stress (cf. Halle and Chomsky, to appear) or Japanese intonation (McCawley,

---

[1] The rule is transformational in the sense that its domain is defined not by a string of symbols but by a phrase marker or set of strings which provides a labelled bracketing of the terminal string of morphophonemic symbols. One of the reasons stratificational phonology cannot allow rules which refer to Surface grammatical categories is an apparently a priori decision that all linguistic rules must operate exclusively on single strings. Hence transformational rules are excluded.

1965), etc. are considered, this conclusion is strengthened almost without limit.[2] It is rather significant, I believe, that in the course of making extraordinary claims for the adequacy of stratificational phonology, stratificational writers have failed to discuss any such cases.

FEATURE PROPERTIES

Not all syntactic properties are represented by constituents. Such 'selectional' properties as Animate, Human, Count, etc. are evidently of a quite different nature and will be represented in the syntactic structures of a generative grammar as <u>syntactic features</u> (for discussion and justification of this kind of syntactic structure cf. Chomsky, 1965). Such features are also relevant for phonological rules in many, perhaps all, languages. However, in considering syntactic features it is necessary to distinguish at least two fundamentally different kinds. On the one hand there are syntactic features which play an independent role in the syntax, that is, are relevant for syntactic rules. Such a feature in English is Pro, associated with nouns like 'one,' 'thing,' 'it', etc. This feature is relevant for many syntactic rules and it also serves as partial environment for the stress shifts and reductions which account for the differences between sentences like:

(6.18) I saw Mars

in which <u>saw</u> is not as strongly stressed as <u>Mars</u>, and those like:

(6.19) I saw it

in which the verb is more strongly stressed than the object. Similarly, in Mohawk it is such syntactically relevant features as Animate, Human, etc. which partially define the environment for the rule of reduplication (which yields forms like [gwe'sgwes] 'pig,' [gi'tgit] 'chicken,' etc.). That is, reduplication is possible

---

[2] It is at least conceivable that simple cases of category reference such as those discussed in the text can in fact be described by a sufficiently complex and ad hoc statement without category reference. But for complex cases involving cyclical application of rules with category reference this is out of the question. This is argued in McCawley (1965b).

in a subset of [+Animate, −Human] nouns.

On the other hand, however, there are syntactic features which are not independently required or justified by the syntax, features only relevant to the phonology. These are the features which determine divisions of the vocabulary, divisions often corresponding to distinct historical sources of the vocabulary. It may seem confusing to speak of such features as 'syntactic.' Let us therefore introduce the special terminology of <u>morphological feature</u> for such elements. It must be noted, however, that such features share certain properties with independently justifiable syntactic features. Like such syntactically relevant properties as Animate, Count, etc., the properties I am now referring to are properties of entire morphemes, not of individual phonological segments of them. Furthermore, all such properties can apparently be treated as indicating membership or not in categories, so that a +, − notation is feasible for both sorts. Finally, the fact that both must be referred to in the same kinds of phonological rules is a relevant similarity.

The fact that morphological features are not independently required by the syntactic rules raises very important questions as to why they are recognized or posited by the current theory of systematic phonemics. In discussing categorial properties like Noun, Verb Phrase, etc., or properties like Animate, Pro, etc., which are relevant for the statement of the phonology, one can criticize a theory like stratificational phonemics for not making use of structure which the syntax necessarily assigns and which is thus available for the phonological component of the grammar if it is properly formulated. That is, a theory like stratificational phonology is wrongly forced to set up special morphophonemes, allomorphs, or both, just to avoid reference to structural information which must be present in the structural description regardless of how the phonology is formulated. And this structural information is in fact necessarily one to one associated with the ad hoc morphophonemes or other apparatus required. But no such argument can be given in the case of morphological features, which are not justifiable independently of the phonology.

The question is, therefore, why should morphological features be allowed instead of the alternative of stating all alternations and differential behavior not explicable in terms of independently justified Surface Syntactic Structure (either features or categories) in terms of differential strings of morpho-phonemes?

Let us make this question more concrete. In Mohawk, stress is, for most words (in fact for an infinite class of words), correctly assigned in large part by a rule which accents the penultimate vowel in a word, where 'penultimate' is defined over a representation derived from the systematic phonological matrix by independently justified rules (like the rule mentioned above which drops a vowel before another vowel). However, there is a class of a few dozen words, almost all of them French borrowings, which have final stress. An example is [razo's] 'gravy.' On all other grounds but stress placement, one would assign such a form the systematic phonological matrix we can abbreviate as #rasos#. But this predicts penultimate stress. The question is, must such a form be assigned a different phonological matrix, or can the phonological matrix be given as above with the form differentiated from penultimate stressed forms by morphological features? In other words, can the vocabulary be divided into subparts with morphological features and can separate stress rules be recognized which have domains partially determined by these morphological divisions? Current systematic phonemic theory insists that the recognition of *syntactically* unjustified morphological features which divide the vocabulary is right in such cases, and assignment of contrastive phonological matrices (morphophonemes) is wrong. What is the justification?

The answer to this is rather easily seen in the Mohawk example we have chosen. Its general basis lies in the Naturalness Condition. Suppose one *were* to attempt to differentiate final stressed words from penultimate stressed words in Mohawk in terms of their phonological feature matrices. How would one do it? Remembering that the phonological matrices are systematically related to phonetic form, it is clear that there is no non-arbitrary assignment of phonological matrix structure which will serve to differentiate the two classes of forms.[3] One could, of

---

[3] It should be emphasized that marking vowels in the dictionary with the feature Stress itself is quite out of the question. No vowel in any morpheme in the language is inherently either stressed or not. This is completely a function of position in the *word* and is hence determined by the morphological structure of the infinite class of words of the language. Stress must therefore be assigned by rules of some kind. Cf. later discussion.

course, assign all vowels in French words [+Pharyngealized] vowels, all vowels in native forms [−Pharyngealized] vowels, and then define the stress rule over the feature of Pharyngealization. But such an assignment of structure is entirely ad hoc and without independent motivation. In addition to complicating the phonological representations of all vowels, it requires a special rule to switch the French vowels back to [−Pharyngealized]. Furthermore, and most crucially, the choice of feature here is totally arbitrary. One could just as well have picked Rising Tone, or Tense, etc. In short, these are really cases where the phonological rules require a structural differentiation of forms given neither by independently generated syntactic properties nor by the phonological matrices which are justifiably assigned in terms of the phonetic and *general* morphophonemic properties of the language. These are cases, in other words, of arbitrary and ad hoc (but not completely as will be seen below) categorizations of forms.

But now we are in a position to see exactly why it is a mistake to represent phonological differences like that between Mohawk final and penultimate stressed words in the same way as one represents such differences as, for example, that between Mohawk words with [t] and [s]. Representing such contrasts in the same way asserts that they are the same kind of contrast. But this is not the case. The latter is one in which the choice of phonological matrix structure is not at all arbitrary and is given by a host of completely general phonetic and morphophonemic facts. In the former, the choice would be arbitrary. Therefore, to represent this kind of difference within linguistic theory, systematic phonemics recognizes two different kinds of apparatus. Phonological matrices, that kind of structure discussed at length earlier in connection with our specification of the Naturalness Condition, represent those phonological properties of forms which are systematically related to phonetics in terms of general and independently justifiable structures. But there are relatively ad hoc and arbitrary divisions of forms which have phonological relevance, and these are represented by morphological features.

An important empirical claim involved in such a differentiation should be stressed. Phonological features are only properties of *segments of morphemes*, but morphological features are properties of *morphemes as a whole*. In other words, the claim is being made that all such relatively arbitrary divisions in the vocabulary can be given by dividing morphemes into subsets and without providing subanalyses of *parts* of morphemes. In Mohawk, morphemes are marked [+Native] or [−Native] in the lexicon, but individual segments are not. Or to put it another way, every segment in a morpheme must have the same value for any morphological feature. That is, the claim is made that the reduction in the number of features which is achieved by recognizing only single feature specifications over whole morphemes, as against many feature specifications for the individual segments of morphemes (as implied in the ad hoc Pharyngealization approach to Mohawk final stressed forms and all analogous cases) will never fail. Such a reduction can succeed because, although both terms of the structural differences represented by phonological features may appear within the same morpheme, this is not the case with differences represented by morphological features. Hence the same morpheme in Mohawk may contain both [t] and [s]. But no morpheme may undergo both the penultimate and final stress rules, if this contrast is represented, as I have claimed, in terms of morphological features. Notice that this is by no means a logical necessity. It is quite possible, logically, that the French words might, for example, have had *two* strong stressed vowels, one penultimate and one final. The empirical fact that this is not the case is an important piece of evidence confirming the whole-morpheme versus individual-segment distinction being claimed. An approach like stratificational grammar which represents all alternations in terms of segmental morphophonemes thus necessarily misses the generalization involved here. The descriptions it allows must provide useless *segmental* distinctions. Important evidence showing the mistake of representing all morphophonemic properties as properties of particular segments is provided by the phenomenon of vowel harmony. Cf. the discussion at the end of Chapter 8.

Another important formal advantage ensues from the recognition of morphological features and their use in place of arbitrary phonological feature contrasts. Because of the Naturalness Condition, use of ad hoc phonological matrices like those including [+Pharyngealized] vowels for Mohawk final stressed words requires special language-particular rules to eliminate the [+Pharyngealized] markings which do not exist phonetically, after they have served for the relevant rule differentiations. However, in positing morphological features, no such rules are required in particular grammars, because it is a general fact, statable within linguistic theory, that morphological features, like independently justifiable syntactic features, have as such no phonetic consequences. Hence if we assign a morpheme like Mohawk [razo's] the morphological features [−Native, +French], in contrast to a native morpheme which is assigned [+Native], or to an English borrowing which is assigned [−Native, −French], no special Mohawk rules are needed to avoid erroneous phonetic consequences. Therefore the recognition of morphological features permits the elimination of all such ad hoc rules from the grammars of individual languages and their replacement by a general principle within linguistic theory. But the entire goal of linguistic theory is to incorporate general principles which permit the elimination of ad hoc features from particular grammars. The ad hoc character of rules like that which would be needed to eliminate [+Pharyngealized] in Mohawk and the absence of any basis for choice of the phonological differences on which they are based is straightforward indication of the mistake of representing arbitrary vocabularly divisions with contrastive phonological matrices. For this claims in effect that such divisions require special phonological correction rules in individual languages, and this is not the case.

What is really being said above is that there are, at least in the majority of languages, important *limitations on the scope of the structure determined by the Naturalness Condition.* This condition claims, in effect, that the systematic phonemic representation of forms is a function of phonetic facts, independently justified syntactic and morphophonemic facts, and the general rules of the language these require. But this is not entirely the case. There are, in a vast number of languages, arbitrary divisions of forms with respect to their behavior under some phonological rules. That is, many rules are valid not for the vocabulary as a whole or for independently characterized subsegments of it, but only for largely arbitrary subportions. This fact cannot be avoided. However, in view of the enormous contribution of the Naturalness Condition, the vast savings which it permits in every description, the phonological universals for which it provides the basis, its role in providing insight into language learning, etc., it is necessary to represent this fact of arbitrary limitation on phonological rules while still maintaining this condition. This can be done by allowing morphological features, that is, properties of morphemes as a whole, whose function is to delineate those classes of items which behave specially under various rules, where this is necessary. It is important to emphasize, however, that the arbitrary divisions represented by morphological features are in every language in the minority. That is, if one considers the entire class of rules in the phonology and the behavior of every morpheme under all relevant rules, then most of the behavior of most morphemes is correctly predicted by the phonological feature matrices of the phonetic forms determined by the Naturalness Condition in connection with simplicity considerations. It is only a small portion of this behavior which is unpredictable in such terms and which requires positing of morphological features. Hence it is important not to exaggerate the extent to which phonological structure is phonetically arbitrary. For discussions of actual cases involving morphological features in English, French, Russian, Japanese, Mohawk, and Spanish, cf. Halle and Chomsky (to appear), Schane (1965), Lightner (1965), McCawley (1965), Postal (to appear c), and Foley (1965), respectively.

We can then underline another error of stratificational grammar or any other theory which allows no equivalent of morphological features and which attempts to handle all differential morphophonemic behavior in terms of special morphophonemes. Such theories mistakenly fail to distinguish those aspects of systematic representation which are naturally related to phonetic form from those aspects which are not. By insisting on representing all alternations with atomic, phonetically arbitrary morphophonemes, such theories claim in effect that all alternations are linguistically of the same character. That is, they cannot represent the difference between a phonetically nonarbitrary morphophonemic contrast like [t]-[s] in Mohawk and one like the phonetically arbitrary contrast between penultimate and final stressed words. Such theories thus fail to explain why the latter types of contrast cannot occur in the same morpheme while the former can, and why contrasts of the latter type are much more difficult to learn.

Independent evidence of the validity of the distinction drawn by systematic phonemics but ignored by stratificational phonology is, of course, provided by the fact that the morphological divisions generally correspond largely, though seldom entirely, to the historical origin of the forms. In other words, morphological features are largely a synchronic representation of the fact that vocabulary may be borrowed and that when languages borrow large bodies of vocabulary they very often borrow nonnative phonological matrices and/or phonological rules along with them. Thus Mohawk has not only borrowed several dozen French words, *it has also borrowed a rule of final stress*. Similarly, at the beginning of this millennium English not only borrowed a number of French words but also their Latin stress rule along with them.[4] Hence there is a good historical and sociolinguistic reason why there should be arbitrary divisions of vocabulary, divisions not given by the Naturalness Condition. These distinctions are largely the synchronic residue of past historical contact between languages.[5]

An independent justification for morphological features comes from the fact that apparatus of just this type is required in many languages to indicate which inflectional pattern a particular stem falls into, i.e. to handle phenomena like 'conjugation classes.' In such cases, the shapes of particular inflectional elements fall into mutually exclusive sets, and which shape a stem takes is at least partially unpredictable in terms of independently motivated syntactic and phonological properties of the stem. For example, in Mohawk the aspect suffixes yield a conjugation class structure with the shape of serial and perfective aspects determined lexically. Verb stems must be marked in the lexicon to indicate the particular shape of perfective or serial with which they may occur. These divisions of stems into inflection-shape classes seem exactly analogous to the divisions of the vocabulary required for more general phonological rules. The relation between divi-

---

[4] And most crucially, this rule was generalized beyond the words of French origin to ultimately apply even to Germanic vocabulary. Cf. Keyser and Halle (to appear); Halle and Chomsky (to appear).

[5] This contact is not always of the direct, person-to-person kind. Many morphological divisions are a function of the borrowing of 'learned' vocabulary at least partly through writing systems. This is, for example, true of the 'erudite'-'nonerudite' distinction in Spanish (Foley, 1965).

sions required on inflectional grounds and those we have spoken of previously is brought out even further by the fact that in some cases choice of inflectional form is *partially* determined by the independently required phonological form of the stem. (It is evidently a linguistic universal not yet precisely built into linguistic theory that the shapes of lexical morphemes may, in part, determine those of grammatical morphemes but not vice versa.) For example, in Mohawk the choice of serial aspect shapes s̲ versus ha̲ʔ is in general unpredictable from the form of the stem. But apparently all stems ending with p̲ take ha̲ʔ. Hence this fact need not be listed for each stem in the dictionary. Rather, there is a redundancy rule which predicts the + value of the morphological feature determining the ha̲ʔ shape in terms of stem final p̲.

Less clear is the role which morphological features may play in the description of the combinatorial facts of derivational morphology, i.e. of such facts as that there is English telephone, telegraph, telegram, photograph but not *phonophone, *phonogram. Since there is no serious proposal about how such facts are to be described, no conclusions can be drawn. But that morphological features must play a role in determining the *shape* of derivational morphemes is quite clear on the same kind of grounds as for inflectional ones. Thus in English some verbs take the nominalizer tion (detention), some ment (development), some al (recital), some null (win), etc. in a generally unpredictable way so that vocabulary divisions are required.

While there are a host of important questions which remain open about the description of these derivational and inflectional alternation facts, it is clear that they both involve vocabulary divisions essentially identical to those required for the prediction of such phonological facts as final stress in Mohawk French borrowings, or softening of stop consonants to [s]-[š] before systematically front vowels in parts of the English vocabulary. Such facts justify the utilization of morphological features for the latter tasks by showing that such apparatus is required by linguistic theory in any event.

Stratificational phonemics, with its insistence that morphophonemic structure is exhausted by a string of morphophonemes, shares the general assumption of autonomous phonemics that the entire vocabulary of a language must be treated homogeneously. Since it is clear that many morphophonemic and phonological rules have domains limited by synchronically arbitrary divisions of the vocabulary, this is an obvious error. The failure of stratificational phonemics to avoid this mistake is another indication that it in no way can be taken as a theory which 'saves' autonomous phonemics, and is another indication of the exceptional degree to which it deviates from known linguistic reality.

We have discussed morphophological features, and 'nonphonetic' properties generally, in very informal terms. We have not specified such structures explicitly nor indicated how phonological rules are to take account of them. These are important and interesting topics which are, however, highly complex and technical. For discussion cf. Halle and Chomsky (to appear), Postal (to appear c). I would, however, briefly like to indicate here how morphological features, as well as the exception features discussed in the section following, are in part to be handled. A dictionary entry for a morpheme consists of an association of three basic kinds of properties: semantic, syntactic, and phonological. For discussion cf. the first part of Chapter 8. Morphological features are a subtype of syntactic properties, features of the whole morpheme. Phonological properties, on the other hand, are features of individual segments of a multisegment matrix. Chomsky has proposed, however, that phonological rules can take account of morphological and syntactic features in a very natural way. It is only necessary to assume that at the beginning of the phonology each (or more likely some well-characterized subset) syntactic and morphological feature of a morpheme $\underline{m}$ is assigned to every phonological segment of $\underline{m}$. Thus all segments of the same morpheme will necessarily be marked with the same value for each morphological and syntactic feature. This 'projection' of grammatical features into the phonological segments embodies the claim that such features are features of whole morphemes in terms of the assumption that each segment receives the same value for all such features. Under this assumption, phonological rules which take account of syntactic and morphological features need have no difference in form from those which refer to phonological features. That is, we can now formulate a stress rule for the final vowels of French forms in Mohawk essentially as follows.

$$(6.20) \quad \begin{bmatrix} -\text{Consonantal} \\ +\text{Sonorant} \\ -\text{Native} \\ +\text{French} \end{bmatrix} \longrightarrow [+\text{Stress}] \text{ in } - \left\{ \begin{matrix} +\text{Consonantal} \\ -\text{Sonorant} \end{matrix} \right\}_0^n \#$$

And such a rule can only apply to the final vowel of morphemes which are morphologically [−Native, +French], since only these will have these features 'projected' to their final vowels. The crucial point here is that this suggestion of Chomsky's shows how very natural is the functioning of morphological features in phonology. The relevance of such properties in fact requires no changes or complications of the phonological rules at all. These are exactly the same in form as they would be if morphological features played no role in determining the pronunciation of sentences. Without going into details, I note that exception features of the type discussed immediately below are also properties of whole morphemes and are similarly projected to each phonological segment of the morpheme. This incorporates the claim, suggested by M. Halle, that one will never find a morpheme part of which is exceptional with respect to a rule but another part not.

EXCEPTION PROPERTIES

In considering morphological features it was claimed that they represent largely, though not completely, arbitrary divisions of the vocabulary with respect to behavior under phonological rules. No content was, however, given to this claim of 'largely though not completely.' Our intention is, however, to draw a very important distinction between morphological features which do not involve totally arbitrary divisions and exception features which we shall claim do involve such divisions. The distinction has to do with the fact that morphological features mark vocabulary divisions which are relevant for predicting the behavior of morphemes under *several* phonological rules. This is illustrated by the example of Mohawk final stressed forms.

The morphological divisions given by the features Native

and French are relevant for several rules. First of all, these features are relevant for the two stress rules. That is, [−Native, +French] predicts not only the *application* of the final stress rule but also the *nonapplication* of the penultimate stress rule, while [+Native] predicts the opposite. As pointed out earlier, these two facts are logically independent.[6] Furthermore, there are other properties of the final stressed forms which have not been mentioned. For example, unlike the native forms, these may contain the labial consonants [m], [b], [p], so that special behavior under several rules involving phonological feature constraints is represented by the morphological features. In other words, morphological features are not quite as ad hoc as might have appeared at first, because they are posited not for special behavior under a single rule but for correlated special behavior under a number of rules. The chief fact here is that a class of morphemes which behaves in a unique way under rule j also behaves specially under rules k, l, etc.

It is logically possible, however, that there could exist completely isolated behavior of single morphemes, i.e. special behavior of a morpheme under a single rule, behavior correlated with no other properties. A hypothetical example would be a Mohawk native word which received no stress whatever on its penultimate vowel (and also none on the final vowel). Notice that such a case would involve special behavior under a single rule. However, one need not be content with hypothetical examples since real cases are found in abundance. These are of two formally different kinds. On the one hand, there are cases in which the application of a rule is predicted by the otherwise motivated phonological matrices and independently assigned syntactic structure *but the rule does not apply*. On the the other hand, there are cases where the nonapplication of a rule is predicted *but the rule does apply*. A Mohawk case of the latter sort derives from a rule which turns a palatal fricative (itself derived by previous rules from systematic s (+)y) into a dental affricate (essentially [dz]) *except after h*. But there are a handful

---

[6] Real examples illustrating the distinction can be found. For example, it is an ad hoc fact about some native Mohawk particles, but not all, that they simply do not take the stress. Hence while these fail to undergo one stress rule they have no special rule of stress associated with them. They are simply exceptions of the type discussed later.

of morphemes which undergo the switch to [dz] even though an h̲ precedes. An example is [ohdza':naʔ] 'hand, palm' which, if regular, would be *[ohša':naʔ]. Cases of the *former* sort seem much more frequent. An example is given by violations of the Mohawk rule which turns a stressed vowel followed by a glottal stop to a falling tone vowel and defines the environment for another rule which deletes the glottal stop. There are a handful of morphemes which do not undergo this rule, one of which is yo̲ʔtʌ 'to work.' Thus one finds [royo'ʔdeʔ] 'he works' instead of the predicted but impossible *[royô':deʔ].

Such cases are to be handled, it is claimed, by some version of an extremely insightful device suggested by Chomsky (unpublished). Namely, it is necessary to recognize morphological features (features of whole morphemes not of segments) which refer directly to the applicability and application of individual phonological rules. By using such features one makes such remarks about morphemes as 'although the application of rule k̲ is predicted in context U, no segment of this morpheme can̲ undergo k̲ in U,' and 'although the nonapplication of rule k̲ is predicted̲ in context U, relevant segments of this morpheme under k̲ in U.' Exactly how to formalize such features and how to construct̲ the formalism of phonological rules to take advantage of them is a highly technical topic and one far from completely understood. We shall not go into it further here (cf. Halle and Chomsky, to appear; Postal, to appear c). It is worth noting that special behavior of a completely exceptional sort is also found with respect to the transformational rules of the syntax. Here also it appears that features of morphemes which refer to the applicability and application of particular grammatical rules will be required.

It is important to specify much more precisely than we have yet done, formal differentia of morphological features and exception features. Thus far they have been distinguished only rather vaguely in terms of relevance for a single rule versus relevance for several. I suspect, however, that one may in addition say at least the following. Morphological features may serve as (partial) environments for phonological rules, i.e. they may actually be mentioned in such rules. Exception features may not. For example, about half of the final stressed forms in Mohawk begin with a sequence [ra], residue of the old French article la̲.

It seemes correct to treat this as partially predictable by setting up a morphological feature, let us call it L, and predicting these occurrences of [ra] in terms of [+L] by a prefix rule. But while [−L] is unpredictable in [+French] morphemes (i.e. within this class there is a contrast), it is predictable in [−French] and [+Native] ones, which are all [−L]. In other words, the [ra] prefix rule is relevant only to a subset of [−Native, +French] morphemes. [+French] morphemes will therefore be listed with some value of the feature L, but all others need not be since the value can be predicted by a redundancy rule in the dictionary. But exception features cannot be part of the environments of any such redundancy rules. The assumption is that, while morphological features in general may predict other lexically relevant properties, exception features cannot.

It is, however, apparently necessary to allow redundancy rules which predict exception features in terms of other kinds of dictionary features, and also phonological rules which predict exception features in terms of phonological matrices. The Mohawk rule that word final stops drop in nouns is not applicable in reduplicating animal names. The morphological structure which determines the reduplication rule thus also predicts the exceptional behavior under final stop truncation. In fact, both the application of the reduplication rule and the nonapplication of the stop truncation rule involve exception features, since the former is a rule which in general does not apply. This one small class of forms thus illustrates both general types of exception: failure of application when the normal situation is for the rule to apply, and application when the normal situation is for the rule not to apply.

Prediction of exception features by phonological rules is necessary to formalize statements which in ordinary language would involve the terminology 'except in the environment X.' Thus in Mohawk all consonants are voiced before a vowel except for the single segment [š]. Use of the device of predicting exception features from phonological matrices permits the voicing rule to be perfectly general with the special fact handled by its own highly restricted rule. The exceptional property here cannot be handled by redundancy rules in the dictionary because [š] is not present in the dictionary. Rather, it is derived by previous phonological rules from the systematic sequence <u>s(+)y</u> (and the y̱ may be epenthetic and not from the dictionary). It has been suggested by Halle and Chomsky (to appear) that phonological rules which specify exception features can be strictly limited to predicting exceptional behavior with respect to the very next rule in the ordering. But this claim seems to me incompatible with one of the most interesting supports for such rules. Namely, one finds cases where 'except in the environment X' statements can be removed from two or more different rules. Thus in Mohawk an epenthetic [y] is inserted between s̱ and following i̱ except when ẖ precedes the s̱. Similarly, [š] becomes a dental affricate except when preceded by ẖ. Here then is a case where a single rule can predict nonapplication of two other rules in the environment ẖ. The two rules are, it should be noted, necessarily not contiguous in the ordering. Between them must lie the general consonant+y̱ mutation rule which in fact derives the instances of [š] which are relevant for the second rule and derives them from sequences which include those s̱y̱ produced by the first rule. Proper constraints on such rules must, it seems to me, therefore be regarded as unclear.

The fact that some instances of exceptionality are partially predictable by rules does not alter the basic fact that the chief function of exception features is to indicate completely unpredictable properties of morphemes in the dictionary, properties which predict nothing and which are correlated with nothing.

One should investigate the possibility of giving an even stronger characterization of morphological features in terms of relations between those subcategorizations of morphemes given by the set of morphological features and the set of phonological rules. The strongest requirement here would be to insist that every such subclass have at least one phonological rule defined over it. This condition is met by some of the vocabulary divisions discussed for Mohawk. Thus [+Native] forms involve at least rules which exclude [p], [b], [m]; [−Native, +French] forms involve the final stress rule. However, [−Native, −French] forms, i.e. English borrowings, do not seem to involve any special rules since they have the penultimate stress of native forms. Thus this condition is too strong. But it is suggestive, and perhaps some weaker variant along the same lines will add further content to the notion 'morphological feature.' For example, perhaps one can only require that those subdivisions defined by positive values of morphological features have rules uniquely associated with them. Such a constraint would indicate that the choice between features like Native and Foreign is not merely notational.

There is an additional difference between morphological and exception features which does, however, not bear upon whether a particular phenomenon is to be described with one or the other. Namely, linguistic theory defines an exception feature for every phonological rule so that in a sense these features are partial universals. Morphological features are, on the other hand, largely particular to individual languages. In other words, the class of exception features in a language is determined completely by the class of phonological rules of that language, but the class of morphological features is subject to no such constraints. It goes without saying that the terminology of French, English, Native,[7] etc. is simply mnemonic and has no cross-linguistic significance. As has been emphasized several times, morphological feature divisions do not correspond *completely* to historical antecedents. Thus the Mohawk form for 'cat,' [dago's], has final stress and must today be represented as [−Native, +French]. But this is certainly not a French borrowing.

In view of the differential arbitrariness of exception features and morphological features, and of morphological features and phonological features, it seems incorrect to consider them on a

---

[7] A feature like Native is quite possibly an exception to this ad hoc character of morphological features. It is likely, I think, that the Native-non-Native distinction is universal. Furthermore, in terms of the notions of Marked and Unmarked discussed in Chapter 8, it is probably right that [+Native] forms are Unmarked and [−Native] ones Marked. Since only Marked values have a cost, only the borrowed vocabulary will require specifications with expense. In other words, the assumption would be that unless a special remark is made about a morpheme it is [+Native]. Additional content would be given to the notion of Native by assuming again that, unless a special remark is made, all rules apply to [+Native] forms (and possibly fail to apply to [−Native] ones). That is, a rule without special markings will follow these constraints. Therefore not only borrowed morphemes but also borrowed rules will require special apparatus. The notions of Markedness would therefore make such claims here as that in general the number of [+Native] forms is larger, that the number of rules restricted to [−Native] forms is smaller than that applying to [+Native] forms, etc. Morphological features for phenomena like vowel harmony are also exceptions to the nonuniversal character of morphological features. Cf. latter part of Chapter 8.

par from the point of view of simplicity considerations. In other words, in considering the representation of individual morphemes in the dictionary part of the grammar, it is likely that differential cost should be assigned to features of different types. This differential cost would represent the increasing arbitrariness of categorization and decreasing predictability of phonological behavior from independently available syntactic and phonetic facts. Linguistic theory might then embody the hypothesis that the cost hierarchy of features from the point of view of phonology is the following:

(6.21)   Least Arbitrary . . .   Phonological Features (binary
                                       projections of phonetic features)
                                       Morphological Features[8]
            Most Arbitrary . . .   Exception Features

In determining a way of weighting such features differentially, arbitrary manipulations of numbers must be avoided. That is, there is no basis for counting phonological feature specifications as 1, morphological specifications as 2, exception specifications as 3, rather than 1, 5, 9, or 1, 6, 36, etc. It is more natural and certainly less arbitrary to establish the weighting by imposing an order for evaluating grammars.[9] When evaluating $\underline{n}$ proposed dictionaries for the same language, one would first pick that set whose members contain the smallest number of exception features. Then among all those with the same number of exception features, those with the smallest number of morphological features would be picked.

Finally, the theory would pick from among all those dictionaries remaining that one with the fewest phonological feature specifications in the dictionary entries of morphemes. In this way the theory of language which includes the order of dictionary evaluation principle would maintain that exception features are

---

[8] Independently justifiable syntactic features are not included in this hierarchy, since they must by definition be present in dictionary entries independently of any phonological facts. Therefore, in representing a form in the dictionary, such features cannot be eliminated on phonological grounds. Hence they are, as it were, not 'in competition' with the three types of features hierarchically listed in the text.

[9] This proposal owes its essential features to suggestions of George Lakoff.

the least desirable and most costly, i.e. only to be posited as an absolute last resort; that morphological features are next least desirable and only to be resorted to when phonological feature matrices fail, etc. The theory would thus incorporate an empirical claim about the assumptions underlying a child's learning of phonological structure.

Unfortunately, such an order of evaluation principle cannot stand by itself as stated since it would suggest, if nothing further is said, that the best dictionary is one which represents all morphophonemic properties in terms of phonological matrices regardless of type. In other words, we spoke above of appealing to morphological properties when phonological matrices 'fail,' or to exception features 'as a last resort,' but no characterization was given of these notions. What has been left out, obviously, is some way of relating complexity *in the dictionary* to complexity *in the set of phonological rules*. Clearly the grounds for resorting to the more abstract types of features are the preservation of regularities which are not fully statable in terms of independently justified properties. Use of morphological and exception features thus has desirable effects on the set of rules, namely, it permits statement of regularities over maximum domains without insisting that these be total or completely justified independently. In other words, such highly expensive features are resorted to in order to prevent the exclusion of regularities simply because they are not more regular than they are. It is therefore evident that in general one is driven to morphological and exception features in the dictionary even though the order of dictionary evaluation makes such features exceptionally costly because the alternative reduces the phonological rules to chaos or even prevents their statement at all.

This is clear in the case of Mohawk stress. Stress must be predicted by rule because it cannot be listed in morphemes as such. That is, we cannot simply give up and mark the French morphemes with stress on the final vowel in the dictionary. These forms receive no stress on this vowel unless this is the final vowel of a word. Thus compare [dago's] 'cat' with [dagosgo':wah] 'mountain lion.' Hence stress in Mohawk words must be assigned by rule, and this is only possible if morphemes are classified into nonphonetic, nonphonological classes of the type given by morphological features. But a fully precise and explicit theory of phonological evaluation will not be statable until principles for weighting dictionary complexity against rule simplicity and vice versa are determined, and until the theory contains principles which force a definite choice of type of representation in every case. And we are today rather far away from enough understanding of the form of language to be able to state such a theory.

As pointed out by Chomsky as long ago as 1958, one of the most obvious objections to the theory of autonomous phonemics is that it cannot allow exceptions to phonological rules (1962:156–157). This follows because exceptions to such rules yield superficial contrasts. For example, imagine a language in which voicing is predictable for stops between vowels so that [p] and [b] do not contrast, [b] occurring between vowels and [p] elsewhere. One exceptional morpheme which does not undergo the voicing rule, i.e. a morpheme like [tepa], creates an apparent contrast between [p] and [b]. Hence instead of leaving voicing unmarked and adding the voicing rule, the autonomous phonemicist is necessarily forced to set up contrasting phonemes and to mark voice everywhere in labial stops. This instead of the right solution of marking [tepa] as an exception to the voicing rule.

The distinct views of systematic and autonomous phonemics make interestingly contrasting claims here. In the presence of even a single exception like [tepa], the autonomous phonologist claims that voice is unpredictable in all labial stops. The theory of systematic phonemics, with its recognition of the pervasive role of nonphonetic properties in phonology, claims in such a case that voicing is everywhere predictable except in [tepa]. Assertions like this permit testing because the two theories involve inconsistent claims about possible but nonexistent forms. The systematic view claims that a *possible* but *nonexistent* form of the language which contains an intervocalic labial stop must have a voiced stop. The autonomous view claims, on the other hand, that voice is unpredictable in such cases. This claims in effect that there are possible but not actual forms [. . . VbV . . .] and [. . . VpV . . .]. It is evident in a wide variety of cases that the autonomous claim of possible contrast is simply false.

For example, in English morpheme initial clusters such as those found in 'sphere,' 'sphinx,' 'sphincter,' etc. are exceptional since obstruent clusters in general consist of s plus voiceless stop. That is, these forms exist only because they contain at least

one exception feature in their systematic descriptions. Hence it
follows that the systematic theory claims that there are no possible but nonexistent words with morpheme initial [sf]. In other
words, the systematic description will claim that it is impossible
to make up new English words like [sfɔ′rm], [sfI′l], [s′fe′kt], etc.
The autonomous view must claim that these are possible, i.e.
are no different from true gaps in the lexicon like [blI′k], [sto′m],
etc. But this is obviously not so. More generally, in contrast to
autonomous phonemics, systematic phonology insists that there
are four possible types of forms in phonological terms:

(6.22)   possible and actual . . . English <u>big</u>
(6.23)   possible but not actual . . . English [plIg]
(6.24)   impossible but actual . . . exceptions like English <u>sphere</u>
(6.25)   impossible and not actual . . . English [fnes]

The autonomous phonemic claim that phonological rules
can have no exceptions amounts to the requirement that regularities be given up if they are not complete. This means that
where a systematic grammar lists the exceptional facts and predicts the rest by rule, autonomous phonemics insists on listing
everything. In the hypothetical voicing case above, systematic
phonemics thus lists [tepa] in the dictionary as an exception to
the voice rule, but predicts voice in every other labial. Autonomous phonemics insists on listing the voicing in [tepa] and also
listing it in every other labial. Besides the obvious objections to
such a view, one must point out that if it is true that phonological
rules have no exceptions, this is the only domain of grammar
where this is the case. It is widely recognized that syntactic
rules, morphological rules, etc. are burdened with exceptions. It
is significant that advocates of autonomous phonemics have never
attempted to defend this consequence of their position or to
provide any explanation of why phonological rules are unlike all
other linguistic rules. That is, as Chomsky (1962:156) asked,
why does the existence of an exception to a voice rule like [tepa]
force the rule to be thrown out of the grammar, but exceptions
to the plural rule (like 'teeth,' 'feet,' etc.) not cause the plural
rule to be excluded? In other words, why are morphological
exceptions allowed but phonological ones not? The answer is
that this follows from the assumption that only phonetic informa-

tion is relevant to the construction of the phonological level. But it is just this assumption which has never been justified. The fact that it yields this arbitrary restriction on the way exceptions are to be treated is interesting evidence of its erroneous character. Stratificational phonology necessarily assumes this no-exception-in-phonology position of more traditional autonomous phonemics, which is then another piece of evidence indicating the failure of this recent view to overcome the inadequacies of the more standard approach.

I return to the question of exceptions to phonological rules in Part II, where it is argued that they are relevant to the description of phonological change. In particular, contrary to the Neogrammarian position on sound change which is, in a natural sense, the historical corollary of autonomous phonemics, it is argued that 'regular' phonological changes have exceptions.

7

RULE ORDERING AND STRATIFICATIONAL PHONOLOGY

BACKGROUND

Like many other aspects of the current theory of systematic phonemics and the overall theory of grammar developed within the framework of generative grammar, phonological rule ordering is not a completely new idea. Rather it is a necessary aspect of linguistic descriptions which modern taxonomic linguistics, especially autonomous phonemics, has forgotten, overlooked, and/or obscured. Rule ordering was, for example, an explicit feature of Bloomfield's phonological practice (1939a) and is implicit in many of Sapir's phonological discussions (1933). Contemporary systematic phonemics should, therefore, be looked upon in this regard as well as others as developing further and making more precise insights of traditional linguistic work which were temporarily lost. The reintroduction of ordered rules into phonological and morphophonemic description, which was initiated by Chomsky (1951) as long ago as the beginning of the 1950's, is thus by no means a radical departure when seen in the larger context of the whole development of linguistics. It is the intermediate period of some quarter century, from the early 1930's to

140

the 1950's, which stands out as a deviation from the general history.

Nothing reveals more completely or clearly the failure of stratificational grammar to provide a serious theory of phonology than the extraordinary assumption, fundamental to this view, that linguistic rules are unordered (Lamb, 1964b:111–116; Gleason, 1964:93). What is more significant is the complete lack of empirical justification for this position. Stratificational writings have treated this question largely as one of abstract philosophy, as if the assumption of rule order or not is without empirical consequences in particular descriptions. The failure of this approach to consider the actual consequences of unordered rules is only one evidence of the more or less speculative character of its linguistic notions. This is correlated with a failure to even attempt the reasonably complete description of a significant fragment of the phonology[1] of any real language in such terms. As I will argue briefly in the following sections, it is only in the absence of such that the claim of unordered rules can be maintained.

THE MEANING OF RULE ORDER

Let us go over briefly what is involved in assertions that phonological rules are ordered or not. Given a set of systematic structures and a set of phonological rules, there are two fundamentally different ways in which the rules may apply, sequential or simultaneous (for some discussion cf. McCawley, 1965a).

In sequential application some rule will apply to an input structure A and convert it to a distinct structure B; another rule will apply to B and convert it to a new structure C; a third rule will convert C to D, etc. This continues until the derivation terminates according to some specified condition. A logically pos-

---

[1] The failure to apply stratificational notions to linguistic data other than isolated examples is even more true in syntactic and semantic domains. This has not in any way impeded the most extraordinary claims for this approach, however. Thus Gleason (1964:90–93) gives more than three pages of *claims* for the superiority of stratificational grammar as against the theory of transformational grammar. These three pages exceed by several all published analysis of relevant syntactic data in this framework.

sible convention for termination is that the derivation continues, and new structures are derived, until no more rules are applicable. Following McCawley (1965a), let us refer to the rules in this case as <u>random sequential</u>. Another possible condition, and in fact the one which systematic phonemics claims is actually characteristic of human languages, is that the rules are assigned a (partially) fixed order, that they apply in this order, and that the derivation terminates with the structure N, which is the output of the final rule in the ordering.[2] In this case the rules can be said to be <u>partially ordered sequential</u>, or, as is usually said, simply <u>ordered</u>.

A key fact of both random sequential and ordered rules is that the derivation of an output structure from an input structure involves intermediate stages. That is, some, in fact most, of the rules apply not to the original input forms but to structures at least partially 'created' by previous rule applications. The difference is that, unlike ordered rules, random sequential rules can be applied any time in a derivation that they are applicable. In simultaneous application, all rules apply to the original input structure, and there are no intermediate stages (Chomsky, 1964: 53, 88). A derivation therefore consists of exactly two structures, the input and the output.

Stratificational phonology is quite clear on the assertion that all phonological rules are simultaneous (Lamb 1964:111–116).

---

[2] This claim is subject to a crucial additional specification, however. In many languages the ordering is cyclical with the cycles determined by the bracketing of sentences provided in the set of Surface Syntactic Structures. In particular, the cycle of rule applications begins with the smallest constituents and moves successively to larger and larger ones. That is, the rules are applied as described in the text but only within each cycle. At the end of each cycle, the construction of the derivation begins again with the first relevant rule. Derivations thus end not after one pass through the rules, but when there has been one pass for each of the domains of constituents, including the final constituent, or whole sentence. For discussion cf. Halle and Chomsky (to appear), Chomsky (1964b). It is apparently the case that in some languages only one cycle is relevant (at least if intonation is ignored), namely, that defined by the domain of *words*. In other words, it is only necessary (and possible) to run through the rules once. Mohawk seems to be an example of this kind, as does another American Indian language, Hidatsa (Matthews, 1965).

This is, therefore, the position dealt with explicitly below. However, all of the arguments given in effect disconfirm the random sequential assumption as well. In fact, random sequential rules are rather pointless since the advantages of sequential application reside entirely in the possibility of constraining rule applications to certain stages, which is impossible with random application.

A SET OF ORDERED RULES IN MOHAWK

Comments

It is important to investigate some of the empirical consequences of the stratificational assumption of simultaneously applied unordered rules. Let us do this in a hitherto unexplored domain, by considering a set of six ordered rules in Mohawk and certain consequences for the grammar if this ordering must be eliminated.

Since interest here is in the order of rules and not their other properties, all of the rules will be stated in a very informal and technically quite inadequate way. In addition, certain refinements and special facts not bearing on ordering will be ignored (cf. Postal (to appear c) for complete discussion). In this informal statement I shall utilize the following abbreviations:

$\underline{V}$ any vowel

$\underline{C}$ any consonant, resonant or not, including systematic $\underline{w}$, $\underline{y}$

$\underline{D}$ any nonvowel, i.e. consonant, or $\underline{h}$, $\underline{?}$

$\underline{R}$ any resonant, i.e. $\underline{w}$, $\underline{y}$, $\underline{n}$, $\underline{r}$

$\underline{\emptyset}$ the null or identity element

$\underline{X}_0^n$ 'from $\underline{o}$ to $\underline{n}$ successive occurrences of X'

$\left\{ \dfrac{\underline{A}}{\underline{B}} \right\}$ 'either $\underline{A}$ or $\underline{B}$'

$\underline{\#}$ word boundary

$\underline{'}$ Stress

$\underline{\wedge}$ Falling tone

$\underline{:}$ Length

The Rules

Truncation	V	$\longrightarrow$	$\emptyset$	in ___V
Prothesis	$\emptyset$	$\longrightarrow$	i	in $(\#\underset{\text{verb}}{\underline{\qquad}}D_0^n\ VD_0^n\ \underset{\text{verb}}{\#})$
Stress	V	$\longrightarrow$	V'	in ___$D_0^n\ VD_0^n\ \#$
Stress Jump	$VD_0^n\ \not{V}'$	$\longrightarrow$	$V'D_0^n\ \not{V}$	
Tone	V'	$\longrightarrow$	$\hat{V}'$	in ___$\left\{\begin{array}{c}?\\ hR\end{array}\right\}$
Length	V'	$\longrightarrow$	V':	in $\left\{\begin{array}{c}\underline{\qquad}CV\\ [\quad_\wedge\ ]\end{array}\right\}$

It is claimed that these rules are strictly ordered. The rules will now be briefly explained and justified, and consequences of eliminating the claimed order will be discussed.

The Truncation rule drops one vowel directly in front of another (ignoring morpheme boundaries; cf. footnote 12 of Chapter 4). The Prothesis rule is that which inserts an [i] in the front of verbs containing less than one vowel. It was discussed at length in Chapter 6. The operation of the Truncation rule can be illustrated by such forms as:

(7.1)	[ra':gʌs]	'he sees her'	hra+kʌ+s
(7.2)	[ro':gʌh]	'he has seen her'	hra+o+kʌ
(7.3)	[re':zaks]	'he looks for it'	hra+esak+s
(7.4)	[ge':zaks]	'I look for it'	k+esak+s
(7.5)	[wahoyoʔʔdʌʔ]	'he worked'	waʔ+hra+o+yoʔtʌ+ʔ
(7.6)	[royoʔʔdeʔ]	'he works'	hra+o+yoʔtʌ+eʔ

Consider now the order of Truncation and Prothesis rules. Since the latter involves appeal to categorial structure, it is in any event impossible in a stratificational system. But since this has been discussed earlier it can be ignored here in favor of concentration on ordering. Truncation must precede Prothesis because of cases like that already given in Chapter 6:

(7.7)	[i'deneks]	'You and I eat it'	t+ni+ek+s

After the Truncation rule eliminates the first vowel, the structure meets the 'one vowel' condition of Prothesis in verbs. But without the ordering, it is necessary to modify the Prothesis rule to apply not only if there is one vowel in a verb but also when there are two vowels *which are contiguous* (except for intervening morpheme boundary). That is, structural facts which are completely predicted by the Truncation rule, namely, that at one stage two contiguous vowels behave like a single vowel, must be redundantly built into another rule, in this case Prothesis.

The stress rule we have given is the penultimate accent rule relevant for multivowel native words. Truncation-Stress ordering is also crucial. If Stress applies at a point where Truncation has not, it is not possible to specify stress placement in terms of penultimate position alone. As (7.7) shows, it is then necessary to reformulate the rule of accent placement to stress the penult *or the antepenult if the penult directly precedes another vowel.* As in the Truncation-Prothesis case, eliminating the order again means that generalizations are lost and linguistic information which one rule predicts must be redundantly listed in another.

Prothesis-Stress ordering reveals exactly the same fact. In all cases where it applies, the Prothesis rule actually introduces the vowel which receives the stress. But this means that in terms of simultaneous application, it is impossible for this stress to be assigned by the stress rule. The only possibility in a stratificational-like system is to complicate the Prothesis rule by having it introduce not a vowel unmarked for stress but one with stress specified. This is, in effect, to make the claim that the penultimate stress of these prothetic [i] is *accidental* (i.e. not a function of the general penultimate rule of the language).

The Stress-Jump rule is required because of certain epenthetic a vowels which will not bear the stress when penultimate. In such cases the accent is displaced to the antepenult. Thus consider:

| (7.8) | [gatga′hthos] | 'I look at it' | k+atkahtho+s |
| (7.9) | [niganu′hzageh] | 'houses' | ni+ka+nuhs+ke |

The a in (7.9), unlike the one in (7.8), is of the special nonstress-bearing sort, indicated by ą in the rules.[3] Observe first the con-

---

[3] There are, of course, fundamental questions of Mohawk phonology concerning how such vowels are to be introduced, how they are to be represented, and especially how they are to be distinguished from stress-bearing a vowels. These questions have, however, no direct bearing on the question of ordering. For discussion cf. Postal (to appear c).

sequences of having Stress-Jump and Stress rules simultaneous. If this is the case, the latter rule can no longer appeal for part of its environment to the stress of a vowel $\acute{\alpha}$. Instead, the jump rule itself will in addition have to mention all that structure which predicts stress on the penultimate $\acute{\alpha}$. In effect, the jump rule will have to incorporate the environment of the Stress rule to indicate which antepenult vowels before penult $\acute{\alpha}$ are to be stressed. But this will not be sufficient. Such a modification does not guarantee that the Stress rule will not accent the $\acute{\alpha}$. In other words, modification of the jump rule alone does not preclude specification of both penultimate accent and antepenultimate accent. The only way to prevent this is to modify the Stress rule as well, specifying that it does not apply to vowels of the type $\acute{\alpha}$. Hence predictable structure must be added to both of these rules if they are simultaneous.

The Tone rule specifies a stressed vowel as a falling tone vowel in front of ? or h before a resonant. A subsequent Laryngeal Deletion rule drops the ? or h in most such cases. Compare:

(7.10)   [ranǔ':we?s]   'he likes it' $\overline{hra+nuhwe?+s}$
(7.11)   [ronuhwê':?uh]   'he has liked it' $\overline{hra+o+nuhwe?+u}$

If the Tone rule does not follow the Stress rule, then the stress of a vowel cannot indicate the context of tone specification. But only stressed vowels have tone. Hence the Tone rule will have to be modified to include the environmental structure which specifies the position of stress. This will include not only the environment of the Stress rule but also that of the Stress-Jump rule since tone is also introduced on antepenult vowels stressed by the latter:

(7.12)   [wahayâ':dago?] 'he picks bodies' $\overline{wa?+hra+ya?\,t+ko+?}$

The amount of predictable structure which must therefore be redundantly listed is hard to exaggerate. This is even more true for simultaneous rules in the case of Tone-Prothesis ordering. It was already pointed out that, without order, the latter rule must be reformulated and complicated to indicate stress specification. But if prothetic [i] are introduced in the environment __hR they of course have the tone:

(7.13)   [ï':raks]   'he eats it'   hra+k+s

However, since the vowel which receives the tone is not in the
input representation, under the simultaneous application assumption, it cannot receive the tone from the Tone rule or any modification of it. Therefore the Prothesis rule will have to be complicated further to contain part of the environmental specification of the Tone rule, namely, __hR. The Prothesis rule is
now really a pair of rules sharing part of their context but not
all, and introducing a stressed [i] with tone in one case but
without it in the other.

The Length rule specifies length in a stressed vowel before
a single consonant or in a vowel which has already received tone.
Consider first the most trivial ordering and the consequences
of eliminating it. If Length and Stress rules are simultaneous, as
per stratificational assumption, stress cannot serve as environmental indicator of which vowel to lengthen. Therefore the
Length rule itself must contain that part of the environmental
structure of the stress rules which specifies the position of a vowel
to be stressed. In other words, exactly like the Tone rule, the
Length rule will have to contain as part the contextual structure
of both the Stress and Stress-Jump rules. The latter is required
because an antepenult vowel stressed by the jump rule lengthens
under exactly the same circumstances as a stressed penultimate
vowel:

(7.14)   [yehawɔ':naraʔs] 'he speaks to her' ye+hra+wʌn+raʔ+s

Observe that the structure to be added to the Length rule is not
just that which the environments of Stress and Stress-Jump rules
have in *our* formulation above, which presupposes strict ordering. Rather, it must be this plus the additional structure these
rules require by virtue of not being ordered with respect to the
Truncation rule. In addition, consider the ordering of the Length
and Prothesis rules. We have already seen how with simultaneous
rules this latter must in fact be reformulated as a pair of rules
incorporating environmental structure from both the Stress and
Tone rules. But actually it will at best have to be a triple of rules
since the structure of the Length rule must be incorporated into
prothesis description because of such contrasts as:

(7.15)   [i′sraks]   'he eats it again' $\dfrac{s+hra+k+s}{}$
(7.16)   [i′:geks]   'I eat it' $\dfrac{k+ek+s}{}$

That is, the prothetic vowel is long when introduced in the environment of the <u>Length</u> rule. But since a simultaneous <u>Length</u> rule cannot predict such a fact, this also must be added ad hoc to the <u>Prothesis</u> rule.

It was remarked earlier that marking stress in the output of the <u>Prothesis</u> rule claims that the penultimate stress of these vowels is accidental, i.e. not a function of the penultimate stress regularity of the language as a whole. But now we see that in stratificational terms the output of the <u>Prothesis</u> rule must contain length and tone specifications and indications of the environments which determine them. This claims that the fact that these vowels have these properties in the contexts they do is also accidental. In other words, although in fact the stress, length, and tone properties of prothetic [i] vowels follow in every respect the general rules of the language required for all other vowels, a stratificational grammar must treat them as unpredictable accidents and list them in its version of the <u>Prothesis</u> rule, actually a set of three rules. That is, the stratificational grammar would be far simpler if the prothetic vowels were <u>exceptional</u> and had constant stress, length, and tone properties regardless of whether or not they were in the proper environments for stress, length, and/or tone (i.e. if they were, for example, always unstressed, short, and level toned). This is the sense in which such a grammar cannot incorporate the regularities which predict the real, perfectly nonexceptional stress, length, and tone properties of prothetic vowels.

CONSEQUENCES

Some consequences of reformulating six Mohawk rules in stratificational terms as simultaneous operations without order have been investigated. The effects are quite clear. Almost every generalization which the six ordered rules embody is necessarily lost and cannot be represented in the simultaneous grammar. A mass of perfectly predictable facts must be listed, and in fact listed several times. Properties which are consequences of linguistic regularities must be listed and treated as exceptional. More formally, eliminating the ordering requires that important parts of the same rule be repeated over and over as parts of other rules. It was shown, in fact, that eliminating the order requires that part of the <u>Truncation</u> rule be built into the <u>Prothesis</u> rule, part of the <u>Truncation</u> rule into the <u>Stress</u> rule, part of the <u>Stress</u> into the <u>Prothesis</u> rule, part of the <u>Stress</u> rule into the <u>Stress-Jump</u> rule, part of the <u>Stress-Jump</u> rule into the <u>Stress</u> rule, part of both the <u>Stress</u> and <u>Stress-Jump</u> rules into the <u>Tone</u> rule, part of both the <u>Tone</u> and <u>Length</u> rules into the <u>Prothesis</u> rule, and finally part of the <u>Stress</u> and <u>Stress-Jump</u> rules into the <u>Length</u> rule.

Compare these empirical results with the unsupported comments by Lamb (1964b:115–116):

In other words, each rule must be placed into the ordered sequence in such a way that (1) no preceding rule has already altered the conditioning environment of e$_i$ and (2) e$_i$ will not be part of the conditioning environment in any following subrule. It is this property of rewrite rules which makes it essential that they be ordered and which evidently also accounts for various other complications in process descriptions. Thus much of the complexity seen in a transformational grammar is the result not of complexity in the language, but of an artificial restriction imposed by the type of rule being used.

It is necessary to keep clear the meaning of these results and why they amount to a complete empirical disconfirmation of the hypothesis of simultaneous rule application. It is quite wrong to interpret such results as showing simply that, without order, phonological rules must be formulated with many more symbols. Although this is true, it is not the real point. This is crucial in view of confusions which recent stratificational writings have introduced. For example, Lamb (1964b:114–115) remarks after the comparison of two ordered rules with two simultaneous rules of the type he advocates:

At this point we can expect that the champion of replacement rules (ordered rules:PMP) will say, "Aha! You have had to use an extra symbol in the statement of the conditioning environment, namely #." To which my reply would be, "Aha! *You* have had to use *two* extra symbols in your rules, namely the digits 1 and 2!" Those digits cannot be ignored. They are technically an integral part of the ordered rule, since the ordered rule is ordered. In other words, the ordering is not free, when we are computing degrees of complexity by counting symbols. An ordered set is a more complex object than an unordered one and, in particular each rule of a set of ordered rewrite rules is, formally speaking, paired with a positive integer. So every rewrite rule has an extra symbol, namely the rule number.

There are two absudities here, one theoretical, the other factual. First, Lamb maintains without any justification that there is some a priori notion of simplicity which can be appealed to in linguistics, a notion defined by the total number of symbols of all kinds appearing in a linguistic description. This measure is, he implicitly claims, absolute in the sense that it need not be tested in terms of empirical consequence and that it even governs choice among descriptions based on different theories, for example between one allowing ordered rules and another not. There is no more reason to accept such a measure than any other. That is, why should this be the absolute measure rather than the opposite (best grammar is one with most symbols), or any of a thousand others which might be proposed? Quite clearly the absolute number of symbols in a description is, as such, of no linguistic significance whatever. There are, for example, obviously meaningless and arbitrary ways in which this may be reduced. For one, in a language with no consonant clusters, some one vowel may be arbitrarily chosen and removed from the representation of all forms. Then a 'rule' may be given which inserts this vowel between all the unique consonant clusters which its deletion yields. By Lamb's assumptions not only is this a *possible* description, it is the *necessary* description since it saves symbols. Thus stratificational grammar makes the incredible assumption that, phonemically, there are no languages without consonant clusters. Many other equally absurd cases can be constructed. I shall not discuss this point further since the confusions in Lamb's assumption of an absolute, empirically independent, cross-theory simplicity metric are discussed in great detail in Chomsky and Halle (1965).

But second, suppose one adopted this unfounded proposal about absolute number of symbols. As our results above show, this would unquestionably lead to choice of ordered rules since the number of symbols which must be added to reformulate the six ordered Mohawk rules discussed exceed by many times the six required in Lamb's terms to specify their order. And this result is perfectly general and typical of all cases of ordered rules. Lamb has avoided this consequence, which is inconsistent with his theory, only by failing to attempt to construct a set of simultaneous rules for any significant part of a real language, i.e. only by keeping the approach speculative and treating isolated two-rule examples of a restricted sort.

What our original arguments show, then, is not that the number of symbols must be increased if ordering is eliminated, a fact which is, as such, of no significance. What is crucial is that, without ordering, the *same* facts must be stated again and again, *predictable* facts must be listed, etc. In short, without order, linguistic generalizations are necessarily lost. It is not the fact that symbols must be added which is important as such, but rather that the same contextual limitations must be stated again and again, that properties governed by regularities must be listed as exceptions, etc., all of which reveals the total empirical inadequacy of simultaneous phonological rules.

The incredible loss of generalizations involved in eliminating the order of only six rules, a tiny fragment of the total class of ordered rules in Mohawk phonology, is something of a measure of the mistake involved in the claim, to which current stratificational grammar is strangely wed, that phonological rules (among others) are simultaneous in application and hence unordered. It should be emphasized that as one expands the class of rules which one considers, that is, as more and more of the language is treated, the consequences we have documented of course compound extraordinarily. More and more parts of more and more rules must be built into each other, more and more generalizations must be given up and replaced by listing, etc. Anyone who attempts to construct explicit rules specifying the phonetic properties of any reasonable portion of the forms of a real language can easily document this conclusion for himself.[4] The fact that

---

[4] Phenomena incompatible with simultaneous rules have been brought forward in the literature on generative grammar long before recent stratificational discussions. It is thus significant, as Chomsky and Halle (1965:110–11) point out about the ordering discussion in Lamb (1964b), that:

"How can one decide between mutation systems and realization systems? Obviously, one must turn to questions of empirical import. One must try

unordered rules are grossly incompatible with real linguistic generalizations is obvious quite early in the attempt to formulate an explicit phonology. This is further evidence that the stratificational claim of simultaneous application has never been tested by application to real linguistic material. It is thus no accident that the only attempts to reformulate real ordered rules which stratificational or taxonomic linguists generally have ever given to my knowledge, involve only a depth of two rules. Naturally, if such a limited aspect of the facts is considered, the linguistically disastrous consequences are partially (but importantly only partially) concealed. This is perfectly expectable of course since, as one narrows the domain of linguistic fact of any kind which theories of description or particular descriptions must account for, one increases the number and kind of distinct, incompatible theories and descriptions which are compatible with the data. It is for this reason that those who are seriously interested in linguistic truth will seek to test their conceptions against the widest possible bodies of data both within a single language and cross-linguistically.

---

to discover phenomena that can be adequately described by one of these systems but not the other. For example, it has been pointed out by Chomsky that although certain examples of descriptive order can be handled by realization systems . . . such systems are inadequate for slightly more complex examples of a sort easily found, and illustrated there. Lamb does not try to show how these defects can be overcome (in fact, he makes no reference to the earlier discussion of realization systems); nor does he show how certain phenomena can be handled by realization systems that are beyond the scope of mutation systems. In short, he does not attempt to deal with the question of empirical import."

Hence the kind of untenable consequences which simultaneous rules were documented to have in Mohawk are neither a new revelation nor an isolated phenomenon. The current stratificational insistence on unordered rules thus involves not only a failure to consider actual linguistic data, but also a neglect of documented inadequacies in the previous literature.

8

MARKED AND UNMARKED IN PHONOLOGICAL STRUCTURE

SOME COMMENTS ON DICTIONARY ENTRIES

Part of any linguistic description must consist of a lexicon which specifies the vocabulary of morphemes[1] of the language. Such a lexicon, if properly constructed, should provide a list of all those sets of unpredictable associations of properties. The relevant properties are evidently of three types: semantic, syntactic, and phonological. Some entries may, however, be without properties of either the first, third, or conceivably even both sorts. For example, elements like 'be' in English have no semantic properties, and elements like the <u>causative</u> verb, present as the main verb in the Deep Structure of sentences like 'Schwartz enabled Jack to leave,' are without phonological properties.[2]

---

[1] This is of course a simplification, since many lexical items are not single morphemes but complexes of morphemes. In other words the whole problem of idioms, nonproductive derivation, etc., is ignored here. Although these matters involve important and fundamental questions which bear heavily on the correct formulation of lexicons, they do not materially affect the points made in the text here.

[2] I am assuming, that is, that the Deep Structure of causative sentences of this form is with irrelevant simplifications:

However, all entries must have syntactic properties.

The list character of the dictionary is required simply because some associations of properties are wholly arbitrary and unpredictable. That is, some associations are governed by no rules, universal or particular. To take an example, consider the English element written 'dog.' This has syntactic properties which include [+Noun, +Animate, −Human, +Countable, +Concrete,] etc. It has phonological properties which include beginning with a consonant, ending with a consonant, being monosyllabic, having no Implosive segments, etc. It has semantic properties which can be grossly abbreviated as (Physical Object), (Animal), etc. If one considers the total set of all such properties manifested by 'dog,' it is clear that some are unpredictably associated with the set, while the presence of others is predictable by principles relevant for other entries as well. For example, no regularity predicts that an element which is [+Noun] is monosyllabic, or refers to animals, or is [+Concrete], etc. Compare 'elephant,' 'car,' 'time.' On the other hand, some properties are

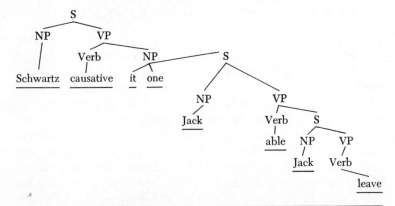

There is then an obligatory rule which substitutes the verb of the embedded sentence for the main verb, accounting for the fact that the main verb never occurs in Surface Structures, i.e. accounting for the absence of phonological properties. The prefix en (normally a suffix as in 'lighten,' 'tighten,' 'soften,' etc.) cannot be regarded as the phonological representative of the causative verb. Often it is not even present in causative sentences. Consider 'Schwartz moved the car.' Thus en is a derivational element added after the embedded verb is substituted for the main verb; added only in lexically determined cases; and sometimes moved to the front, also a lexically determined operation.

predictable. For instance all [+Animate] nouns in English (in all languages?)[3] are [+Concrete] and [+Countable]. Similarly, all segments of all morphemes in English are Non-Implosive. Hence, the presence of these properties and others in the set is predictable by rules, either of English or language generally. They need not, therefore, be listed as part of the class of unpredictable associations in the lexicon proper. A dictionary entry may therefore reasonably be defined in the most general and vague terms as a collection of three types of properties whose associations are unpredictable by linguistic rules, either universal or particular. The entries thus represent Saussure's famous 'arbitrary association of form and meaning' where, however, syntactic properties are abstracted from both 'form' and 'meaning' as a distinct kind of linguistic feature.

Backtracking a little, one must inquire more precisely into the role of phonological information in dictionary entries. The basic function[4] of the phonology as a whole is to describe how each sentence, that is, each Surface Syntactic Structure, generated by the syntax is to be pronounced, i.e. to assign each such entity its phonetic representation or set of phonetic representations in cases of free variation.[5] A priori it is conceivable that the minimal

---

[3] The universality of such a relation would of course at once require and in part justify considering at least a subset of syntactic features like Animate, Concrete, and Countable as universals, that is, as properties characterized within linguistic theory.

[4] Other functions include the specification of <u>free variation</u> and <u>contrast</u> as discussed in Chapter 1 and 2; the characterization of the notion <u>possible morpheme</u> (i.e. specifying in English that [krʌk] is a possible morpheme but that [tmok], [atde], etc. are not; and possibly the specification of phonologically possible word).

[5] Some terminological lacks are obvious here. It would be desirable to have short, simple terms differentiating 'single phonetic representation' and 'set of phonetic representations.' Suppose these were respectively <u>A</u> and <u>B</u>. Such terms would then permit one to say that the <u>phonetic interpretation</u> of a sentence consisted of a <u>B</u>, and that a sentence possesses two freely variant pronunciations just in case the <u>B</u> contains more than one <u>A</u>. These would be analogous to the terms suggested by Katz and Fodor (1963) for semantics. They define the notion <u>semantic interpretation</u> of a sentence as consisting of a set of <u>readings</u>, where each reading is a single semantic object characterizing one 'meaning.' However, they proposed no term for 'set of readings.' It would also be desirable to have a terminology in phonology corresponding to 'ambiguous' in semantics. That

syntactic elements or morphemes,[6] i.e. the parts of words, which the syntax enumerates might have as such no inherent (unpredictable) phonetic properties whatever. It is possible, that is, that all of the phonetic properties of every phonetic representation could be totally a function of general rules which operate across the lexicon. This would mean that no inherent phonetic information has to be given about how forms like 'dog,' 'gun,' 'eat,' 'remember,' etc. are to be pronounced, and that this is entirely predictable by general rules. However, this is in fact obviously not the case. Although many properties of the pronunciation of all forms are predictable by general rules, every form has some pronunciation properties which are completely unique.

In other words, if it is insisted that items come out of the syntax with *no* phonological information and that all of their pronunciation features be predicted by rule, one will necessarily find that almost every individual item requires a special rule. Furthermore, since there are no independent synatactic or semantic features which distinguish many distinct lexical items, these will have to be distinguished by ad hoc assignments of properties which have no other function than to indicate distinctness in pronunciation. Thus compare 'Paul' and 'George.' The independently motivated entries for these in terms of semantic and syntactic features are identical. If there are to be phonological rules to predict fully the pronunciation of such items, the environmental contrasts which the relevant rules require can only be given ad hoc. There are therefore two senses in which at least some information about morpheme pronunciation is not governed by rule. On the one hand, there will be for the overwhelming majority of morphemes a special 'rule' relevant only

---

is, it would be nice to have a term $\underline{C}$ which could be used in contexts of the form: 'this sentence is $\underline{n}$-ways $\underline{C}$' where this meant that the sentence had $\underline{n}$ distinct phonetic representations in free variation.

[6] Within a transforational grammar of the kind here being assumed to provide the input to the phonology, one must distinguish two sorts of terminal elements. There are the terminal elements of the Deep Syntactic Structures and the terminal elements of Surface Syntactic Structures. I would prefer to distinguish these nonidentical sets terminologically as <u>morphemes</u> and <u>formatives</u> respectively. But to avoid too great a conflict with traditional usage I have, in the text, utilized 'morpheme' for the minimal elements of Surface Structures, i.e. for the minimal <u>segmental</u> syntactic elements which are phonologically relevant.

for it. On the other hand, much of the structure which these ad hoc 'rules' require as a basis is not independently motivated, i.e. is entirely ad hoc as, for example, the syntactic properties which would have to be assigned to differentiate 'Paul' and 'George.' The assumption that all pronunciation properties must be predicted by rule means in effect that every morpheme would have to be assigned a distinct integer and there would have to be a set of 'rules,' one for almost every integer (exceptions being only those cases like the causative verb above), of schematically the form:

$$(8.1) \quad
\begin{aligned}
1 &\longrightarrow X_1 \\
2 &\longrightarrow X_2 \\
&\cdots\cdots\cdots\cdots \\
N &\longrightarrow X_n
\end{aligned}$$

where X_i is the abbrevation for those generally unpredictable associations of pronunciation features. Such 'rules' obviously represent no linguistic generalizations. They are nothing but a misleading way of listing unpredictable phonological properties.[7]

All theories of systematic phonemics, past and present, therefore insist that such 'rules' have no place in the descriptions of natural languages. Instead of dictionary entries of the form: [Semantic Features+Syntactic Features+Arbitrary Integer], all systematic phonemic dictionary entries replace the arbitrary integer with the relevant set X_i of unpredictable phonological properties. Otiose 'rules' like those in (8.1) are eliminated. The question then arises as to the nature and proper form of these associations of phonological properties.

One possibility might appear to be simply to list for each morpheme a complete phonetic representation. The phonological part of the dictionary entry of a lexical item would then consist of a two dimensional phonetic matrix of the kind we have dis-

---

[7] The untenable approach to dictionary entries just rejected is actually implied in essence by the assumptions of stratificational grammar. In fact, an even worse position is entailed by this approach, since such a view of linguistic structure is incompatible with any notion of lexicon or dictionary at all. The fundamental feature of a lexicon is that it provides for associations of properties of <u>different kinds</u>, especially semantic and phonological. But this is just what is not allowed under stratificational assumption. Cf. the appendix to this Chapter.

cussed earlier (Chapter 4). This is, however, quite impossible for two different reasons. First, it is an empirical fact that in most languages an enormous number of morphemes have several different pronunciations in various different contexts. The plural is not pronounced the same in 'dogs,' 'cats,' and 'foxes'; the stem 'corrode' is not pronounced the same in 'corroded' and 'corrosion,' etc. Second, and equally disconfirming of this hypothesis about phonological dictionary information, it fails to disinguish those properties of the pronunciation of a form that are predictable by general rules operating for whole sets of morphemes from those which are entirely idiosyncratic. Even for a morpheme like 'dog,' whose pronunciation is perhaps always phonetically uniform, such an approach makes the claim that every aspect of its pronunciation is as unpredictable as every other. This is simply false. It is, for example, not an idiosyncratic fact at all that every segment of 'dog' is non-Implosive, non-Glottalized, non-Pharyngealized, etc., etc., for these are features of every segment of every English morpheme. Hence even in those cases of no alternation where it is conceivable, indentification of phonological dictionary information with a single completely specified phonetic representation makes the false claim that features which are in fact predictable are unpredictable. Such a theory of descriptions would wrongly claim, for example, that, in learning a new form, an English speaker must memorize whether or not any segment is or is not Gottalized, Pharyngealized, etc.

It should be observed that the second argument just given disconfirms not only the hypothesis that the phonological part of a dictionary entry is a *single* phonetic representation. It also falsifies the slightly more flexible view, which one might be led to in order to handle alternations, that the information is a *set* of pairs of phonetic representations with specifications of the context in which each may be used. Such a position is, in effect, the exact opposite of the arbitrary integer hypothesis which in essence is accepted by stratificational grammar. The latter gives as such *no* information about pronunciation in the dictionary and attempts to predict all phonetic facts by rule. The former attempts to eliminate all rules and give all phonetic information in a list.

The list proposal is, in effect, a slightly more extreme version of the approach to morphophonemic alternation which actually developed in modern American taxonomic linguistics, an approach which has variously been called the 'method of allomorphs' or 'morpheme alternants' (Lounsbury, 1953:11) or the 'item and arrangement' approach (Hockett 1954). In this approach, each morpheme is assigned a set of allomorphs plus a set of associated statements indicating the context in which each allomorph must be used. Most crucially, there is no systematic or morphophonemic representation, and each allomorph is a sequence of autonomous phonemes. This view then differs from that given at the beginning of the previous paragraph in that *some* predictable phonetic features have been eliminated from dictionary listing. But only a few, namely, just that small set which distinguishes autonomous phonemes from phonetic elements. These are, as has been mentioned several times before, just those phonetic features which can be predicted by rules operating on purely phonetic environments.

The allomorph or item and arrangement approach is thoroughly disconfirmed as a hypothesis about human linguistic structure on several grounds. This is not easy to discuss, however, since the approach is unfortunately quite vague. The vagueness resides in a failure to ever give any precise account of how the environments in which different allomorphs occur can be specified, what kinds of properties these statements may appeal to, etc. But without such an account there really is no precise theory. Disconfirmation is possible, however, because the fundamental intention is clear. This is to list for every morpheme all alternations (phonological properties) which are not predicted below the phoneme level; that is, to list all those properties and their distributions which are not expressible in terms of general rules with purely phonetic environments. This amounts to the denial that there are any general rules without phonetic environments. A good illustration of the incompatibility of this approach with even relatively trivial linguistic generalizations is provided by Mohawk stress, briefly discussed in Chapter 7.

Stress is contrastive in autonomous phonemic terms. The allomorph approach must then indicate stress position in the allomorphs of every morpheme. The majority of morphemes will have stressed and unstressed variants, that is, variants with at least one stressed vowel or not. Compare, for example, variant words formed with the stem <u>ket</u> 'to scrape'.

(8.2)	[ragé':das]	'he scrapes it'	hra+ket+as
(8.3)	wahá':gede?]	'he scraped it'	wa?+hra+ket+?
(8.4)	[ɔhageda'shege?]	'he will be scraping it repeatedly'	ʌ+hra+ket+as+hek+?

Sometimes the stress is on the stem vowel, other times before it, other times after it. These facts are, of course, all automatic and trivial consequences of the penultimate stress rule, which operates on the systematic phonemic representation, or subrepresentations derived from it by previous rules in the ordering. But it is exactly the function of allomorph descriptions to avoid such abstract representations,[8] and this elimination of any morphophonemic representation is one of the most incredible regressions in modern taxonomic linguistic work.[9] Therefore, in entering a

---

[8] The reasons for this wish had to do with a priori methodological ideas about 'mentalism,' 'objectivity,' 'rigor,' etc. For some discussion cf. Postal (to appear b).

[9] In Postal (to appear b) it is pointed out how this led, for example, to an actual decline of very serious proportions in the adequacy of descriptions within Iroquoian. In particular it is shown how this forced the account of Oneida in Lounsbury (1953) to be less adequate in crucial respects (stress placement) than that in Lounsbury (1946). Another example of even greater time depth is relevant. Barbeau (1915:223, 23) pointed out a number of general rules of Mohawk-Oneida (which, to be sure, he interpreted basically as historical) including one which yields an affricate from systematic sy:

". . . causes the transformation of the preceding s into ts according to the general Iroquoian phonetic law: SY > TS."

Compare Mohawk:

[zatga'hthos]	'you look at it'	s+atkahtho+s
[dzʌ'thos]	'you plant it'	s+yʌtho+s
[i'sraks]	'he eats it again'	s+hra+k+s
[dza'geneks]	'someone and I eat it again'	s+ya+k+ni+ek+s

Exactly analogous alternations are found in Oneida with [dž] cognate to Mohawk (that is, Caughnawaga Mohawk) [dz]. Yet in Lounsbury (1953) /s/-/j/ (this was Lounsbury's phonemicization) alternations were listed for individual morphemes as if they were idiosyncratic and unpredictable (for example, 1953:44). The rule roughly given by Barbeau four decades before was ignored. It should be emphasized that the rule was omitted not because it was unknown to the author, but rather because in terms of the 'item

stem like 'scrape' in the lexicon of Mohawk, it will be necessary for such an approach to list both autonomous phonemic /ket/ and /ke't/ and *to indicate in what contexts each may occur.* But here is the fundamental difficulty. Although the presence or absence of stress on a vowel is a relatively simple function of the structure of words in systematic phonemic representation, it cannot be defined at all in terms of autonomous phonemic sequences. This follows, for example, from the fact that epenthetic vowels like the final ones in (8.3) and (8.4), which are irrelevant for the stress count, are *absent* from the systematic representation of words, although necessarily present in the autonomous ones, since the epenthetic vowels are phonetically identical with other nonepenthetic vowels. Therefore, to really indicate the position of stress in the item and arrangement approach, it will be necessary to list for every stressed allomorph like /ke't/ all those morpheme (sequences) which may intervene between final word boundary and the allomorph. Since those morphemes which have stressed allomorphs include the vast majority, such a list will be part of the allomorphic statement for most morphemes in the language.

The key point here, of course, is not simply the expansion in absolute number of symbols or the like which the avoidance of systematic representation entails. The real objection is that such a theoretical framework makes the untrue claim that stress position is unpredictable and must be listed in terms of morpheme sequences for each morpheme. Stress position is fundamentally predictable by the penultimate stress rule and several minor subsidiary stress principles. The method of allomorphs thus makes such false claims as that a Mohawk who learns a new stem must memorize the morpheme sequences before which it will have stressed variants and those before which it will not. This method also maintains that, given a hypothetical word whose morphemic structure he does not know, a Mohawk will have no idea about where to place the stress. All such assertions are, however, easily disconfirmed. Knowledge of stress placement in such cases is exactly what the systematic rules predict. These conclusions of course generalize to other examples in other

and arrangement' approach accepted in 1953, such a generalization and the systematic structures it required were considered methodologically unacceptable ('fictitious').

languages. Completely contrary to what the item and arrangement theory maintains, speakers have an enormous amount of general knowledge about how to pronounce morpheme sequences, knowledge which is neither limited to particular morphemes nor restricted to information statable in purely phonetic terms.

Just as the proposal that dictionary entries contain sets of *fully phonetic representations* makes the false claim that predictable facts cannot be predicted, the slightly more abstract proposal about lists of *autonomous phonemic representations* makes quite analogous false claims. And it is obvious why this must be so. The extreme or phonetic theory lists everything. The allomorph theory lists everything not predicted by purely phonetic rules. But this still leaves an enormous mass of phonetic facts, which are predictable in terms of rules with more abstract environments, scattered in a gigantic set of lists restricted to individual morphemes. In fact, the class of facts listed in allomorph representations is in the majority, since most phonological rules do not have purely phonetic environments. Thus the representations allowed by the allomorph approach in particular languages are actually closer to those which would be permitted by lists of purely phonetic representations than they are to the representations in systematic phonemic terms which contain no predictable information whatever. As a consequence of this, lexicon entries in autonomous phonemic notation will in the vast majority of cases involve several different phonemic sequences, i.e. very few morphemes will have a single base form.

In systematic representation, on the other hand, the situation is the reverse. Most morphemes will have single base forms with all alternative phonetic realizations predicted by general rules. Only cases of true, unpredictable suppletion will require multiple phonological sequences in entries (cases like 'be,' 'am,' 'is,' etc.). It is therefore possible to state the objection to the allomorph hypothesis in terms of the notion of suppletion. The allomorph approach fails to distinguish true suppletion, in which the alternants are totally idiosyncratic, from alternations which can be predicted by rules with nonphonetic environments. In short, it treats all alternations like suppletions. Obviously then, autonomous phonemic representations, either singly or in sets, cannot serve as the representations utilized in the dictionary entries of a grammar which truly describes the linguistic knowledge of speakers. And this is one of the most important senses in which such structure is an artifact that fails to qualify as a level of linguistic structure.

In view of the facts just discussed, the theory of systematic phonemics naturally insists that the phonological part of a dictionary entry must consist of some kind of morphophonemic representation, that is, a representation which lists only those completely unpredictable aspects of the pronunciations of the morpheme. And the character of these representations has been extensively discussed above, most of it, however, in terms of what I shall call 'the early theory of systematic phonemic dictionary representation.'

THE EARLY THEORY OF SYSTEMATIC PHONEMIC DICTIONARY REPRESENTATION

In the early theory of systematic phonemics, the dictionary entry of a form is a segment-feature matrix in which the cells contain three possible markings $+$, $-$, and zero. The first indicates the presence of the feature in that segment, the second its absence, the third gives no information. In the simplicity metric associated with this theory, equal cost was assigned to both $+$ and $-$ markings, and no cost whatever to zero. In this early version of the theory it is zero markings which, within the dictionary, represent linguistic regularities, $+$ and $-$ markings which indicate unpredictable properties of lexical items. That is, the zero will be later specified as either $+$ or $-$ in the appropriate contexts by general rules. Thus, for example, in this theory all segments in all English morphemes would be marked [0Glottalized], and a general rule of English would specify all segments as [$-$Glottalized]. This theory is in a clear sense symmetrical. The presence or absence of a property contribute equally to the cost or complexity of the dictionary. No value of any feature is more 'natural,' 'normal,' 'dominant,' or inexpensive than any other. The only cost savings which can be achieved are those obtainable by showing that feature values are predictable and hence replaceable in the dictionary by zero markings. Such a theory underlies all published work on systematic phonemics to this date.

Another aspect of this early theory should be mentioned. It was assumed that the set of phonological rules had a natural division into <u>morpheme structure rules</u> and <u>phonological rules proper</u>. The former rules were restricted to filling in zero markings within the dictionary by appropriate + and − values. That is, they were restricted to operate within morphemes (not across morpheme boundaries) and could not permute, delete, or add segments, etc. It was never assumed that morpheme structure rules filled in all zero markings, but attempts were made to discover some formal constraints on the output of such rules (Halle, 1959:38). The function of morpheme structure rules was to represent those language-particular predictable constraints on the possible combinations of feature specifications both within a segment and sequentially. It has often been assumed that the systematic phonemic proposal of morpheme structure rules is little more than an equivalent in a new notational system for the phonotactics of ordinary autonomous phonemics. But this is not the case. The phonotactics of autonomous phonemic descriptions was never concerned to do more than provide a compact representation of the observed facts. Thus, at best, such a system makes a two-way distinction between observed sequence and nonobserved sequence. But within the theory of morpheme structure rules it was insisted that formal grounds be provided for determining when a rule could or could not be added to the set. That is, it was required that precise criteria be given within linguistic theory for projecting the observed distinction between actually occurring morpheme and not actually occurring morpheme in many languages to the internalized knowledge which subdivides the latter morphemes into possible and impossible. In other words, systematic phonemics was interested in providing an explanation for the fact that there is an important distinction between [kwun] and [fun] from the point of view of the knowledge of an English speaker. Although neither is an actual English element, the second but not the first is possible. Systematic phonemics was interested in explaining how an English speaker knows this kind of fact. For extensive discussion of this point and its significance, cf. Chomsky and Halle (1965). For lengthy treatment of the formalism of morpheme structure rules and problems in their formulation, cf. Stanley (to appear).

Although the original theory of systematic phonemics is a

vast improvement on any previous or competitive view of phonological representation, further investigation has shown that it cannot be accepted as such. Certain remarks made in earlier chapters have already suggested this and indicated certain aspects of a newer and modified theory which incorporates many but not all of the features of this earlier view.

FUNDAMENTALS OF THE MARKED-UNMARKED ASYMMETRICAL THEORY OF PHONOLOGICAL REPRESENTATION

Several different sorts of difficulties suggest that the early systematic theory is not adequate. First, there are important formal difficulties caused wholly by the necessity of having rules apply to matrices containing zero markings. These are discussed in great detail by Stanley (to appear) who proposes a rather different solution than that treated in this section which is basically due to Chomsky and Halle. Second, although there appears to be a clear notion of 'hierarchy of features,' the early theory does not provide an adequate reconstruction of it, nor does the hierarchy appear to play any real role in descriptions. In particular, the 'trees' of phonological features which accompany many systematic descriptions, for example Halle (1959:46) and Postal (1964a:277), are neither actually a function of any phonological rules nor derivable in any systematic way from the grammar. Nonetheless, they appear to represent some real facts about the relevant languages (Halle 1959:34). Furthermore, 'trees' of different languages appear to have much, if certainly not everything, in common, so there are universal facts about language here.[10] Third, and most fundamentally, the claim of symmetry of feature values is just not born out. In fact the symmetrical assumption is sharply deviant from the actual phonological-phonetic situation in the languages of the world.

As already illustrated at some length in the latter part of

---

[10] For example, all such 'trees' have features like Sonorant, Consonantal, and/or Vocalic at the top, have features like Grave and Diffuse above Abrupt Onset, all of these above Voice, etc. No 'trees' draw the fundamental distinction in consonants between Nasal and Non-Nasal with all other distinctions subordinate, etc.

Chapter 4, there is a mass of very clear universal properties of language which reveals a striking asymmetry of feature values in particular contexts. For example, as noted earlier [+Glottalized] consonants are definitely 'nonnormal,' or less 'natural' than [−Gottalized] consonants. Hence, they are not found in many languages, are a minority in those where they are found, etc. But no way of expressing such facts exists in the older theory. Basing their proposal on earlier, fairly vague Praguian and Jakobsonian ideas about marked and unmarked values, Chomsky and Halle have recently proposed an extremely interesting and powerful way of capturing such generalizations which, significantly enough, appears to eliminate many other difficulties with the early +, −, 0 system, and which seems to provide a wide variety of other new insights and generalizations about phonological structure.

Consider the problem of representing facts like the 'subordinate' character of [+Glottalized] consonants. If dictionary representations are given in terms of +, − and 0 markings, rules to represent such facts are impossible. It is not possible, for instance, to give a universal rule simply saying that all segments are [−Glottalized]. This would embody not the true generalization that [+Glottalized] segments are 'subordinate' and 'unnatural,' but rather the false generalization that they do not exist at all. In a language with a Glottalization contrast, such a rule would wrongly merge [+Glottalized] consonants with [−Glottalized] ones. Nor is it possible to represent all [−Glottalized] consonants as [0Glottalized] and give a universal rule to turn these [−Glottalized]. For this amounts to treating 0 not as an indication of no information, but as a value distinct from both + and −. (Cf. Stanley, to appear.) Nonetheless, while rules like this cannot be allowed in a +, −, 0 system, they do suggest something of the right solution. The proposal made is as follows.

Instead of a single level of dictionary representations in terms of equally costly + and −, and costless 0, there are now distinct levels. On the deeper, or more abstract level, features have only two possible values, M(arked) or U(nmarked). U markings are without cost, M markings have a cost. Thus where the early version of the theory allows dictionary matrix cells with three states for a given feature, presence, absence, or no information, the current version allows only two 'normal' and 'not normal.'

There is, in addition, a less abstract level of matrix representation in which every cell contains either a + or − marking. But the crucial and fundamental assumption is that this level is entirely the function of *universal* rules which operate on the level of M-U representation to successively derive + and − markings. At no stage are there any 0 specifications. Thus, where the early version of dictionary theory claimed that for every feature the + and − values were of equal cost, and that savings could be achieved only where the values could be predicted, the present theory claims that in every context some value is 'natural' and costless, the other 'unnatural' and with a cost. The new theory therefore assimilates the cases of natural value and no information (predictability) and specifies them both as U.

Consider what this means in terms of neutralization, the phenomenon where in a certain context only one of the possible values of some feature (set of features) occurs. For instance, in English there is a Voice contrast in consonants after sonorants, but in another position, such as after an obstruent, no contrast. In the early systematic theory this class of facts would have been represented as follows, illustrating with velars:

(8.5) k in Sonorant _____ = [−Voice]
     g in Sonorant _____ = [+Voice]
     k,g (the archiphonomene of k and g, i.e. the set of feature
        specifications they have in common)
     in Obstruent _____ = [0Voice]

A special rule of English would then have specified the value of Voice in the neutralized position. This rule would have represented an enormous saving since, although it itself costs only a few features, it permits the saving of one feature in each morpheme internal neutralized sequence within the dictionary. The rule thus represents the generalization that the value of Voice is predictable in such a position in English, i.e. need not be memorized as part of lexicon entries like contrastive features.

In the Marked-Unmarked theory, assuming that in general voiced consonants are Marked,[11] such a set of facts would be represented as follows:

---

[11] A poorly understood limitation on this, having to do with intervocalic positions in languages without a Voice contrast, is discussed later.

(8.6) k̲ in Sonorant _____   = [UVoice]
       g̲ in Sonorant _____   = [MVoice]
       k̲,g̲, in obstruent _____ = [UVoice]

A universal rule will then interpret both occurrences of [UVoice]
as [−Voice][12] because they are in consonant segments. The
present theory therefore assimilates the neutralized case to the
'natural' term in the contrastive position. It is important to recognize, however, that such a theory does not claim that in *every*
case the Unmarked phonetic element will actually occur in the
position of neutralization. It claims only that this will be the
case in the majority of instances since, if it is, no special, language
particular rule is required. But it is possible for a language
to have special rules which yield Marked segments in positions
of neutralization.[13]

Such a Marked-Unmarked theory incorporates the claim that
underlying the particular phonological system of every language
there is a universal phonological structure involving, in particular,
universal rules which convert the input matrix of M-U values
into an output matrix containing + and − values. Accepting
such a theory commits one to determining for each feature value
in each context grounds for a nonarbitrary choice of M or U
representation. That is, accepting such a theory involves the
responsibility for discovering the right class of universal rules
interpreting M and U representations as + and −. This is a vast
undertaking. At the moment, from the point of view of a completed system, our knowledge along these lines is limited. But
there is already a great deal of knowledge, and many M-U
decisions can be made with some confidence. In fact a large
set of such decisions is implied in the list of asymmetrical gen-

---

[12] It is remotely conceivable that, instead of *replacing* M and U values
by + and − values, such rules will form complex values of features of the
form M+, M−, U+, U−. This would be the proper formulation if generalizations could be discovered showing that + or − values coming from
Marked entries behaved regularly in many cases in different ways than
+ or − values of the same feature coming from Unmarked cells.

[13] The theory claims that, in a large proportion of the cases where
Marked values show up in morpheme internal neutralized positions, this
is a function of independently required rules operating across morpheme
boundaries. Cases of this sort are discussed below.

eralizations given in the latter part of Chapter 4. Thus it is clear that in [+Sonorant] segments [+Voice] is [UVoice], that in vowel segments [−Nasal] is [UNasal], that in all segments [−Glottalized] is [UGlottalized], etc.

It should be emphasized that the comments made after the underlined assertions (4.4) through (4.15) in Chapter 4 to support claims of 'naturalness' or asymmetry among several types of phonetic entity are by no means the only sorts of arguments which can be brought forward as to which value of a feature is Marked in an environment. Each of these remarks was an assertion about relative generality in distribution among the entire class of languages. Other relevant types of fact include: Relative frequency and differential predictability within particular languages. For example, among the facts showing that nonStressed rather than Stressed vowels are normal, and hence Unmarked, is that in all languages the more strongly stressed vowels are in the minority. Furthermore, in stating the rules which predict placement of differential stress, it is always the case that the rules must specify the position of strong stress and not weak stress. It is always simpler to specify that all vowels are unstressed and then to specify the positions of strong stress rather than to specify that all vowels are strong stressed and then specify which must be made nonStressed. As even traditional descriptions reveal, languages have Stress rules, not nonStress rules.[14] Again there is a special kind of asymmetry and the deviant case, that for which special remarks must be made in individual languages, is the case of strong stress. Similar arguments can be given showing the 'normality' of short, not long segments; of nonAspirated, not Aspirated ones; of level tone, not rising or falling tone vowels, etc.

Another relevant type of fact is appearance in position of neutralization. Compare Trubetzkoy (1936:191–192):

. . . jenes Oppositionsglied, welches in der Aufhebungs-stellung zugelassen wird, ist vom Standpunkte des betreffenden phonologischen Sys-

---

[14] This is even true in cases which might appear to be contrary, as for example the extremely weak stress of English shwa. In fact this is an automatic consequence of the assignment of strong stress to other vowels and does not require special 'nonstressing' rules. Cf. Halle and Chomsky (to appear).

tems merkmallos, während das entgegengesetzte Oppositionsglied merkmaltragend ist.

For example, in English morphemes before other true consonants within morphemes only one consonant can appear, [s]. This supports the assignment of 'normality' to [s]-type and not [θ] type dental fricatives. It goes without saying that we cannot and do not accept Trubetzkoy's much too narrow and unjustified following remarks:

Es muss besonders betont werden, dass merkmallose and merkmaltragende Glieder nur bei aufhebbaren phonologischen Gegensätzen bestehen. Nur bei diesen hat der Unterschied zwischen merkmallosen und merkmaltragenden Oppositionsgliedern ein objecktives phonologisches Dasein, und nur in diesem Falle ist man wirklich imstande, das Merkmal des phonologischen Gegensatzes mit völliger Objektivität und ohne Heranziehung ausserlinguistischer Forschungsmittel zu bestimmen. Ist ein phonologischer Gegensatz konstant, so lässt sich das Verhältnis zwischen seinen Gliedern manchmal wohl als Verhältnis zwischen Merkmallosen und Merkmaltragendem denken, dies bleibt jedoch nur eine logische oder psychologische, nicht aber eine phonologische Tatsache.

This shows at once too little faith in the role of universal considerations and lack of awareness of the range of facts beyond neutralization which bear on the assignment of Marked or Unmarked status.

Other arguments can be derived from facts of phonological change and dialect variation. One would expect, for example, that given two series of related segments, one of which is of the Unmarked type, that sound change will frequently merge the Marked with the Unmarked, or change the Marked in some other way. Hence one would expect to find dialects differing in that, for example, one had two series of consonants, one Glottalized and the other not, while the other had only non-Glottalized consonants which were cognate with both these series in the former, etc. But opposite situations in which there is loss or merger of 'normal' to 'nonnormal' types should be extremely rare or nonexistent.

Ultimately, perhaps some of the strongest evidence for assignment of Marked or Unmarked status will come from physiological and perceptual investigations. Although one must avoid overly simplistic assertions about 'ease of articulation' or the like, it is evident that articulatory and perceptual factors of this sort are behind the linguistic structuring of Marked and Unmarked. It has been pointed out by M. Halle (personal communication), for example, that the Unmarked status of voicing in Sonorants but Marked status of voicing in non-Sonorants is due to the fact that non-Sonorant articulations build up back pressure on the vocal cords. But this does not happen in sonorant articulations. This means that vocal cord vibration is impeded in non-Sonorant segments. But in Sonorant articulations without back pressure the passage of air will, all other things being equal, naturally lead to voicing. Hence in a rather clear sense it takes a special instruction to voice non-Sonorants or to devoice Sonorants. And this is what the M-U representation indicates.

Similarly, if we consider the normality of Apicality in the dental position, but its unnatural character in labial, palatal, and velar positions, we cannot fail to be struck by the fact that the dental region is the closest to the tip of the tongue *starting from the rest position of the apparatus.* One also cannot fail to be struck by the fact that it is the + value of many of the 'secondary' or 'modification' features which is either always or generally Marked (Palatalization, Rounding, Velarization, Glottalization, Pharyngealization, etc.). But the phonetic realizations of the value of these features involve the performance of extra articulatory gestures not required by the − values in these cases. Thus we have good reason to suspect that there are good articulatory and/or perceptual[15] grounds for Marked-Unmarked status. Much of Jakobson's work is highly suggestive along these lines. At the same time, I think, we must frankly recognize the enormous limitations on the ability of present day linguistic and phonetic theory to give a serious account of such neuro-physiological bases.

---

[15] A good example of the relevance of perceptual considerations here is given by the obvious Markedness of [+Nasal] segments in most contexts. But articulatorily it requires an extra gesture to prevent nasal articulation, i.e. to close off the nasal pharynx. The Markedness of nasalization must then be due to the perceptual consequences of nasal resonances, quite likely their strong tendency to obscure other aspects of the signal. The well-known greater difficulty in discriminating [m], [n], [ŋ] as against [b], [d], [g] is relevant here.

Finally, one must agree with Jakobson (especially 1962:317–401) that important evidence on this topic as well as many others of linguistic, and especially phonological, significance comes from the study of both first language learning and language pathology. One rightfully expects, for example, that Marked phonolgical elements will be acquired later in the process of language learning and lost first in certain pathologies. And there is limited evidence, emphasized by Jakobson, which supports such claims. To quote only one example (1962:31):

Les oppositions relativement rares dans les langues du monde sont parmi les dernières accroissements du système phonologique enfantin, et le R sibilant (ř), phoneme excessivement rare dans les langues du monde, termine d'ordinaire l'apprentissage phonologique des enfants tchèques; dans les diverses tribus indiennes faisant usage des consonnes glottalisées les enfants tardent a les acquérir, et les voyelles nasales n'apparaissent chez les enfants français et polonais qu'après tous les autres phonèmes vocaliques.

The new theory which allows only M and U markings in the dictionary representations of morphemes eliminates those formal difficulties caused by the need to have language particular rules apply to matrices containing zeros. These difficulties concerned various spurious simplifications which could be achieved (cf. Stanley, to appear). But in the new theory the only rules which apply to M-U representations are universals. Language particular rules apply only at the stage when all values are + and −.

One of the crucial additional contributions made by this new theory is that it serves to eliminate a large proportion of previously required morpheme structure rules. Each such rule in each language was, in effect, a representation of one or more neutralizations of one kind or another. But in the new theory neutralizations will be treated by U markings in the dictionary and these will be converted to the 'normal' values by completely universal rules. If the 'normal' values are actually those occurring, nothing more need be said in particular grammars. Special rules will then be needed only in cases where 'nonnormal,' or Marked, values appear in these positions (and are not a function of independently required statements). It is a very important question to determine just what proportion of morpheme internal phonological constraints in particular languages are eliminated and accounted for by the universal M-U interpretation rules. To the extent that this theory is right, one would expect to find that a great majority of such restrictions will be predicted, and that many others will be correcly handled by independently needed phonological rules which operate across morpheme boundaries (as mentioned in footnote 13), i.e. one would expect that very few language particular rules will be required for morpheme internal constraints.

Brief examination of certain facts in Mohawk seems to support this view. For example, important two-segment sequential constraits in morphemes include the following:

(8.7) consonant+n̲ sequences are not allowed although consonant +r̲ sequences are

(8.8) consonant+w̲ sequences are not allowed although consonant+y̲ sequences are

(8.9) p̲[16] and w̲ are not allowed before o̲, u; y̲ and k̲ are not allowed before i̲, although p̲, w̲ occur before i̲ and k̲, y̲ before o̲, u

(8.10) y̲r̲ and y̲y̲ are not allowed, although w̲r̲ and w̲y̲ are

If we consider these constraints, which are in effect complex neutralizations, we find that most of them are a function of universal marking principles. That is, if those elements which do occur are given the relevant U representations, the phonetic facts are predicted by universal rules without special Mohawk rules or, where this is not the case, the required rules have independent motivation.

In (8.7) the occurrent consonant+r̲ sequences involve a neutralization of the r̲-n̲ contrast after consonants. Under the clearly justified assumption that [+Nasal] is Marked, we can specify the r̲ in these clusters as [UNasal], and the [−Nasal] feature will be predicted by the marking principles. No special

---

[16] The systematic element p̲ is represented phonetically as either [gw] or [g]. Evidence for recognizing a special consonantal element here is quite strong. Some of it is discussed in Chapter 11. Evidence showing that this element must be treated systematically as a labial (i.e. [+Grave], [+Diffuse]) is not lacking, but is much more tenuous. The issue is discussed in some detail in Postal (to appear c). Cf. also footnote 7 of Chapter 11.

diffuse = anterior
grave = - cor.

Mohawk rule is required. In (8.8) there is an exception, since I would assume that p̲ w̲ are Unmarked[17] as against k̲, y̲.[18] That

---

[17] This is not quite the same as Jakobson's view (1962:377, 491) that the plain labial stop is the *optimal* consonant. First of all, the claim I am making here is restricted to the domain of Grave consonants. It is not so clear that the labial position, which is Grave, should be Unmarked as against the dental position, which is not Grave. In other words, while it is clear that the maximally Unmarked position is [+Diffuse], either labial or dental, it is not so clear what the value for Grave should be. Evidence in favor of the dental region can be derived from the clearly Unmarked character of the dental nasal as against the labial. Where there is only one nasal in a language this is almost without exception dental (ignoring assimilations), and languages with more than one nasal always have a dental nasal (Hockett, 1958:99). On the other hand, an interpretation of Jakobson's position to claim maximal Unmarkedness for the labial position, at least in stops, may be derived from a combination of the formalism of Markedness rules and the assumption that the palatal position is most Marked (this latter follows of course from Jakobson's minimal *p-t-k* consonant 'triangle.' Cf. 1962:324, 379, 493). The two features relevant for defining the four major positions are Grave and Diffuse. Assuming that the labial position is maximally Unmarked the situation would be as follow:

	p	t	č	k
Grave	U	M	M	U
Diffuse	U	U	M	M
Grave	+	−	−	+
Diffuse	+	+	−	−

The rules would then be that within the domain of true consonants (i.e. excluding resonants) [UGrave] is [+Grave] and [UDiffuse] [+Diffuse]. The Marked values, as always, would be opposite. If, however, the Markedness specifications of Grave for the labial and dental positions were to be reversed, the rules could not be given. Notice, incidentally, that justification of the structure given for labials bears upon our claim that the element p̲ in Mohawk is actually a labial. If the labial position is truly [UGrave], [UDiffuse], the assignment of labial status is the most inexpensive and hence most highly justified. This is a good illustration of the way universal assumptions bear on particular descriptive decisions.

A second difference between the claim made here and those of Jakobson is that I am extending the claims beyond stops to include other labials as well, both true consonants and liquids. For the liquid consonant character

is, I would assume, at least within the domain of [+Grave]
consonants, that the front, or [+Diffuse] ones are normal. Some
evidence for this decision can be derived from the fact that languages which have two nasal consonants ordinarily have [m]

---

of phonetically non-Consonantal [w] and [y], cf. the following footnote.
How these wider claims are to be made compatible with the Unmarked
character of the dental nasal is not clear.

[18] Although the phonetic manifestations of y̱ are exclusively palatal, it
is necessary on a number of grounds to treat y̱ systematically as a velar.
A good deal of the basis for this is given by the facts described in the text
showing how y̱ behaves with ḵ. An interesting piece of evidence supporting
the claim of a velar (i.e. [+Grave], [−Diffuse]) characterization of
Mohawk and Northern Iroquoian y̱ is the fact that, in Wyandot, proto-
Iroquoian ḵ went to y̱ under certain conditions (Barbeau, 1915:24). A
direct shift from a velar, interrupted consonant, to a palatal glide seems
highly implausible to say the least. But according to the phonological
representation being proposed here, the relevant features for ḵ are

$$\begin{bmatrix} +\text{Consonantal} \\ -\text{Sonorant} \\ +\text{Grave} \\ -\text{Diffuse} \end{bmatrix}$$

and those for y̱ the same except for [+Sonorant]. In other words, y̱ is
being treated systematically as a velar liquid consonant. Under this assumption, the Wyandot sound change is simply a one feature switch of a type
documented again and again in the study of sound change.

The question arises whether both the velar status of y̱ and the systematic [+Consonantal] status of y̱ and w̱, which is needed on a large
number of grounds, require ad hoc rules in Mohawk to derive the correct
nonvelar and non-Consonantal phonetic variants (significantly enough, w̱
does have [+Consonantal] realizations also, namely [f]). I believe that the
answer to this is negative, and that both the switch of velar to palatal and
of [+Consonantal] to [−Consonantal] are a function of universal rules.
That is, it would appear that no phonetic elements exist which have the
properties:

$$\begin{bmatrix} +\text{Consonantal} \\ +\text{Sonorant} \\ -\text{Vocalic} \\ +\text{Grave} \\ -\text{Diffuse} \\ -\text{Nasal} \\ -\text{Lateralized} \end{bmatrix}$$

Hence a universal rule to switch the value of Consonantal is possible. It
is not clear, however, that the resulting segment is phonetically possible
so that a universal rule to switch the value of Diffuse may also be possible
(this would be the rule which insures that phonetically there are glides
only in the labial and palatal positions (i.e. [w] and [y]). Similarly, in the

and [n], which are both [+Diffuse]. Hence the universal rules predict that in these Mohawk clusters [UDiffuse] will be [+Diffuse]. That is, they *wrongly* predict *Cy and Cw instead of Cy and *Cw. A special Mohawk rule to switch to [−Diffuse] in these cases is therefore required.

However, under this assumption of Unmarkedness for [+Diffuse] in Grave consonants, the facts in (8.9) provide a striking support for the theory being outlined. The Diffuse distinction in Grave consonants is neutralized before o, u, and i. Therefore, in these positions in the dictionary, the markings will be [UDiffuse] and the universal principles will predict [+Diffuse] in all cases. Schematically, this yields *po, *pu, pi, *wo, *wu, wi instead of the correct representations ko, ku, pi, yo, yu, wi, apparently either disconfirming or at least not confirming the assumptions. But the crucial fact is that, independently of morpheme internal constraints, Mohawk must have a rule operating across morpheme boundaries which, before o and u, turns p to k and w to y.[19] Compare:

---

labial position there would appear to be no phonetic elements with the properties:

$$\begin{bmatrix} +\text{Consonantal} \\ +\text{Sonorant} \\ -\text{Vocalic} \\ +\text{Grave} \\ +\text{Diffuse} \\ -\text{Nasal} \end{bmatrix}$$

so that the same universal rule which works for the velars can switch the value of Consonantal here to yield phonetic [w]. It is this rule which, it is claimed, accounts for the 'ambiguous' behavior of [w]; that in some cases it behaves like a consonant but in others like a glide or vowel. Therefore, the claim is that because of these rules, it is possible for a language to represent both [w] and [y] as liquid consonants ([+Consonantal], [+Sonorant]) without special cost, and that [y] may be represented as velar ([+Grave], [−Diffuse]), also without any need for special, language particular rules. These matters will be discussed in greater detail and against the background of a deeper justification for the solution in Mohawk in Postal (to appear c).

[19] It is quite impossible to formulate these alternations in the opposite way, i.e., by letting k and y appear in the output of the neutralized positions and specifying the morphophonemic rule as one which turns k, and y to p and w respectively before i. For in fact neither k nor y switches to a 'labial' element before i across morpheme boundaries.

(8.11) [rahdahgwi':zaks]	'he looks for shoes'	hra+ahtahp+isak+s
(8.12) [rahdahgu':nis]	'he makes shoes'	hra+ahtahp+uni+s
(8.13) [rashuwi':zaks]	'he looks for holes'	hra+shuw+isak+s
(8.14) [rashuyu':nis]	'he makes holes'	hra+shuw+uni+s

But the operation of this rule will automatically turn morpheme internal *po, *pu, *wo, *wu into the correct sequences with k and y. Thus the neutralized positions can utilize the [UDiffuse] representations without addition of an ad hoc rule, even though the elements which appear before o and u have Marked values for Diffuse. This is exactly the kind of thing one would expect to find if the marking theory were correct, and it provides a striking, if limited, confirmation of both the marking theory in general and the assignment of Unmarked status to [+Diffuse] in Grave consonants. The facts in (8.10) also reveal a neutralization of the Diffuse distinction in Grave consonants. But in this case the Unmarked elements occur phonetically so the [UDiffuse] representation plus the universal rules predict the output phonetics without any Mohawk rules at all.

Therefore, the entire web of Mohawk morpheme internal restrictions in (8.7) through (8.10) is predicted from costless Unmarked dictionary representations at the cost of at most one special rule. At least five morpheme structure rules would have been required in the old theory. Thus, with respect to these facts at any rate, the Markedness theory apparently has built at least eighty percent of what superficially appear to be special, ad hoc Mohawk restrictions into the general theory of language.

It is important to inquire how this new theory characterizes the notion 'possible morpheme' in particular languages. In the earlier, or zero marking theory, 'possible morphemes' could be simply defined as those sequences of underlying segments which pass through the morpheme structure rules. That is, the possible

[wagi':da?s]	'I sleep'	wa+k+ita?w+s
[ganɔyi':yo?s]	'nice stones'	ka+nʌy+iyo+?s

Furthermore this would mean treating stems which show [w]-[y] and [kw]-[k] alternations with basic y and k, which is impossible, because the 'labial' forms show up not only before i but also before all other elements except o, u.

[rahdahgwage':das]	'he scrapes shoes'	hra+ahtahp+ket+as
[rahdahgu':nis]	'he makes shoes'	hra+ahtahp+uni+s

phonological matrices of morphemes in a language L were defined as that set which was the result of applying the morpheme structure rules of L to arbitrary phonological matrices. Thus in English an arbitrary matrix of, schematically, the form kmol is not possible, since application of English morpheme structure rules would have specified the first element as s, and the output would be [smol] which is possible. But in the new theory there are, for the most part, no morpheme structure rules. Thus, as we have seen in the Mohawk examples discussed above, there is no Mohawk morpheme structure rule which prohibits °yr and °yy. Then how is it to be predicted that morphemes containing such sequences are impossible in Mohawk? This is a difficult question to which we propose the following partial and tentative answer.

Observe that it is necessarily the case that for any dictionary position X____Y, if the Marked value of a feature F_j occurs in X____Y in the phonological representations of some morphemes, the Unmarked value of feature F_j must occur in X____Y in the representations of some morphemes. In other words, Marked values entail a contrast. Wherever there is no contrast, U markings must occur. Therefore, in every language the mapping from the level of M-U markings to that of +, − representations involves *every* single interpretation rule for U values of features but only *some* rules for M values. It therefore follows that the phonological matrices of the class of actual morphemes in a language select a certain subset of the set of all universal interpretation rules for M values of features, namely, just those which are required to interpret the actual M markings in this set of morphemes. It should be the case, therefore, that the notion possible morpheme in language L with a set of actual morphemes S can be defined as that class of M-U matrices which can be fully specified as +, − matrices without making use of any universal interpretation rule for M values which is not used in interpreting the M-U matrices of S.[20] Thus, for example, a

---

[20] It is of course only possible to test claims about 'possible morpheme' against phonetic forms. And these must be determined not only by the output of the M-U interpretation rules, but also by the full set of language particular phonological rules. Therefore the statement in the text must be revised to claim that the phonetic forms of possible morphemes are determined in the way suggested in conjunction with the application of

sequence with a +, − matrix containing [+Glottalized] or [+Pharyngealized] markings is not the phonological representation of any possible morpheme in English, since such specifications would require utilization of interpretation rules for [MGlottalized] or [MPharyngealized] and these rules play no role in the +, − interpretation of any *actual* English morphemes. This proposal about 'possible morpheme' seems to me to be directly in line with the fundamental assumption of the entire theory of Markedness. For what it comes down to is the assumption that a language cannot have a Marked sequence unless it has the corresponding Unmarked sequence (or unless there is a special rule to change the values). Therefore, the impossible phonological matrices are necessarily those which involve M specifications for features in positions where all actual morphemes contain only U specifications.[21]

This discussion of phonologically possible morpheme is also relevant to the question of how one might reasonably define

---

all relevant phonological rules. The necessity for this is obvious in the Mohawk p̱, w̱ cases discussed earlier. It was pointed out that many morphemes will come out of the interpretation rules with sequences like °p̱o, °w̱u, etc. However, this does not claim that there are possible morphemes in Mohawk with the phonetic forms [. . . gwo . . .] or [. . . wu . . .], etc. These are eliminated by the p̱, w̱ dissimilation rule before rounded vowels, which is also relevant for determining the phonetic forms of possible morphemes, i.e. which determines in such cases that the phonetic forms must be [. . . go . . .], [. . . yu . . .], etc.

[21] Difficult and poorly understood questions are raised by relations between M-U markings and morphological features as discussed in Chapter 6. It seems clear that possible morpheme is defined for native vocabulary only, or, more precisely perhaps, only for certain subparts of the vocabulary as defined by morphological features. In Mohawk, for example, it seems clear that possible morphemes do not include those with actual phonetic [p], [b], [m], etc. even though these occur in French and English borrowings and would involve M markings not found in the native vocabulary. This kind of fact is further evidence of the point made in footnote 7 of Chapter 6 that morphological features like Native may be universals and have formal and functional properties beyond those of providing an ad hoc division of forms. To the extent that it is true that intuitions of 'possible morpheme' are defined for speakers only for a subportion of the vocabulary, this is enormous additional evidence of the validity of morphological features (and exception features) which provide these divisions, that is, additional evidence of the total incorrectness of representing all alternations by segmental morphophonemes as in approaches like stratificational phonology.

the notion 'systematic phoneme' in terms of a theory involving M-U matrices. What would be involved substantively is the idea that somehow the relevant segmental elements of English, for example, do not involve Glottalization, Pharyngealization, etc., but do involve Voice, Grave, Strident, etc. Taking roughly the kind of considerations relevant for defining phonologically possible morpheme as above, it is not difficult to give a natural characterization of the notion 'systematic archiphoneme' of which systematic phonemes are a special subtype. What is involved in these notions is contrast. Not contrast exclusively in terms of superficial phonetic environment, as in autonomous phonemics, but rather contrast within the cells of M-U matrices. As pointed out, all contrasts are given by the presence of M markings. It is therefore simple to determine, for particular positions, those sets of features which involve contrasts, and these define the archiphonemes of those positions. The phonemes can then be defined in terms of the maximal set of distinctions found in all positions. The definitions can then be given on the M-U matrix type, the $+$, $-$ type, or both. Since nothing of principle is involved in these definitions, we shall not bother to give them in detail.

An important result of this new theory is that it provides a basis for the hierarchy of features which linguists in general (and most notably Jakobson) have recognized but not precisely characterized. It turns out that the rules which interpret M and U markings cannot be stated in random order. That is, the values of some M and U markings are determined by contexts defined over $+$ and $-$ values of other features but not M and U values. The contextually relevant features must, therefore, have their $+$ and $-$ values determined before the other M and U values may be interpreted. A good example is given by the interpretation of [UVoice]. In vowels this must clearly be specified as [$+$Voice]. This environment will have a simple formulation in terms of $+$ and $-$ values, say for argument,[22]

---

[22] The proviso here is indicative of a feeling, partly the result of considerations of Markedness, that the present set of features does not characterize the vowel-nonvowel distinction correctly. I suspect that there should be a single feature, say <u>Vowel,</u> which does so, this being primary both phonetically and phonologically. Furthermore, use of the feature Sonorant, which is necessary in a variety of cases, largely renders the Jakobsonian feature Vocalic unnecessary. One important advantage of

$$\begin{bmatrix} -\text{Consonantal} \\ +\text{Sonorant} \end{bmatrix}$$

But because of the differential Markedness of various consonant and vowel clusters, in terms of M and U representations vowels do not have any common properties as such. Thus such sequences as CVC, VVC, and CCV will have the following Markedness representations in terms of the feature Consonantal:

	C	V	C	V	V	C	C	C	V
Consonantal	U	U	U	M	M	U	U	M	U
Consonantal	+	−	+	−	−	+	+	+	−

(8.15)

Notice (8.15) asserts that the maximally Unmarked sequence consists of consonant + vowel + consonant, and that vowel sequences are less Marked than consonant clusters. The former assertion seems well-founded since it can provide the explanation for the universality of the CVC pattern. The latter is more controversial but seems right to me. It is, in any event, basically ir-

---

assuming Vowel, Consonantal, and Sonorant to be the three major features is that it becomes possible to characterize generally which elements can be syllabics. That is, segments may be syllabics (whatever this means exactly) if they are [+Sonorant] and have opposite values for the features Consonantal and Vowel. Thus vowels ([+Vowel], [−Consonantal]), nasals ([−Vowel], [+Consonantal]), and [r] and [l] sounds ([−Vowel], [+Consonantal]) may all be syllabics since they are [+Sonorant]. But true consonants like [p], [s] and nonresonant glides like [h] and [ʔ] cannot be because they are [−Sonorant] and resonant glides [w], [y], etc. cannot be because, although [+Sonorant], they fail the condition of Vowel-Consonantal value nonidentity. The suggestion would then be that elements which are [+Vowel] are universally specifiable as [+Sonorant] (and possibly [−Consonantal]). In other words, there is no M-U contrast possible in [+Vowel] segments for these two features. The U values which must occur take on positive values by virtue of principles in linguistic theory. The [r]- and [l]-like sounds would be distinguished from nasal consonants by the feature Nasal and from each other redundantly by Lateralization and Retroflexion.

relevant to the present point. But given the representations in (8.15), if the rule to interpret [UVoice] is to be maximally general, it must be stated in terms of contexts defined by + and − values of features like Consonantal. Hence, as is traditionally recognized, such features are higher in the hierarchy than Voice. The 'traditional recognition' was, of course, most often implicit only. It consisted in such facts as that, in describing phonemic systems, no linguist would ever make a fundamental division into voiced and voiceless phonemes, with a subsidiary division of the voiced elements into consonants and vowels, etc. Ultimately, it seems that with the growth of knowledge of Marked and Unmarked values, the order of interpretation rules will define precisely the (partial) hierarchy among phonological features and provide a principled basis for the descriptive practice of linguists in this regard.

It goes almost without saying that a theory as new, powerful, and comprehensive as that of phonological Markedness must necessarily involve a host of unsolved problems. A hierarchy of features provides part of the basis for explaining certain impossible phonological *systems*. For instance, there clearly can be no consonant system which consists exclusively of palatal elements, i.e., in which there is a set of elements that can be abbreviated:

(8.16)   ť   ď
         tš   dž
         š   ž
         ľ
         ř
         ň
         y

Such a system provides eleven consonantal elements, which is more than some languages have, so numbers are not the difficulty here (Mohawk has only eight consonantal elements). It is evident that part of the deviance of such a system consists of making use of very low features in the hierarchy, Voice, Nasal, Abrupt Onset, Abrupt Offset, etc., at a point at which higher order distinctions, in particular the fundamental positional properties of Grave and Diffuse, have not been utilized. A further deviant factor is that the only major position represented is palatal, which is actually the most Marked of the four major positions for consonants. But this is far from accounting for everything.

There is no doubt that besides a hierarchy of features there are certain obligatory contrasts. In other words, not only must dictionary segments be composed of M and U values determined by certain hierarchical arrangements, so that for some features no M may appear unless there are M markings for other features, for some features there must be some M markings in the dictionary. Thus although it is not necessary for a language to have a Voice contrast, or an Aspiration contrast, or any of the tone contrasts, or a Lateralization contrast, it must have a contrast between vowel and consonant, between high and nonhigh vowels, between several[23] different major consonantal positions, etc. Many other properties are so commonly contrastive as to raise suspicions. For example the stop-fricative and true consonant-liquid contrasts are reported lacking in only a tiny number of cases, suggesting perhaps that they are phonologically present and only missing phonetically. This means that there is a kind of minimal phonological system for all languages (Jakobson, 1962:319) with the varying actual dictionary systems of different languages a function of differential uses of various optional contrastive possibilities which are lower in the hierarchy.

Just as there are obligatory contrasts, so also there appear to be prohibited contrasts. The present writer is convinced, for example, that there can be no Voice contrast in vowels, probably no Abrupt Onset contrast in nasals, no Nasal contrast in laterals, etc. It is far from clear at the moment, however, how either obligatory or prohibited contrasts should be built into the formal system of phonological theory. A number of possibilities suggest themselves, but it seems too soon to propose and certainly far too soon to justify firm ideas on these topics. What is clear is

---

[23] Although the gross phonetic facts would suggest that as few as two positions may exist, since there are languages without labials or without velars, I suspect that in systematic terms the minimum number of distinctions is three with labial, dental, and velar contrasts being obligatory. That is, in those cases where only two contrasting positions appear to exist, I suspect that structurally there are three with phonetic merging. This is what appears to be the case in Mohawk with its systematic labial p merging with velars phonetically.

only that the problem must be considered in light of the general conception of Marked and Unmarked values and the universal interpretative rules these require.[24]

Another unsolved problem concerns the fact that the notions of Marked and Unmarked must doubtlessly be extended beyond dictionary representations to cover phonological rules as well. This is shown rather clearly, for example, by such well-known phenomena as word final devoicing of consonants, which is found in a large number of diverse languages (Russian, German, Turkish). In all of these cases this phenomenon extends beyond mere dictionary Markedness, since even dictionary voiced consonants (i.e. [MVoice]) are devoiced when word final. What needs explanation is the fact that in the context_____# the rules always devoice rather than voice. That an account of this must be based on notions of Markedness is obvious, since [−Voice] is of course the Unmarked member in non-Sonorant segments. A similar and related problem is given by the distribution of consonant voicing intervocalically in languages without a Voice contrast. It appears that in general in such a case the consonants will be voiced. In both this and the final devoicing case there is something of the kind of asymmetry of feature values in particular contexts which the M-U theory was largely designed to handle. What is crucially different, however, is that in these cases the contexts are not dictionary contexts but environments at least in part determined by language particular phonological rules.

It is likely that a treatment of such facts will require phonological rules whose right hand sides contain specifications in terms of U values as well as + and − (something required on other grounds as well; see below). The interpretation would then be that after the application of the rule introducing the U value, the U is interpreted by the universal principles, but now in terms of the relatively late phonologically determined context in which it is found. However, although necessary, such a proposal would by no means be sufficient. It fails, for example, to handle the intervocalic voicing of consonants in languages with-

---

[24] It should be evident that, given a system of phonetic features, a rich system of obligatory and prohibited contrasts makes an enormous contribution to the ease of language learning (as does the hierarchy of features) by vastly decreasing the number of possible phonological systems possible for fixed phonetic facts.

out Voice contrast since it is certainly not true in general that [UVoice] is [+Voice] in consonants occurring between vowels. This is at best the case only where there is no Voice contrast. It seems then that here a difference between two different kinds of [UVoice] may be showing up. [UVoice] appears to behave one way in a context X____Y if there is a contrast in X____Y, but another way if there is not. How this is to be handled is far from clear. Proposals to allow Markedness values in phonological rules raise many questions. Should both M and U be allowed? Can all + and − values be eliminated? (This seems dubious.) What kinds of combinations of the various values can occur in the same rules? How are these possibilities related to special properties of different features? And so forth. To none of these can we offer serious answers at the moment.

Other problems with Markedness in rules are easily found. It was pointed out earlier, for instance, that no language has all [+Glottalized] consonants. Making [+Glottalized] the Marked member automatically specifies all consonants as [−Glottalized] unless there is a dictionary contrast with M specifications. However, assuming no contrast, the cost of specifying all consonants or some large subset as [+Glottalized] with a late phonological rule is not very high. Yet such rules would yield situations not actually found, situations in which languages without a Glottalization contrast had predominantly [+Glottalized] consonants. It follows that some important constraints must be added to the rules, constraints which in some way either prohibit or vastly increase the cost of phonological rules which specify segments with Marked values (of at least a wide variety of features). But again, exactly how such constraints should be formulated is not known.

I remarked above that rules which introduced U values were required independently. This was a reference to the remarks made in footnote 19 of Chapter 4. There we discussed the rule which accounted for [t]-[s] and [k]-[s] alternations in English pairs like 'pirate-piracy' and 'opaque-opacity.' If we consider these alternations, in particular the latter, we are struck with the relatively large number of features which differentiate the alternating segments. Thus, at the end of the universal rules for interpreting M and U values k̲ would be a set of specifications including:

(8.17)

$$\begin{bmatrix} +\text{Consonantal} \\ -\text{Sonorant} \\ +\text{Grave} \\ -\text{Diffuse} \\ -\text{Apical} \\ +\text{Abrupt Onset} \\ +\text{Abrupt Offset} \\ -\text{Strident} \end{bmatrix}$$

On the other hand the natural set of binary features to determine phonetic [s] would be:

(8.18)

$$\begin{bmatrix} +\text{Consonantal} \\ -\text{Sonorant} \\ -\text{Grave} \\ +\text{Diffuse} \\ +\text{Apical} \\ -\text{Abrupt Onset} \\ -\text{Abrupt Offset} \\ +\text{Strident} \end{bmatrix}$$

These two segment types thus differ in at least six feature specifications. The question arises whether each of these changes must be made ad hoc by the rule of English which accounts for the [k]-[s] alternations. The answer is very likely not. Many of them can be predicted from Markedness considerations if the rule simply specifies the features in question as U. In fact, I suspect that the only features which must be specified directly in the English rule are Abrupt Onset and possibly Grave and Diffuse. The English rule would then at worst specify these with + and − values on the right hand side, but would specify Abrupt Offset, Apical, and Strident simply as U. Their values are then determined by a return to the universal principles which, in particular, must indicate that [U Abrupt Offset] is [−Abrupt Offset] in a segment which is [−Abrupt Onset]; that [UApical] is [+Apical] in [−Grave], [+Diffuse] segments; and that [UStrident] is [+Strident] in [+Diffuse], [−Abrupt Onset] segments.[25] What is crucial here is again the hierarchy of features. Involved is ap-

---

[25] These remarks are essentially congruent with Jakobson's position about the universal structure and relations of pure stops, fricatives, and affricates except that they implicitly deny the Jakobsonian claim that affricates are strident stops. This is too simple for the quite elementary reason that there exist nonstrident affricates. Cf. the discussion later in the text.

parently the fact that as feature values are changed by the rules it is possible to allow features subordinate to those changed in the hierarchy to take on their Unmarked values. In many cases this will lead to changes of values for them also, as here. Thus the theory of phonology is to be constructed in such a way that when a feature value is changed from + to − or vice versa, the cheapest thing which can happen is for subordinate feature values to take on their Unmarked values. Rules of this type and the alternation facts which they describe are therefore an additional important source of evidence about the proper establishment of the feature hierarchy.

The possibility of utilizing the hierarchy for switching subordinate features to their Unmarked values automatically, without language particular apparatus, builds a vast variety of special facts into the theory of grammar. Consider for example the not uncommon shift of stop consonants to glottal stops. With the subordinate switching assumption it will be necessary to specify in the language particular rule only a shift of one feature, Consonantal. However, the particular stop involved might be:

(8.19)
$$\begin{bmatrix} -\text{Grave} \\ +\text{Diffuse} \\ +\text{Apical} \\ -\text{Tense} \\ \text{etc.} \end{bmatrix}$$

All of these are the opposite of the specifications defining glottal stops. However, these facts are predictable from U values in [−Consonantal], [−Sonorant] segments, so that by specification of U in the rule which shifts consonantality they will occur automatically.

It is being assumed in this discussion, of course, that the cost of specifying a feature in a rule as U is less than specifying it as + or −. A natural proposal would be that U is without cost, + or − each of cost 1. If M specifications had to occur in rules, these would probably be even more costly than + or − values. But in fact there is no ground for such occurrence. It is necessary to allow rules which yield segments not only with Unmarked subordinate values but also with Marked ones. In other words, there must be rules which, in effect, not only turn [t] to [s] (as in English) where Strident takes on its Unmarked value, but also rules which turn [d] to [ð] (as in Spanish) where Strident has its Marked position. But such contrasts do not require M values in rules. It is sufficient to take rules like the former to have [−Abrupt Onset], [UStrident] on the right hand side; rules like the latter to have [−Abrupt Onset], [−Strident]. In other words, if features take on Unmarked values this is predicted by the costless device of U values on the right hand sides of rules. If they take on Marked values this is accounted for by specifying the relevant + or − values on the right hand sides of rules with, of course, the associated greater cost this entails. That is, there is only a two-way contrast in values, not a three-way contrast. Values are either predictable by underlying universal marking principles in which case U specifications suffice or they are not, in which case the appropriate + or − value suffices. It is this actual listing of + or − values in rules which indicates that the relevant values are in fact Marked. Although there are important insights obviously involved in the use of Markedness values in phonological rules, it should be apparent that this must raise a variety of difficult and fundamental questions which cannot be answered at the moment. For further illustration and discussion of these matters against the background of the facts of English cf. Halle and Chomsky (to appear).

A short digression on the description of stops, fricatives and affricates, revealing differences between the present approach and that of traditional Jakobsonian distinctive features, is perhaps in order since these matters have figured in our examples.

Given a fixed position, let us use dental for illustration, Jakobson's framework distinguishes four contrasting types of segments in terms of two features, <u>Interrupted</u> and <u>Strident</u>:

(8.20)	plain stop	[t]	[+Interrupted],	[−Strident]
	noisy fricative	[s]	[−Interrupted],	[+Strident]
	quiet fricative	[θ]	[−Interrupted],	[−Strident]
	affricate	[ts]	[+Interrupted],	[+Strident]

The fundamental claim is that affricates are strident stops. However, this is not tenable for the quite simple reason that there exist non-Strident affricates, for example, [tθ] which bears the same relation to [θ] as [ts] does to [s]. These exist in many North American Indian languages, for example Chipewyan (Li, 1946:398). Such facts have led Halle to propose the addition of a new feature, <u>Abrupt Offset</u> in addition to Jakobson's <u>Inter-</u>

<u>rupted</u> (my terminology: <u>Abrupt Onset</u>) and <u>Strident</u>. This yields
+, − representations as follows:

(8.21)

plain stop	[t]	[+Abrupt Onset],	[+Abrupt Offset],	[−Strident]
noisy fricative	[s]	[−Abrupt Onset],	[−Abrupt Offset],	[+Strident]
quiet fricative	[θ]	[−Abrupt Onset],	[−Abrupt Offset],	[−Strident]
noisy affricate	[ts]	[+Abrupt Onset],	[−Abrupt Offset],	[+Strident]
quiet affricate	[tθ]	[+Abrupt Onset],	[−Abrupt Offset],	[−Strident]

In other words, <u>Abrupt Onset</u> groups plain stops with affricates,
<u>Abrupt Offset</u> groups affricates with fricatives.

However, in addition to an analysis of stops, fricatives, and
affricates in terms of values for a feature of onset and noisiness,
Jakobson (1962:320, 364, and elsewhere) also insisted on a
hierarchical relationship among these three types which definitely
implied greater Markedness for affricates than for fricatives and
for fricatives than for stops (1962:320):

L'acquisition des constrictives suppose l'acquisition des occlusives et,
parallèlement, dans les systèmes phonologiques du monde, l'existence
des premières implique celle des dernières. Il n'y a pas de langues san
occlusives, mais d'autre part on trouve maintes langues, en Oceanie, en
Afrique et dans l'Amérique du Sud, completement depourvues de
constrictives . . .

L'acquisition enfantine des mi-occlusives opposées aux occlusives cor-
respondantes suppose l'acquisition des constrictives de la même série;
egalement dans les langues du monde l'opposition d'une mi-occlusive
et d'une occlusive dentale, labiale ou vélopalatale implique la présence
d'une constrictive dentale, labiale ou vélopalatale.

In terms of the developing theory of Markedness we can attempt
to represent these facts as follows.

A hierarchy among the features is recognized with Abrupt
Onset primary, Abrupt Offset secondary, and Strident tertiary.
Furthermore, we specify that there is no Strident contrast for
plain stops, i.e. that the combinations of features which define
these determine [UStrident], and that there is no Abrupt Offset
contrast for elements with a [−Abrupt Onset] value. That is,
of the four possible combinations defined by two values of the
two 'abrupt' features, only three exist. There is apparently nothing
which would be indicated as [ˢt] or [θt]. We partially represent
these facts with the following assignment of M and U values:

	t	ts	tθ	s	θ
Abrupt Onset	U	U	U	M	M
Abrupt Offset	U	M	M	U	U
Strident	U	U	M	U	M

(8.22)

The universal rules to connect the values of (8.22) to those of (8.21) are elementary. [UAbrupt Onset] becomes [+Abrupt Onset]: [UAbrupt Offset] takes on the *same* + or − value as previously interpreted Abrupt Onset: [UStrident] takes on the value *opposite* to previously specified Abrupt Offset. This then is a very good example of the role the order of interpretation of M and U values plays in defining the hierarchy among phonological features.

Degree of Markedness alone then explains Jakobson's observations concerning the dominance of plain stops over fricatives (and affricates by transitivity). That is, if a language has no contrast along these dimensions, either in all environments or in fixed positions, the universal rules specify a plain stop. However, the degree of Markedness alone does not explain the dominance of fricatives over affricates. This can only be explained by the hierarchical assumption that Abrupt Onset dominates Abrupt Offset, and that a contrast for the latter is only possible in the presence of one for the former. Schematically (with both +, − and M, U, values superimposed):

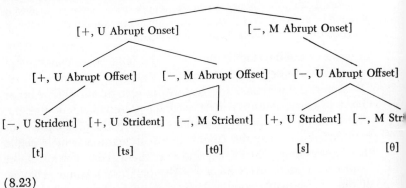

(8.23)

The hierarchical dominance of Abrupt Onset over Abrupt Offset in the theory thus plays a double role. It simplifies the rules mapping M-U representations into + and − values, and it explains the kind of facts discovered by scholars like Jakobson concerning the relative distribution, ontogeny, and loss in speech pathology of fricatives and affricates. It must be emphasized, of course, that this analysis involves all those difficulties of formalization concerned with obligatory and prohibited contrasts which were discussed earlier. In fact, this analysis is an excellent illustration of both phenomena, and is a good demonstration of the need for linguistic theory to ultimately incorporate both kinds.

It should be remarked, of course, that this analysis is overly simple. It implies, for example, that the relative status of plain stops, fricatives, and affricates is identical in all of the major consonantal positions. This is not right. As mentioned before, it seems clear that in the palatal position strident affricates are more natural than plain stops. No doubt many other refinements are necessary. Nonetheless, this description may serve to indicate something of the way in which the theory of M-U values can serve to provide the basis for a formalization of many traditional linguistic insights.

The well-known phenomenon of vowel harmony reveals in a very interesting way relations between the Markedness ideas of the present chapter and the concept of morphological features as discussed in Chapter 6. Furthermore, this phenomenon provides, I believe, important evidence of the essential correctness of both of these features of current systematic phonemic theory.

Vowel harmony exists where the vowels of morphemes must share some property, i.e. they must all be front, or all rounded, or all tense, etc. Vowel harmony is thus, incidentally, an important basis for determining the proper set of features for vowel description in the languages of the world (Jakobson, 1962:635). The harmony may involve more than one feature. In Turkish, to mention an example we shall use as the basis for our discussion, vowels must agree both in the features Grave (front-back) and Rounded. There are morphemes containing Grave Rounded, Grave nonRounded, nonGrave Rounded, and nonGrave nonRounded vowels, but none with both Grave and nonGrave or Rounded and nonRounded.

Vowel harmony is, in a rather clear sense, a phenomenon which lies halfway between the kind of structure provided by the Naturalness Condition and the largely phonetically arbitrary divisions of vocabulary determined by morphological features. The phonetic facts in general predict the classification of forms, and to this extent the situation is in accord with Naturalness. But it is whole morphemes which must be characterized, rather than individual segments, so to this extent the situation is as it is in the case of arbitrary vocabulary divisions. Consider the treatment of this kind of fact within a theory incorporating the notions of Markedness. First, all those features of vowels partaking of the harmony will be represented as U in the dictionary. Thus in Turkish all vowels will be marked [UGrave], [URounded] in the dictionary. The universal interpretative rules will then specify these as the appropriate + and − values. For our discussion here it is not even necessary to consider which values these would be. It is enough to recognize that at this point in derivations, every vowel has the same + or − value for both the phonological features Grave and Rounded. This amounts to the claim that within Turkish the *segmental* distinctions between [+Grave] and [−Grave] and between [+Rounded] and [−Rounded] within vowel segments are neutralized.

However, since some morphemes contain front vowels and some back, and since some contain Rounded vowels and others nonRounded, the treatment of all vowel segments with [UGrave] and [URounded] is obviously insufficient. In addition it is necessary to posit two <u>morphological features</u>, mnemonically, FRONT and ROUND. Therefore, assuming a +, − representation for morphological features, every morpheme taking part in the harmony system will have one value of each of these features. This is still not sufficient, since morphological features have as such no phonetic consequences. These can only be determined by language particular rules. It is therefore necessary to have rules which determine the <u>Marked</u> values of the segmental phonological features Grave and <u>Rounded</u> in vowels. However, the crucially significant fact is that these rules, which are required by our treatment of the distinction with morphological features, <u>are in general needed in the grammar in any event</u>. That is, vowel harmony cases are especially significant instances where morpheme internal neutralizations which have <u>Marked</u> phonetic realizations do not require special, ad hoc rules. This follows because in languages with vowel harmony, and particularly in Turkish, only <u>lexical</u> morphemes have inherent, unpredictably harmonic properties. Grammatical morphemes have variant harmonic properties according to the lexical morphemes of the words in which they occur. Thus, in Turkish, the same grammatical morpheme will sometimes have [+Grave], and sometimes [−Grave] vowels depending on whether the lexical morpheme it occurs with is of the [−FRONT] or [+FRONT] type. This means that vowel harmony languages must, quite independently of how the morpheme internal constraints are handled, contain rules which specify the vowels of grammatical morphemes with features harmonic to lexical morphemes. These rules guarantee the projection of the inherent harmony, which in the dictionary is limited to morphemes, to the superficial harmony of sentences in which the vowels of a *word* are harmonic. But the fact is that these very same rules can be used to predict the Marked harmonic features of vowels within morphemes from the noncontrasting values predicted by the universal interpretation from the U values in the dictionary.

In other words, suppose we assume that the Unmarked values are [−Grave] and [−Rounded]. At the end of the application of the interpretative principles, every vowel in Turkish will therefore be [−Grave] and [−Rounded]. There will then be rules which say, schematically: All vowels in a word containing a head lexical morpheme which is [−FRONT] become [+Grave], all vowels in a word containing a head lexical morpheme which is [+ROUND] become [+Rounded]. In this way the rules which operate across morpheme boundaries to determine the vowel features of grammatical morphemes serve also to predict the Marked values of the harmonic features in lexical morphemes. Hence this kind of fact is a strong support for the Markedness treatment of morpheme internal phonological constraints in exactly the same way as the Mohawk examples treated above. Of course, the description of harmony we have given is oversimplified in many ways irrelevant to the present discussion. An actual description of Turkish would require a number of refinements which need not concern us here.

The chief point of the above discussion of harmony is that the combination of morphological features and Markedness assumptions permits a description of vowel harmony which lists only what is unpredictable and which makes use of only the minimally necessary rules. Each lexical morpheme is listed only with the unpredictable properties which indicate whether it belongs to one harmonic class or the other. Individual vowels are specified without cost as maximally normal for all harmonic features. Nonnormal or Marked values of features are then in large part predicted from the morphological properties plus the independently required morphophonemic rules.

Vowel harmony is a phenomenon which should ultimately contribute important evidence with respect to the determination of Markedness in vowel features. We should expect to find, within particular languages manifesting this feature, some independent grounds for having the morphophonemic rules specify one value or another of the harmonic features. And just these values are the Marked ones. It should also be pointed out that there are some important universal features of vowel harmony not yet accounted for. In particular, our assumption of a largely arbitrary character for morphological features might suggest that languages will be found in which arbitrary phonological features are harmonic. But this is not the case, and there are evidently very strong constraints on which features may enter into harmonic relationships. This means that the class of vowel harmony morphological features must be a universal. However, even this will not suffice unless the class of phonological rules is universally constrained in accordance with the morphological features. If we are to avoid, for example, the possibility of a language in which vowels are harmonic for falling tone, it is necessary not only to constrain the class of morphological features, but also to limit phonological rules in such a way that they cannot mark all the vowels of some words with [+Falling Tone]. How this is to be done is not at all clear at the moment. It is evident, though, that there is some kind of linkage between the morphological features relevant for vowel harmony and certain phonological rules. This is also clear on other grounds from the very fact that all languages with vowel harmony appear to extend the agreement beyond lexical morphemes to the words they occur in. Both of these facts are probably related to the suggestion made in Chapter 6 that morphological features probably were associated with at least one phonological rule, in a sense of 'associated with' which is evidently not well understood. It is perhaps not insignificant, however, that apparently the class of features relevant for harmony in different languages is the same class which permits various kinds of phonological rules, in particular shifts of whole sets of segments, mergings, dissimilations, assimilations, etc.

Similarly, features relevant for harmony appear exclusive with those normally called prosodic, which tend to undergo their own special kinds of rules (cf. particularly that kind called <u>feature jump</u> in footnote 10 of Chapter 14). As with most other phenomena treated in this book, it is also the case with vowel harmony that our knowledge at the moment has rather clear limits. While certain aspects of a correct solution seem clear and can be well justified, other aspects involve poorly understood features of language and shade off into areas where a complete account can only be hoped for as the result of much future investigation of different sorts.

An interesting discussion of Turkish vowel harmony in relation to phonological theory is provided by Lyons (1962). This article is worth brief discussion so that we can relate our ideas to a somewhat larger realm of issues. Lyons argues not unconvincingly for the superiority of the British Prosodic approach to vowel harmony to that of autonomous phonemics. He notes correctly the enormous redundancy of autonomous phonemic representations in cases of harmony. However, this is in a way rather misleading. It overlooks the deeper and more fundamental fact that autonomous phonemic representations are almost always enormously redundant, harmony or not, since they necessarily mark all predictable features whose rules of prediction are not statable in purely phonetic terms. In the Prosodic approach, which Lyons advocates, the description is in terms of two kinds of elements, linear phonematic elements and prosodies. The prosodies are essentially phonetic features with domains of variable length, one phonematic unit, two, etc. which must somehow be indicated. In the treatment of the harmony Lyons extracts four prosodies, F(ront), B(ack), R(ounded) and N(onrounded). Each <u>word</u> is then represented by a sequence of phonematic units in which no distinctions for the harmonic properties are given and also by a pair of prosodies.

It is not difficult to see the advantages of a Prosodic treatment over that required by standard autonomous phonemics, and the Prosodic attempt to represent the intuition that the harmonic features should not be indicated vowel by vowel is obviously correct. However, from the point of view of characterizing the linguistic structure which actually underlies vowel harmony, or other kinds of phonological phenomena for that matter, the Prosodic approach is very far from adequate. In fact, most of the important questions have not even been raised in this approach. In particular, no attempt has been made to integrate the phonological representations with the grammatical structure. By marking each <u>word</u> with the prosodic elements, the approach misses the fact that the harmonic properties are determined by lexical morphemes and are inherent features of these. Secondly, the kind of formal structures represented by Prosodic representations has never been specified. Prosodies are said not to be in linear combination with the strings of phonematic units, but nothing more than this has been said. To this extent no real theory of Prosodic representations exists. As a partial function of this, and most fundamentally, Prosodists have, quite like ordinary autonomous phonemecists, not faced the problem of specifying what kinds of phonological rules map Prosodic representations onto phonetic structures. It is clear, however, that by treating the Prosodies as elements distinct from both segmental phonological elements *and their features,* a theory necessarily raises a host of unnecessary formal difficulties with phonological rules. In addition, the incompatibility of such an approach with notions of Markedness is an enormous loss.

It seems safe to conclude, therefore, that the Prosodic approach, while embodying some correct insights about the redundancy and arbitrariness of autonomous phonemic representation, has not moved very far toward a theory which overcomes these correctly. Many of the particular features of this approach and its gaps seem to come directly from a failure to recognize the componential character of phonological segments, and from a failure to consider how phonological structure fits into an overall grammar which associates semantic, syntactic, and phonetic representations. For more detailed criticism of Prosodic phonology from the point of view of the (early) theory of systematic phonemics cf. Langendoen (1964a, 1964b).

Recognition of the componential character of phonological segments would have meant the realization that redundancies can be eliminated without destroying the natural relation between phonetic and phonological structure given by the Naturalness Condition. Recognition of integration within an overall grammatical description would have meant the acceptance of the fact that phonological properties are the specification of unpredictable pronunciation facts of minimal grammatical elements, i.e. morphemes.

It is therefore interesting that, in large part, Prosodic criticism of autonomous phonemics and autonomous criticism of Prosodic phonology are both right. This is only paradoxical if one assumes that one of these theories must be correct. From the point of view of systematic theory, however, it is not at all surprising, since this view claims that while both of them incorporate correct insights, both contain many errors. Schematically:

(8.24) Prosodic phonology is correct in noticing part of the enormous redundancy of autonomous phonemic structures, in noticing the predictability of features from grammatical structure, in noticing the arbitrariness of certain segmental distinctions, in noticing that the same set of contrasts is not found in all positions, and in noticing that the same phonetic entity may have very different phonological statuses in different contexts.

(8.25) Autonomous phonemics is correct in noticing the chaotic character of Prosodic representations, i.e. their lack of specifiable formal structures in comparison to the string structure of autonomous structures, in noticing a certain arbitrariness in whether phenomena are to be treated as prosodies or segments, in noticing a lack of interest in generalizations, and in noticing a failure to maintain a natural relation between phonetic and phonological structure.

Both theories are inadequate because of a failure to deal with the question of the form of phonological rules and a consequent failure to specify the nature of phonological structure with sufficient precision; both miss the fact that phonological structure is essentially 'morphophonemic' in character, i.e. that it is concerned fundamentally with the question of how the pronunciation of whole sentences is predicted from the inherent phonological properties of individual morphemes; both miss almost entirely the asymmetrical properties involved in Markedness; both are much too little interested in phonological universals in general and hence necessarily burden particular descriptions with universally statable facts. Finally, because of all these limitations both of them have failed to arrive at empirical descriptions which take advantage of all the structural possibilities in particular languages for predicting phonetic facts.

APPENDIX: THE INCOMPATIBILITY OF STRATIFICATIONAL GRAMMAR AND A LEXICON

In the stratificational view of linguistic structure, it is assumed that there are four distinct strata, each of which is an independent system with its own generative rules (tactic rules) and its own basic vocabulary of primitive elements (which are uniformly indicated with the suffix -on). The four current properly linguistic strata are, in hierarchical order from 'top' to 'bottom,' the sememic, the lexemic, the morphemic, and the phonemic. On each stratum there are complex entities, terminologically indicated by the suffix -eme. It is apparently the function of the tactic rules on a particular stratum X to generate both the class of X-emes and the possible combinations of X-emes. Fundamental to this approach is the assumption that the vocabularies of each stratum are totally distinct and completely ad hoc to the particular language of description, and that no elements of one stratum automatically carry over in the rules to the next. Each X-on on each stratum must be realized (technical term) as zero, one, or more elements (X-1-emes) on the stratum one below by special rules (realization rules).

Unfortunately, this so-called theory is in large part empty, merely a terminology, because the nature of the highest, or sememic, domain has never been specified beyond metaphor. No precise account of the nature of structural objects on this level has ever been given, no description of the tactic rules required to generate these unspecified entities has been offered, and no discussion of the form of realization rules between this stratum and the one below (lexemic) has been presented. Of course, without a precise description of the kinds of structural objects being assumed, questions about either the tactic or the realization rules cannot even be raised. Essentially all that we have been told about the sememic level is that its objects are 'networks' involving 'multiple connectedness' and that 'linear order' is not characteristic of this domain (Lamb, 1964:70; Gleason, 1964:81–82, 85–87). In addition, it is claimed (Lamb, 1964b:110) that all tactic rules are statements about class membership. But rules generating things which could reasonably be called 'networks' and which have some linguistic interpretation have never been described so that this is not very helpful. The emptiness here is almost admitted by Gleason (1964:94) who remarks that ". . . the best form of statement for the semotactic rules has not yet been established." There are many other fundamental ways in which this approach fails to provide a reasonably clear theory, some of which have been discussed in earlier chapters. There seems no need to go into this further here.

In spite of the vagueness and extensive emptiness of the stratificational view, it is easily enough disconfirmed further in terms of what is clear. In particular, the requirement of vacuous rules in place of a dictionary, which it cannot allow, is obvious. Because each X-on must be realized on the stratum one below by special rules, there cannot be any single entity (lexical item in the sense of Dictionary Entries) which consist of an association of three types of properties. Rather, the situation must be as follows. (I utilize an example partially discussed by Lamb, 1964a:62). What a traditional linguistic view would treat as the lexical item 'man' has, in stratificational terms, no meaning. Instead, there are different objects on several different strata related by 'rules.' In particular there is a sememe ^{S}/man/ which is a combination of some sort of semons given by the 'network':

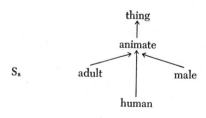

(8.26)

Each of the words here presumably names a semon. The meaning of the geometry, the arrows, etc. in terms of linguistic interpretation has never been explained. It is far from obvious. How, for example, would the empirical claims about 'man' differ if some or all of the arrows were reversed, if positions of symbols were interchanged, if both, etc., etc.?

On the next or lexemic stratum there is one lexeme which is of maximally simple structure, i.e. consists of a single lexon ᴸ/man/ which, it must be emphasized, is a single unanalyzable symbol (Lamb, 1964a:63). There are now some important unclarities. We are told several times that the X-ons are the elements which relate to the X-l-emes, for example, Lamb (1965: 45, diagram). But it is obvious here that to realize such a sememic structure as (8.26) as the lexeme ᴸ/man/ it is necessary to talk about the whole sememic network. For no part of it really has anything to do in particular with ᴸ/man/. If we take a slightly different sememic 'network' in which the semon 'male' is replaced by the semon 'female,' we find that this network must be realized as a totally distinct lexeme (i.e. single arbitrary symbol). The similarities in semon composition of these two networks can therefore play no role at all in the operation of the realization rules. And this must be a general fact about such 'networks.' In other words, while the idea that the X-ons are related by realization to X-l-emes may make some sense between lexemic and morphemic strata, or morphemic and phonemic strata, it makes no sense at all between sememic and lexemic strata. The fact that this yawning difficulty has never been noticed by advocates is some indication of the extent to which this is a serious theory being applied in actual linguistic descriptions.

I cannot imagine what any realization rule for (8.26) would be like, and since nothing has ever been proposed, there is no particular reason to think there is any type of rule which would reasonably do the job. Ignoring this, however, let us represent the relevant hypothetical realization rule as:

$$(8.27) \quad S_a \quad \overset{R}{===\!\!\!\Rightarrow} \quad ᴸ/man/$$

It is now necessary to relate this lexemic structure to the next lower level, that of morphemes. On the morphemic stratum the minimal elements are morphons, i.e. traditional atomic segmental morphophonemes, which occur in linear order. Hence the realization rule in this case between the lexon ^{L}/man/ and the stratum below is a rule which says that a single symbol on the Lexemic stratum is realized as a sequence of three morphophonemes. Schematically again:

$$(8.28) \quad ^L\text{/man/} \quad \overset{R}{===\Rightarrow} \quad ^M\text{/man/}$$

Unlike the input, the output here is therefore not a single symbol. At this point the rules achieve some generality since these same morphons will realize many other lexons. Hence the rules which realize these as sequences of phonemes on the lowest linguistic stratum are not ad hoc. They do, however, suffer from the flaws involved in autonomous phonemic theory in general and the special defects of stratificational phonology, with its violations of Naturalness, absence of ordering, lack of sensitivity to syntactic structure, etc., etc. which were discussed at length earlier.

Instead of a dictionary giving unpredictable associations of properties, stratificational grammar is committed to useless 'rules' like (8.27) and (8.28), 'rules' with no linguistic function whatever. Observe that the intermediate, or lexemic, stage here obviously gives no information at all, since the representation on this level is simply an arbitrary symbol unrelated except by ad hoc rules, including (8.27) and (8.28), to any other elements in the grammar. Nonetheless, this stage cannot be skipped for any item. Unbelievably, in his latest work, Lamb (1965:42–48) makes this intolerably bad situation exactly twice as bad by introducing within each stratum a new division between basic X-emes and X-emes proper. And he insists that in each case this difference be mediated by special realization rules. Hence now instead of a single lexical item 'man' consisting of an association of unpredictably combined properties of different sorts, Lamb is committed to having a basic sememe, a rule (rules?) to realize this as a sememe proper, a rule to realize this as a basic lexeme, a rule to realize this as a lexeme proper, a rule to realize this as a basic morpheme, and finally rules to realize the basic morpheme as a sequence of morphons. In cases like 'man,' all of these intermediate stages are completely useless and contribute no information since the representations are simply arbitrary symbols. They are entirely artifacts of the underlying assumptions which they disconfirm.

The reader should try to imagine what it means, under stratificational assumptions, to say that a person learns a new lexical item, say 'gargoyle.' In a reasonable theory one would say that what has taken place is the addition of a single new set of semantic, syntactic, and phonological properties to the lexicon of the relevant speaker. But in stratificational grammar, the claims are that the speaker has had to learn a new basic sememe, a rule to realize this as a sememe (combination of semons), a rule to map this onto the new basic lexeme which has also been learned, a new rule to map this onto a lexeme, a new rule to map this lexeme onto the new basic morpheme which has been learned, and finally a rule to map this onto a new morpheme (combination of morphons). In short, the claim is that in learning 'gargoyle' a speaker must learn at least six new linguistic elements (basic sememe, sememe, basic lexeme, lexeme, basic morpheme, morpheme, and at least five new rules). Furthermore, the intermediate three 'rules' are simply ad hoc mappings of one arbitrary symbol onto another. The fundamental fact is, therefore, that the notion of 'realization' or 'stratification' confuses regular linguistic rules, i.e. true generalizations holding for sets of elements, with arbitrary associations of properties which cannot be predicted and must be listed.

It is important to emphasize that the incompatibility of stratificational grammar with a lexicon and its involvement with such useless, linguistically contentless 'rules' as those just illustrated is by no means an accidental or peripheral fact or one which can be eliminated by some minor change in the theory. It is a consequence of the most fundamental and defining assumptions of this set of ideas, namely, that the strata are totally distinct systems whose relations are mediated only by special rules. The mistake revealed here is, in a way, simply a generalization to all of linguistic structure of those errors revealed in our discussion of the stratificational rejection of the Naturalness Condition.[26]

---

[26] Notice, for example, that analogous to phonetic-phonological relations, Surface-Deep Structure relations are also governed by a kind of 'naturalness' condition. That is, both are the same *kinds* of objects constructed of largely, though not completely, identical vocabularies of elements. Differences between Surface and Deep structures are the minimum required to state the actually existent regularities of particular languages and language generally. Hence, in some cases, Surface and Deep Structures may be

Stratificational writers have totally failed to notice consequences like those just illustrated, and take considerable pride in the fact that their descriptions cannot allow direct associations of semantic and phonological properties. They even go so far as to criticize transformational grammars for permitting this (Lamb, 1964b:116):

Thus in the Chomsky system the phonetic distinctive features are introduced very early in the generative hierarchy even though they are not needed (and in fact are very cumbersome) until near the end; whereas in a stratified generative system the phonons (i.e. components of the phonemes) are not introduced until the time of the morphophonemic rules, and the components present at the top structural stratum are not phonetic but sememic.

This quote, which is only one of several statements to the same effect to be found in recent stratificational writings, reveals a number of confusions and misunderstandings about both the actual intended character of a transformational grammar incorporating syntactic, semantic, and phonological components and minimal requirements for a reasonable linguistic theory. Disregarding the confusion between <u>phonetic</u> and <u>systematic</u>, or <u>phonological</u>, features which is endemic to stratificational discussions, as was shown in Chapter 5, Lamb mistakenly assumes that phonological features are present at the 'highest' level, which is presumably equivalent to his sememic stratum, in so far as this can be said to exist. Actually, however, in so far as anything in a transformational grammar corresponds to the sememic stratum, it is the semantic representations, which are the output of the Semantic Component, and these have no phonological aspect whatever. The real form of a transformational system can be schematically indicated as follows.

---

fairly similar, although in the present writer's opinion the number of such cases and the degree of similarity is far less than the published literature on transformational grammar would indicate. Most crucially, notice that no ad hoc rules of the type required in stratificational grammars (like [8.27], [8.28] above) to map arbitrary nonalternating elements on one level into arbitrary nonalternating elements on the next are required or allowed. In short, rules are required to state linguistic generalizations, not to fill gaps created by theoretical assumptions.

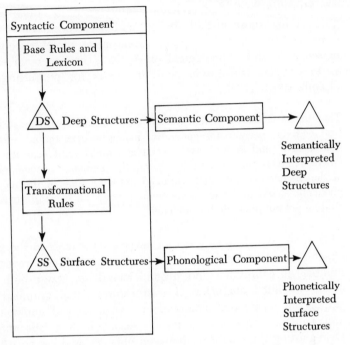

(8.29)

The Base part of the Syntactic Component is the generative source of the description as a whole. The Base generates an infinite class of <u>Deep Structures</u>, which are phrase markers whose terminal elements are lexical items drawn from dictionary entries consisting of complexes of three kinds of properties. Deep Structures are then the input to the Semantic Component, whose rules derive a semantic interpretation (set of semantic representations) for the Deep Structure as a whole, on the basis of its syntactic organization and the inherent semantic properties of its lexical items. Deep Structures are also the input to the transformational rules of the Syntactic Component, which successively derive Surface Structures which are phrase markers. However, in comparison with Deep Structures, Surface Structures are much more superficial and less abstract, and they provide a labelled bracketing of the actual string of words of which the sentence consists. Surface Structures are, then, as we have seen in earlier chapters, the input to the phonological rules, which derive a phonetic interpretation (set of phonetic representations) for the sentence as a whole, on the basis of the Surface Syntactic organization and the inherent phonological properties of those lexical items remaining in the Surface Structures. In a system like this, the Semantic and Phonological components play a purely interpretative role. The productive (recursive) power of the grammar resides entirely in the Syntactic Component.[27]

It is therefore nonsense for Lamb to imply that the 'top' structural stratum in such a system involves phonetic features instead of the appropriate sememic ones. The semantic representations contain no phonological properties. There is not even any reason to assume that the <u>phonological</u> properties of the lexical items in Deep Structures are <u>input</u> to the Semantic Component. That is, one can assume that only the other features make up this input. Since the full Deep Structure mechanically determines a new object which is identical except for lack of phonological properties, this is completely trivial and essentially notational. In the same completely meaningless way, one could insure that no <u>semantic</u> properties were input to the transformational rules.

Is it true then, as Lamb claims without support, argument, or illustration, that properties are present 'where they are not needed'? Obviously not. Phonological, semantic, and syntactic properties are all present in Deep Structures, and in particular in the lexical items these contain, because they are necessary to define those arbitrary associations which exist in the language.

---

[27] The diagram might suggest further that in fact all the productive power resides in the Base part of the syntax. But this is not true. For in fact it is necessary that the Base generate a class of Deep Structures which includes (infinitely) many which underlie no well-formed Surface Structures. It is then the transformational rules which in several different ways 'filter out' those Deep Structures which are not well formed. This is not at all a redundancy or an unwanted feature, since it turns out that in this way the grammar can automatically define the several different types of semi-sentences, i.e. Surface Structures which are partly but not completely well-formed. In other words, in this way the grammar can impose a categorization into types and numbers of <u>violations</u> and can define a <u>sentence</u> as a Surface Structure with no violations of any kind. For introductory discussion of the 'filtering' aspect of a transformational grammar cf. Chomsky (1965): for further discussion and an account of the notion of <u>violation</u> cf. Postal (to appear d), Lakoff (1965).

It is exactly the lexicon which describes these associations. Deep Structures are then those linguistic objects which describe for whole sentences associations between the three kinds of properties, i.e. which provide the information necessary to project to whole sentences what lexical items describe only for individual elements of sentences. And each type of property is necessary for some of the rules which carry out this projection from the information contained in Deep Structures.

Thus if one must speak in terms of the metaphor of 'top,' 'bottom,' etc., it is only correct to say that in a transformational grammar, phonological properties are present in the 'middle' where they are required to indicate unpredictable associations of semantic, syntactic, and phonological characteristics. Part of Lamb's confusion consists in wrongly identifying the level of Deep Syntactic Structure, which is intermediate between phonetic and semantic representations, with his 'topmost' sememic structure. Actually, what Lamb intends for the most part[28] to represent with sememic organization is given by the semantic interpretations of the Semantic Component. For example, the so-called sememe ^{S}/man/ is nothing but a set of unpredictably associated semantic properties or components, 'male,' 'human,' 'adult,' etc. That is, if properly analyzed, these would be just the elements present in the semantic part of the dictionary entry for the lexical item 'man.' But part of Lamb's confusion here, and indeed the major part, consists in failing to recognize the need for some level of linguistic structure where semantic, syntactic, and phonological properties are associated in unpredictable sets. It is just this failing which is revealed by his assertion that phonological features are not needed at a stage before the level of phonological rules.

A basic fact about stratificational ideas is that they allow no real analogue to the Deep Syntactic structures of transformational grammars. Although advocates sometimes speak (Lamb, 1965:38) as if the Lexemic-Morphemic difference corresponded

---

[28] The one real exception would appear to be grammatical relations like subject of, object of, etc., which Lamb indicates in diagrams of the sememic stratum with single symbols. Clearly such relations do not have inherent semantic content. Although the subject relation holds between 'John' and the verb in both 'John received a degree' and 'John refused a degree,' there is no common semantic aspect to both cases.

to the Deep Surface distinction, this is obviously completely false. It is important to emphasize that we have considered only one limitation which this lack imposes. It also prevents, for example, the statement of the mass of syntactic regularities which can be represented in a transformational grammar. But showing this is a complex matter which extends beyond our present concerns. Transformational grammar must be looked upon as completely unique among modern linguistic conceptions in claiming the existence of another level of syntactic structure distinct from both Surface Syntactic properties, which all linguists recognize, and from linguistically structured semantic organization. One part, but only one part, of the failure of stratificational grammar to incorporate such a level of structure is the impossibility of a lexicon or dictionary.

9

NEW TYPES OF ARGUMENT
AGAINST AUTONOMOUS
PHONOLOGY

THE ARGUMENT FROM PHONOTACTICS

In Chapter 3 we considered arguments of the type first presented by Halle, showing that certain linguistic facts require autonomous phonemic descriptions to contain necessarily redundant and generalization-missing rules. It was shown that these useless morphophonemic rules can, in certain cases, be avoided by stratificational-like solutions only at the cost of a mass of other redundant rules; these being required by the absence of any analogue of the Naturalness Condition. However, the extra complexities, ad hoc additions, and loss of generalizations imposed on grammars containing autonomous representations by facts like those uncovered by Halle, are in sheer mass, really quite minor, when compared to the enormous set of useless additions to grammars which the conditions of autonomous phonology force to be included on other grounds.

We are assuming, of course, that any linguistic description must contain systematic representation for reasons like those briefly discussed in the first part of Chapter 8. On the assumption that grammars must also assign autonomous structure, there will be two levels of phonologically relevant structure in addition to phonetic, that is, two levels concerned with the way forms are pronounced. All linguists who recognize autonomous representations are agreed in effect that it is necessary to describe the limitations on combinations of autonomous phonemes, that is, necessary to give some kind of 'phonotactics.' The need for such follows, it is claimed, just because there exists for each language a crucial set of facts otherwise ignored, namely, just what combinations of phonemes in *words*[1] are allowed. Given the need for systematic representation, the exactly analogous argument shows that there must be a set of 'morphophonotactic' rules or their equivalent[2] to describe *the possible combinations of morphophonemes in morphemes.* Otherwise, again there will simply be a set of facts for each language which is ignored. Linguists concerned with autonomous structure have not reached this obvious conclusion because they have often adopted the intolerable assumption that, although morphophonemes are 'necessary' or 'useful,' they are not 'really part of language structure.'[3] Thus

---

[1] Occasionally, of course, autonomous descriptions describe constraints on phoneme combinations within morphemes as well, but this is, strictly speaking, a violation of the autonomy assumption. Indeed, the preference for utilizing words as the domain of phoneme combination is a consequence of the assumption, or at least hope, that words can be defined in purely phonetic terms, i.e. nonmentalistically. This hope is of course vain and has in fact been known to be so for decades. As even Bloomfield (1933: 181) noted, no consistent phonetic properties are associated with every word boundary occurrence in different languages. For further discussion cf. Postal (to appear b).

[2] This amendment is meant to refer to the account of the way many such constraints in particular languages can be built into the theory of language by means of the notions of Markedness as discussed in the previous chapter. I have for simplicity formulated the argument in this section as if all morpheme internal morphophoneme constraints were to be handled by language particular rules. In this case, it turns out that the autonomous phonotactics requires identical restrictions to be stated twice within individual grammars. If, as is ultimately necessary, we take account of the possibilities provided by the Markedness account of morpheme internal restrictions, the criticism is, analogously, that an autonomous phonotactics requires restrictions which are largely specified within the theory of language to be repeated again in each individual language. The strength of the argument is thus unaffected by the insightful revision of systematic phonemic theory along the lines of Markedness.

[3] This position was, for example, very strongly and explicitly maintained by Hockett as late as the beginning of this decade (1961:42). Similar views are implicit in the general American linguistic abandonment of morphophonemic representation.

there is no need to worry about their combinatory restrictions. But this implicit argument is utterly untenable. By exactly identical logic one could conclude that autonomous phonemes are only 'necessary' or 'useful,' but also not 'really part of language structure.' Hence there would be no need for any phonotactics. Indeed the argument obviously generalizes to all linguistic structure leading to the *reductio ad absurdum* that all of linguistic structure is not real and that the whole grammar is unnecessary.

It follows that principles determining the possible combinations of morphophonemes in morphemes must be part of any correct language description, or at least part of the linguistic theory which underlies particular descriptions. But this conclusion immediately reveals that the addition of autonomous phonemic representation incredibly complicates linguistic descriptions by causing masses of essentially identical restrictions to be repeated twice. It goes without saying that morphophonemic and autonomous phonemic structures are not identical and are based on distinct vocabularies of elements. There is a clear sense, however, in which, given a description which embodies autonomous representations, each morphophoneme is specially related to a certain phoneme or set of phonemes, namely, just those it is mapped onto by the morphophonemic rules. For example, in a grammar of Mohawk utilizing both types of representation, the morphophoneme n̲ would always be mapped onto the phoneme /n/ except in word final position in nouns, where n̲ would be mapped onto the null element. This fact is fundamental to the argument which follows.

Let us illustrate this criticism with the consonant elements of Mohawk. The consonant morphophonemes, or systematic elements, are w̲, y̲, n̲, r̲, p̲, k̲, t̲, s̲.[4] The autonomous consonant phonemes would most probably[5] be /w/, /y/, /n/, /r/, /k/, /t/, and /s/. Let us restrict attention to two-element clusters. Two consonant systematic combinations *within morphemes* are as follows:

---

[4] In view of space limitations, I am forced to assert this without detailing any real justification. However, with the exception of p̲, the claim is not very controversial. The system is justified in detail in Postal (to appear c).

[5] Of course, I am not ignoring the possibility of alternative phonemicizations, which would affect the details but not the principles of this argu-

(9.1)

ts	*ss
ks	*tt
st	*kk
kt	*pp
sk	*kp
tk	*pk
sp	*ps
tp	*pt

(9.2)

wy	*yy
ny	*rr
ry	*yr
wr	*nn
nr	*wn
	*rn
	*yn
	*ww
	*yw
	*rw
	*nw

(9.3)

nk	*wp
np	*wk
	*wt
	*ws
	*yp
	*yk
	*yt
	*ys
	*rp
	*rk
	*rt
	*rs
	*nt
	*ns

(9.4)

sr	*pr
tr	*sn
kr	*tn
sy	*kn
ty	*pn
ky	*sw
py	*tw
	*pw
	*kw

sy, ty, ky, py } 6

Thus of the sixty-four two-consonant clusters of systematic elements possible in principle, at most twenty are found. Consider now the possible two consonant clusters of autonomous phonemes in words.

---

ment. To reveal to the fullest extent that I have not, however, set up a straw man, I have picked the phenomicization actually proposed by Lounsbury (1960).

[6] Within morphemes, all of these actually fall together and yield phonetic [dž], so that what really occurs is the archiphoneme of the three stop+y sequences. That is, all those features relevant to distinguishing p, k, and t in positions where they contrast have U markings before y.

(9.5)   /ts/   */ss/   (9.6)   /ny/   */wy/
          /ks/   /ry/   */wr/
          /st/   */nr/
          /kt/   */yr/
          /sk/   */yy/
          /tk/   */rr/
          /tt/   */nn/
          /kk/   */wn/
                                                             */rn/
                                                             */yn/
                                                             */ww/
                                                             */yw/
                                                             */rw/
                                                             */nw/

(9.7)   */wk/   (9.8)   /kw/   */tw/
          */yk/   /sy/   */sw/
          */nk/   /ty/   */ky/
          */rk/   */kr/
          */wt/   */tr/
          */yt/   */sr/
          */nt/   */kn/
          */rt/   */tn/
          */ws/   */sn/
          */ys/
          */ns/
          */rs/

Obviously there are very tight restrictions on two-consonant combinations of autonomous phonemes in Mohawk words. These will therefore require many rules to state. But the extraordinary fact is that in every case the statement of these restrictions by special rules is entirely redundant. There are two subtypes of this redundancy. On the one hand, in a very large set of cases, the restrictions on phoneme combinations simply duplicate the restrictions on morphophoneme combinations which must be stated anyway. And in all the remaining cases, where this is not so, the restrictions on phoneme combinations are completely a function of the grammar and morphophonemic rules. For an example of the first kind, consider the fact that no combinations beginning with systematic y̲ are possible, which correlates completely with the impossibility of sequences beginning with /y/.

Similarly, notice there are no systematic sequences ending with n̲ and no autonomous sequences ending with /n/. These autonomous restrictions within words are fully a function of the morpheme internal restrictions on morphophonemes plus the morphophonemic rules which map n̲ onto /n/ and y̲ onto /y/ and which insert epenthetic [e] between a systematic consonant and a following n̲ across morpheme boundaries. Consider also the fact that in systematic terms no combinations ending with w̲ are possible. The analogue is not quite true in autonomous terms since /kw/ is found, an exceptional sequence in autonomous terms. But in fact there is no real exception here. The morpheme internal [kw] sequences, which the autonomous phonologist must represent as /kw/, are actually automatic results of either p̲ or k̲o̲+vowel by virtue of independently required morphophonemic rules (cf. Chapter 11). The same points are revealed by a mass of other restrictions illustrated in the above lists.

In short, if a description which contains restrictions on the combination of morphophonemes in morphemes plus the morphophonemic rules is embedded in a grammar which defines the combinations of morphemes into words, all possible combinations of phonetic elements in words are necessarily predicted. But if, in addition, such a grammar contains autonomous phonemic representation, all of these restrictions will have to be repeated as part of the phonotactics in order to maintain the autonomous assumption that phoneme combinations must be characterized independently of the rest of the grammar.

The extraordinary degree of extra complexity this will impose on grammars can be partially determined by the reader who analyzes the previous lists of morphophoneme and phoneme combinations in Mohawk, which, it must be emphasized, are only a portion of the restrictions actually existing. Furthermore, this language has a very limited phonological inventory. It is obvious that in an autonomous system simply enormous numbers of facts must be repeated. For example, what are the facts which underly both of the restrictions *y̲t̲ and */yt/? Clearly they are that the phonetic sequences [yt], [yd], etc. do not occur in Mohawk morphemes, and that the morphological and morphophonemic rules do not permit their occurrence across morpheme boundaries. These facts are all predicted from the general condition which disallows *y̲t̲ and the independently required morphophonemic and morphological rules. But in a description based on autonomous phonemic theory, these facts must be repeated as a separate 'phonotactic' restriction on */yt/. And similarly in dozens and dozens of other cases.

We can summarize our argument as follows. Given a phonological description involving a level of morphophonemic structure with conditions determining possible combinations of morphophonemic entities in morphemes, and assuming such a description is embedded in a syntax which specifies the correct combinations of morphemes forming words, the addition of a level of autonomous phonemic structure between the morphophonemic and phonetic levels necessarily involves an enormous mass of linguistically useless and redundant statements because: The addition of this intermediate level necessitates a separate phonotactics involving a description of the possible combinations within words of the autonomous phonemes. Yet every fact which such a separate phonotactics describes is accounted for without the autonomous level by the morpheme internal restrictions on morphophoneme combinations and the morphophonemic rules which must exist in any event. That is, on the one hand, a particular phoneme is essentially mirrored one-to-one by a morphophoneme, as with Mohawk n̲ and /n/, in which case the phoneme and morphophoneme restrictions are almost entirely identical. Or, on the other hand, there is a good deal of morphophonemic-phonemic differentiation (for example, all of Mohawk p̲, ko̲, and k+w̲ would at times be specified as phonemic /kw/) which is, however, always a function of morphophonemic rules. It thus follows that an independent phonotactics is necessarily and in all cases useless and redundant in its entirety. It describes or accounts for not one fact which is not accounted for without it. Clearly nothing could indicate more directly the incredible error involved in the assumption that a grammar contains an independent level of autonomous phonological representation.

It is significant that essentially the same conclusion has been reached by Hale on the basis of his work on Papago (1965:297):

To specify more exactly (e.g., in a phonotactic rule defined over the taxonomic [i.e. autonomous: PMP] notation) which clusters can actually occur, and where, would require paraphrase of a subset of the morphophonemic rules, since the 'possible clusters' in Papago, and their distributions, are automatically specified by a number of very general, independently motivated rules which impose a phonetic interpretation upon the morphophonemic representation.

This is not at all surprising since the argument is independent of the details of particular languages.

In Chapters 3 and 4 it was pointed out that stratificational phonology failed Condition (3.16) in a very serious way. It should be emphasized that, insisting on a separate level of autonomous phonemic structure with its own tactical rules,[7] stratificational phonological descriptions are necessarily subject to all of the useless redundancies which are inherently involved in autonomous phonotactics. This uncovers a whole new dimension of facts which show that this theory fails Condition (3.16), and is further evidence that stratificational phonology in no significant way avoids the evidence which falsifies more traditional formulations of autonomous phonemics.

It was noted at the beginning of Chapter 3 that a systematic grammar claims there are only two *significant* levels of phonological representation, that of systematic phonemics and that of phonetics. It was pointed out, however, that since the rules of a systematic phonological description are necessarily partially ordered, each sentence will receive many additional intermediate representations. In certain cases, but definitely not all, some of these intermediate representations may be identical to autonomous structures or at least to such as would meet autonomous conditions, in so far as these are clear. We are now in a better position to see what is meant by the systematic phonemic denial that these intermediate structures have any real significance, i.e. that they qualify as a significant independent level of linguistic structure. Clearly one important property which serves to define a linguistic level is the existence of a natural set of elements with their own partially independent principles of combination.[8] Thus

---

[7] This is not a minor or irrelevant point. Rather it is one of the fundamental assumptions which advocates of this approach emphasize and consider most significant and characteristic of it. Cf. Lamb (1964b:110, and 1965:39–40, 44); Gleason (1964:77–79, 84).

[8] A possible charge of contradiction should be taken into consideration here. I have advocated a theory in which the only significant level of phonological structure above the phonetic is the systematic phonemic,

it is significant that in claiming there is a significant level of autonomous phonemic structure, both traditional autonomous phonemicists[9] and contemporary stratificational phonemic advocates emphasize the existence of a separate phonotactic statement. Thus by showing that such a phonotactics is totally redundant it has been shown that one of the basic properties generally agreed upon as characteristic of a level of linguistic structure is absent from the putative level of autonomous phonemics. This is then a fundamental part of the evidence for the systematic phonemic claim that autonomous phonemic representations are an artifact descriptive of no aspect of human language.

THE ARGUMENT FROM THE NONTRANSITIVITY OF CONTRAST

Stated from the point of view of phonetic-phonemic relations, the fundamental idea of autonomous phonemics is very simple. As pointed out earlier several times, it is simply that phonemic representation is identical to phonetic except that all those phonetic features are not indicated which can be correctly placed in terms

---

which I equated with the output of the transformational part of the syntax. It might be objected, therefore, that this level of structure is itself completely determined, determined by the transformational rules operating on Deep Syntactic structures. However, the word 'partially' in the text is crucial here. For while the syntactic transformations determine the Surface combinations of morphemes and their associated superficial immediate constituent analyses, they do not determine the morpheme internal phonological constraints among phonological elements, nor the set of elements themselves. These latter properties are independent of the transformational part of the grammar, and hence in a natural sense they define an independent level of structure concerned with phonological features, morphological features, exception features relevant to phonological rules, phonologically possible morphemes, free variation, Markedness, etc. Hence there is no contradiction between the assertion that systematic phonemic structures are the output of the transformational rules and also an independent level of structure. Contradiction could arise only if, counterfactually, the transformational rules determined *every aspect* of Surface Structures. But as we have seen there are unpredictable aspects which must simply be listed in some form in the dictionary.

[9] Cf. for example Harris (1951:150–155); Hill (1965:68–88); Hockett (1958:84–87); Hall (1964:103–107).

of statements whose environments are stated in terms of the complexes of phonetic features which remain. Stated from the point of view of contrast, the fundamental idea is also simple. Certain phonetic feature (combinations) serve to 'distinguish forms,' 'differentiate utterances with different meanings,' 'keep apart separate messages,' etc., while others do not. That is, given the basic categorization of utterances into repetitions and nonrepetitions (cf. Chapter 1), certain features are found to distinguish nonrepetitions, others not. In the simplest case this may be shown by the existence of completely minimal pairs. In other cases more complex considerations indicate which features are to be considered distinctive, considerations involving their nonpredictability from other phonetic features (cf. footnote 11 of Chapter 3).

A completed autonomous phonemic system thus has two fundamental and related functions. On the one hand, it should provide a prediction as to which phonetic representations are repetitions, which not. In other words, it should provide a categorization of forms into free variants and contrasts. On the other hand, it should specify which phonetic features and which combinations of them serve as distinguishers of contrastive forms, which are only in free variation. Both of these functions are served, it is assumed, by providing an autonomous phonemic representation for every form in the language. These representations consist of strings of autonomous phonemes which are phonetically interpreted by an associated set of allophonic statements. These specify the full range of linguistically significant detail for each phoneme in each relevant context, i.e. indicate those phonetic features which are not the distinctive ones, combinations of these latter really being the phonemes themselves. Such an autonomous system predicts free variation and contrast in a maximally simple way. As we have seen before in Chapter 1, two utterances in a language are in free variation if and only if they have identical autonomous phonemic representations. All utterances with nonidentical autonomous representations are contrastive.

It follows then that an autonomous phonemic system predicts free variation and contrast by virtue of identity and nonidentity among strings of phonemic symbols. This fact permits the determination of an important claim which autonomous phonemics makes, a claim which I think has seldom, if ever, been made explicit. Identity and nonidentity among strings of symbols are technically equivalence relations, i.e. relations which are symmetrical, reflexive, and transitive. The first property means that if the relation holds between two terms a and b it necessarily holds between b and a (contrast an asymmetrical relation like 'older than'); the second means that the relation necessarily holds between any term a and itself (compare an irreflexive relation like 'smarter than'); the third means that if the relation holds between a term a and a term b and between b and a term c, it necessarily holds between a and c (compare an intransitive relation like 'son of'). It should be obvious that identity among phonemic strings meets the conditions of symmetry, reflexiveness, and transitivity. By representing an empirical relation, contrast/free variation, with formal structures which meet the conditions of an equivalence relation, autonomous phonemics claims that this relation *is* an equivalence condition. We are not concerned with the claims of reflexiveness and symmetry. It is evident that contrast among forms meets these conditions. That is, every form is in free variation with itself, and if any form A is in free variation with B then certainly B is in free variation with A. What is crucial, however, is the claim which autonomous phonemics makes that free variation is a transitive relation. That is, what is crucial is the claim that it is necessarily the case that if a form A is in free variation with a form B, and B is in free variation with a form C, then A is in free variation with C.[10]

Before investigating the empirical adequacy of this transitivity claim, it should be emphasized that the theory of systematic phonemics makes no such claim. It will be remembered that systematic phonemic descriptions predict free variation not by identity among phonemic strings but rather by the association of phonetic representations with single systematic structures. Thus n distinct phonetic representations are in free variation if they are assigned to the same input systematic phonemic representation by the rules of the phonology. There is, however, absolutely nothing to prevent a situation in which the phonological rules assign to systematic structure A the exhaustive set of pho-

---

[10] It is the logically contingent character of the assumption of transitivity of contrast which motivated footnote 3 of Chapter 1, where it was noted that the claim of disjointness for sets of repetitions is an additional assumption going beyond recognition of the notion of contrast as such.

netic strings p_1, p_2, and p_3, which are thus predicted as free variants, and also assign to systematic structure B the exhaustive set of phonetics strings p_2 and p_4, which are thus predicted as free variants. But in such a case the grammar predicts that although p_2 and p_1, p_1 and p_3, p_2 and p_3, and p_2 and p_4 are in free variation, neither p_1 and p_4 nor p_3 and p_4 are free variants. Systematic phonemic theory therefore claims that free variation is a nontransitive relation, that is, a relation which is neither necessarily transitive nor necessarily not transitive. It follows that the domain of free variation transitivity is one in which systematic phonemics and all varieties of autonomous phonemics, stratificational phonemics especially included, make very clear conflicting claims. It thus will pay to inquire into the actual nature of this relation, for by so doing one can fairly directly determine the truth values of these conflicting conceptions of phonological structure.

In fact, cases which show that free variation is not a transitive relation are not at all difficult to find. One of the most obvious is given by the pronunciation of word initial unstressed vowels, especially before nasals, in English. If we consider the pronunciation of forms like the following in many dialects, including the present writer's:

(9.9)   unless, until
(9.10) intentional, insulting
(9.11) employment, entire
(9.12) antagonize, anticipate
(9.13) amorphous, annul

we find that each word can be pronounced with initial vowels of distinct qualities. Those of (9.9) may be pronounced with an [ʌ] (that of 'cut') or with schwa. Those of (9.10) may be pronounced with an [I] (that of 'bit') or with schwa. Those of (9.11) may be pronounced with an [e] (that of 'bet') or with schwa. Those of (9.12) may be pronounced with an [æ^] (that of 'bad') or with schwa. Finally, those of (9.13) may be pronounced with [æ] (that of 'cat') or with schwa. In each case intermediate vowels between schwa and the other variant may be possible as well, a fact which from the present point of view is irrelevant. The crucial point is that in each case the pronunciation with schwa is in free variation with that in which there is a full vowel. This means that schwa is in free variation in different words with all of [ʌ], [I], [e], [æˆ], and [æ]. However, it is quite apparent that these various full vowels are by no means in free variation with each other. That is, one cannot pronounce the forms in (9.9) with initial [I], [e], [æˆ], or [æ]; one cannot pronounce the forms in (9.10) with any of [ʌ], [e], [æˆ], or [æ]; one cannot pronounce the forms in (9.11) with any of [ʌ], [I], [æˆ], or [æ]; one cannot pronounce the forms in (9.12) with any of [ʌ], [I], [e], or [æ]; and one cannot pronounce the forms in (9.13) with any of [ʌ], [I], [e], or [æˆ]. This is thus a clear case of the nontransitivity of free variation.

Observe that the overlapping of schwa with different full vowels in the examples we have given thus far only involves part of the forms. That is, in terms of the distinction drawn in footnote 11 of Chapter 3, the environments for the merging or nontransitivity of contrast are 'relevant' rather than 'absolute.' Although it is not crucial to our argument, it is worthwhile pointing out that in this case we can find instances where the environments are absolute. Compare such forms as:

(9.14) edition, effective
(9.15) addition, affective

The words in (9.14) may be pronounced with an initial [e] or schwa; the words in (91.5) with an initial [æ] or schwa. On the full vowel pronunciations, the first word of (9.14) is distinct from the first of (9.15) and similarly for the second of each. But on the schwa pronunciation, the words of (9.14) are respectively homonymous with the words of (9.15). In other words, these cases provide a kind of 'minimal pair' illustration of the existence of nontransitive contrasts. Some of the pronunciations in the free variation sets of (9.14) contrast with those in the free variation sets of (9.15). Others are identical.

Other cases of nontransitive contrast are not difficult to find. A number of them revolve around the fact that in many languages, if not all, a majority of word boundaries may be pronounced as a phonetic pause or as phonetic null. Very often phenomena occur at word boundaries regardless of how these are realized phonetically. I discussed such a case almost five years ago without at that time realizing its full implications.[11] In Mohawk, systematic h͟ drops between a consonant and a pause, and a predictable glottal stop is inserted between a pause and a following vowel. But elsewhere in the language both [h] and [ʔ] are unpredictable and hence distinctive. Thus systematic sequences of such forms as: ...rh#vowel... have two alternative pronunciations. On the one hand, they may be pronounced with no pause at the point of the word boundary, in which case a phonetic [h] is present: or with a real pause at this point, in which case the h͟ drops and a glottal stop is inserted before the vowel. But now in every such case the resulting alternative phonetic sequences [...rhv...] and [...rpauseʔv...] are in free variation. In positions where a sequence like [...rhv...] is not a consequence of a phonetically null word boundary, it is of course not in free variation with [...rpauseʔv...]. These facts are thus unrepresentable in autonomous phonemics, which must represent all of the pauseless sequences with the same phonetic representation. But this means that a description of Mohawk based on such a theory claims falsely that the phonetically distinct sequences with pauses and glottal stops are contrastive. Systematic phonemics, on the other hand, handles such cases simply and naturally. Rules must be given to specify the null or pause realization of the word boundary, the insertion of epenthetic [ʔ] between pause and a following vowel, and the deletion of h͟ between a consonant and following pause. Given these rules, a structure like ...rh#vowel... is assigned two different phonetic representations, [...rhvowel...] and [...rpauseʔvowel...], which are thereby claimed to be free variant pronunciations of the input form. On the other hand a structure like ...rhvowel... receives only the phonetic representation [...rhvowel...]. Hence such a systematic structure does not have a variant pronunciation with pause and glottal stop.

This example involving word boundary is quite typical. A similar case from Russian has been described to me by Morris Halle.[12] Others will easily be found.

It is important to point out that although the nontransitivity of contrast has not been, to my knowledge, explicitly noted or

---

[11] In a paper 'Some Phonological Problems in Mohawk' read to the Linguistic Society of America, Chicago, December 1961.

[12] This is briefly discussed in Postal (to appear b).

taken account of for more than a quarter of a century,[13] it is not in fact a recent discovery. Actually, the important kinds of examples were noticed at least once at the very beginning of work on explicit phonological theory in America. The relevant figure is Morris Swadesh. In his famous paper of 1934, 'The Phonemic Principle,' Swadesh not only noticed the phenomenon and illustrated it, but actually coined a name for it, 'phonemic interchange.' Thus he remarked (1934:120):

It sometimes happens that one of a pair of free variants coincides with some other phoneme. Thus Chitimacha wˀ, yˀ, mˀ, nˀ may be pronounced with or without a glottal stricture, coinciding in the latter instance with the phonemes w, y, m, n. Another instance of this phenomenon, which may be called phonemic interchange, is the interchange of initial ð with d in words like the and they in Edgecombe County (near Rocky Mount) North Carolina.

Swadesh is clearly implying in the Chitimacha example that the interchange between glottalized and nonglottalized resonants takes place only in some environments, i.e., only in some linguistic forms and not others, else there would be no need to recognize two contrasting series. In the Southern English example, the implication would appear to be that the free variation between stop and continuant only occurs in (a subset ofˀ) the forms written with initial th. Hence while 'the' and 'they' have variants with both [d] and [ð], words like 'dale' and 'day' would have only [d].

In pointing out that the nontransitivity of contrast was noted by Swadesh more than three decades ago, one should not conclude too much. It seems clear that he did not by any means fully appreciate the implications of the examples he discussed. Thus, in the years that followed, he accepted a version of the theory of autonomous phonemics which claims such examples cannot

---

[13] It is in effect mentioned in passing by Lees (1957:397) but only in relation to its disconfirmation of the view that contrast can be defined in terms of semantic notions.

"The use of such meaning criteria to distinguish free variation from contrast appears even more hopeless when we note the many cases in which two phone types are in contrast in one environment but in free variation in another. This is the case with many pairs of English vocalic nuclei in contrast under strong stress but freely interchangeable under weak stress . . ."

exist. In view of the fact that Swadesh apparently drew no serious conclusions from such examples, it is less surprising that in the theoretical discussions which followed and led to various codifications of autonomous phonemics, linguists ignored these cases and others which can be found and formulated a theory which denied their existence.

Perhaps it is fair to say that the nontransitivity of contrast was implicitly noted even earlier by Bloomfield. In his analysis of English shwa in *Language* (1933:111–113), Bloomfield considered shwa as the unstressed representative of a large variety of full vowel phonemes. In effect he presented an analysis in which unstressed full vowels merge to shwa, essentially what was pointed out above in our initial example of nontransitivity of contrast. Thus he wrote 'away' phonemically as /ewej/, 'domination' as /daminejsn/ although the first vowel in the former and the second in the latter are identical shwas. Similarly he wrote 'a name' as /e nejm/ and 'an aim' as /en ejm/, ignoring in all cases irrelevant stress and other 'modulation' markings which he used.

Again, however, the implications of such facts for phonological theory were not drawn. In fact such cases of full overlapping are completely incompatible with the theoretical account of the phoneme which Bloomfield presents in the same book. In the theoretical account he defines phonemes as complexes of phonetic features actually occurring in sound waves, and assumes that identities and nonidentities among phonemes are determined by phonetic identity and nonidentity. In this regard Bloomfield stated in gross form the basic assumptions of later autonomous phonemics. But such an account makes it impossible, of course, to represent some shwa phonemically as /e/, others as /i/, etc. Hence although Bloomfield gave an analysis which involved recognition of the existing nontransitivity of contrast, he maintained a theory which denied this. This is only one of many different examples of several distinct types which could be brought forward to show the superiority of Bloomfield's linguistic practice over his theorizing. In later developments in linguistics which are often referred to as 'Bloomfieldian,' linguists consistently ignored his practice and based themselves on his theorizing, leading to the inadequate taxonomic linguistics of the 1940's and 1950's, whose phonological aspect we have been criticizing throughout the present study. Therefore, when modern autonomous phonemicists like Hill criticize Bloomfield in passages such as the following (1958:15):

In phonemic theory, perhaps the chief advance has been the elimination of an error on Bloomfield's part. Bloomfield, in his discussion of the unstressed central vowel of English, the schwa, said that the schwa was the unstressed representative of most of the vowel phonemes which appear in stressed syllables. This introduced a theory of phonemic overlapping, which had the unfortunate result of making the boundaries between phonemes arbitrary, and the whole analysis confusing. Bloch is primarily responsible for recognizing this danger, and countering it with the postulate that identical sounds must always belong to the same phoneme.

they are referring to his practice, and their remarks are indicative of the trend toward constructing a wholly consistent autonomous phonemics, i.e. one insisting on the transitivity of contrast. It is also interesting that the criticisms of Bloomfield and the overlapping analysis are nonsubstantive and unsupported. Hill gives no argument or evidence revealing any confusion or arbitrariness. All that he means is that the phonemic analysis of a form is not, in Bloomfield's practice, completely determined by its phonetic form. But the requirement that it must be so determined he never justifies.

Finally, one might note that occasionally advocates of autonomous phonemics have, in relatively recent times, brushed against the problems of complete overlapping and nontransitivity. Thus Hill approaches these questions in his discussion of putative stress contrasts in English (1958a:16–18), observes that many speakers have difficulty in hearing the stress contrasts he posits (cf. the discussion in Chapter 2), but then concludes (1958a:18)

But it is a principle of analysis that sounds are contrastive, even if there is only one pair in the whole system where the contrast is firmly established.

What this means is that if we find a pair of phonetic forms in a language, [. . . X . . .] and [. . . Y . . .], which are not free variants just because of [X] and [Y], then every pair of forms differing by [X] and [Y] must be assumed to be contrastive and so represented phonemically. This is then a rather clear statement of the principle of transitivity of contrast. What is disturbing is the fact, not at all atypical of attempted justification for autonomous phonemics,[14] that this empirical assumption is justified purely by appeal to a priori methodological considerations. No concern is directed toward the fact that it is *logically possible* for contrast to be nontransitive and hence the linguist's job to determine if such cases exist. Rather, an arbitrary methodological principle is brought forward to dictate a wished-for solution. As we have seen in many cases, the principle is simply false. If one assumes what Hill assumes, then phonemic transcriptions will necessarily represent as phonemically distinct sets of forms which are free variants simply because contrast is as a matter of fact a nontransitive relation.

Nontransitivity of free variation/contrast can be stated in other, perhaps more familiar, terms as 'complete overlapping' (Bloch, 1941:280). Complete overlapping or intersection is normally defined as the assignment of the same phonetic segment to different phonemes in the 'same' phonetic contexts. All the cases of nontransitivity are simply cases of complete overlapping. For example, in the first case we described, shwa is assigned to different full vowel phonemes under the 'same' conditions. I have placed the term 'same' in quotes to indicate the vagueness endemic in autonomous discussions of whether environments are 'relevant' or 'absolute,' i.e. whether they are different if there is no minimal pair or whether they may be the same even in the absence of such. This is, in the present context, just the difference between examples like (9.9) through (9.13) on the one hand and (9.14) and (9.15) on the other. Issues related to this problem of environmental specification are, of course, irrelevant to the argument of nontransitivity. Both traditional autonomous phonemics and more recent stratificational varieties are agreed on rejecting the possibility of complete overlapping. The reason for this is obvious. This is incompatible with the assumption of phonological autonomy which is fundamental to the whole view. That is, in cases of complete overlapping it is obvious that

---

[14] The fact that autonomous phonemics is often defended or justified in terms of nonsubstantive, purely methodological arguments is noted by Chomsky (1964b:107–108), who discusses several prominent examples.

something beyond phonetics, in fact the grammar, is determining the representation of forms. Thus Bloch (1941:281) claimed:

Partial intersection . . . can never lead to uncertainty in practice and may therefore be admitted in theory without violating sound phonemic method. The same cannot be said, however, of complete intersection. Examples are rare, and are always the result of an error in the analysis.

We have in fact already quoted stratificational rejections of complete overlapping. For it is exactly this that Lamb refers to by 'neutralization,' which he bans as follows in a passage we partially quoted previously (1964a:75):

In this connection, one of the cardinal principles of phonemic analysis is that it be done so that there will be no neutralization between the phonemic and phonetic strata. In other words (assuming an idealized phonetic representation which is free from noise), it must always be possible to convert uniquely from the phonetic to the phonemic stratum (but this is the only place where conversion to an upper stratum is unique).[15]

But as we have seen, contrary to autonomous assumption, complete overlapping or neutralization is simply a fact of language, demonstrated by the very free variation facts which autonomous phonemics set out to explicate. We can put this differently. Descriptions containing only systematic and phonetic representations are often accused of 'ignoring contrasts' (cf. our discussion of such an accusation by Lamb in Chapter 2). What the cases of nontransitivity of contrast show, however, is that the situation is exactly the reverse. Although all contrasts may be correctly represented in systematic phonemic terms, nontransitive contrasts are necessarily falsely described in a system which excludes complete overlapping.[16]

---

[15] It is interesting that Lamb here notices the fact that the autonomous phonemic level is the only linguiustic area where 'neutralization' is not allowed, i.e. where the 'bottom to top' relation must be unique. He gives, however, no justification or account of this asymmetry and of course there is none. Cf. footnote 2 of Chapter 3.

[16] Recognition of the existence of complete overlapping or nontransitivity of contrast cases eliminates any possibility of defining the class of phonological-phonetic features in terms of transitivity of matching relations,

The fundamental assumptions of autonomous phonemics with respect to the notion of contrast are clear and rather elementary. This view assumes that, having grouped utterances into sets of repetitions, it is possible, making use of only purely phonetic information, to establish a system of phonological representations which represent repetitions with identical phonemic strings and contrasts with nonidentical ones. The autonomous view assumes, in other words, that contrast is a transitive relation definable on phonetic strings and hence independent of grammatical and morphophonemic properties, including word and morpheme boundaries. As we have seen, this assumption is simply not true. The fundamental notion with which modern autonomous phonological thought has been concerned, namely, contrast versus free variation, is a nontransitive relation not definable exclusively in terms of groupings of utterance tokens into disjoint sets. In reality this fundamental notion of phonology is inherently bound up with the superficial syntactic structures which are the input to the phonological rules. Contrast between phonetic strings can only be characterized in terms of the full set of phonological rules which determine whether distinct phonetic forms are assigned to the same input systematic phonemic (i.e. Surface Syntactic) structure. Since the majority of these rules operate at least in part on abstract morphophonemic, boundary, grammatical category, and grammatical feature environments, the fundamental notion of contrast is inherently bound up with the grammatical structure of forms and cannot be characterized without it. This is, as far as I know, the strong-

---

as suggested by Chomsky (1957a:232–233). Chomsky was concerned with suggesting an operational approach to defining linguistic features and excluding nonlinguistic audible features such as rate of speed, absolute loudness, etc. I see no reason today to believe any such operational test exists. Certainly none has ever been proposed. It is perfectly sufficient to characterize this class of features by noting their necessity of inclusion within the universal set defined by phonetic and phonological theory. There is no reason to expect that the child requires an operational test to determine the class of features which his genetic organization provides him with in advance. Or to put it differently, it seems utterly implausible to assume that universal phonetic theory consists essentially of the remark: 'the class of phonetic features is that which meets the conditions of the following operational test' rather than of a rich substantial specification of the class of features, their possible values, possible combinations, Markedness properties, etc.

est argument showing the incorrectness of the autonomous assumption that there is a significant, independent level of phonological structure which can and must be characterized on the basis of phonetics and knowledge of which utterance tokens are repetitions. That is, this is the strongest evidence showing that no level of autonomous phonology with phonemic representations closely linked to phonetics in terms of conditions of Biuniqueness and Local Determinacy[17] is a part of the structure of human language.

---

[17] This term is Chomsky's (1964b). It might better be replaced by 'Phonetic Determinacy' since, as Chomsky noted, the ordinary taxonomic (autonomous) insistence on Biuniqueness really is interpreted by its advocates to mean not literal biuniqueness, but this plus the additional assumption that the phonemic representation of all forms is uniquely determined from the phonetic, given the overall phonemic system.

PART II

On the Mentalistic
Character of
So-called
'Sound Change'

10

THE PROBLEM

FUNDAMENTALS

This second part of the present monograph[1] is concerned principally with sound change. But it must be understood as part of the controversy between autonomous and systematic phonemics which was primarily at issue in Part I. Even more deeply, however, the second part of the present inquiry must be considered against the background of an older and more basic dispute, namely, that between those who hold that linguistics must necessarily be antimentalistic, positivistic, behavioristic, etc., and those who, like the present author and workers within generative grammar generally, hold that linguistics is inherently a mentalistic discipline.

---

[1] Part II is a greatly expanded version of a paper 'Taxonomic Phonemics and Sound Change' which was read before the summer meeting of the Linguistic Society of America, Bloomington, Ind., August 1964. The present version owes a great deal to criticism and suggestion by R. P. Kiparsky, E. Garcia, E. Hamp, S. J. Keyser, and D. Perlmutter, to all of whom I am very grateful.

There are a number of ways to attempt to justify the view that linguistics must be mentalistic. One might, for example, attack the common but seldom defended claim that antimentalism has some justification in terms of the philosophy of science. That is, one could attempt to show that no valid reconstruction of the principles of scientific inquiry generally excludes mentalism. Or one might argue that mentalistic assumptions define a natural, significant field of inquiry in which claims can be justified or overthrown as in other fields, a domain which is in large part explicitly recognized and investigated within the ancient disciplines of traditional grammar and rationalistic philosophy. Similarly, one might argue that various antimentalist, behaviorist, and/or extreme positivistic positions lead to empirically absurd and untenable results. All of these modes of argument have in fact been attempted. This has in effect been the burden of much work on the foundations of generative grammar. Cf. especially Chomsky (1964b), (1959), (1965), (1966); Katz (1964), (to appear); Postal (to appear a), (to appear b). More substantively, one might try to show that some well-established domain of linguistic fact and data can only be understood in mentalistic terms. This is the approach which will basically be followed here.

I shall argue that the domain of so-called 'sound change' can only be understood against the background assumption that a linguistic description describes a mentalistic domain, namely, the internalized linguistic knowledge of a native. Involved in this discussion are the claims that: (1) only the conception of systematic phonemics makes it possible to understand sound change; (2) the facts of sound change support systematic phonemics vis-à-vis autonomous phonemics.

Sound change, it is claimed, can only be understood against the background of a valid conception of language. Too briefly put, one must at the very least assume that a language is an infinite set of sentences, which are triples of phonetic, syntactic, and semantic properties generated by a finite abstract object, or grammar, which consists of a set of partially independent elements called rules and a lexicon, or dictionary. Such grammars are represented in human neural systems and provide implicit knowledge of the languages they define. A grammar is thus in certain ways analogous to a computer program in that it is a formal system partially determining the behavior of a physical system, a formal system which can be represented in hardware of various types but which is in no way identical to any such representation.

Incidentally, it is perhaps worth explaining the emphasis here on the discussion of American positions on sound change in view of the obviously secondary role which American linguists have played in the development of historical linguistics. This emphasis is based on a certain judgement; namely, that in spite of the predominance of European work in the substantial area of diachronic linguistics, it has been American writings which are in the forefront of the attempt to provide a theoretical analysis of the nature of phonological change and to relate the character of this change to theories of synchronic linguistics, to modern developments in phonology, and to methodological assumptions about the proper nature of linguistic inquiry. And these matters are ultimately those on which it is hoped the present discussion may shed some light. It is thus my impression that, although the historical views to be critically discussed here are generally accepted by the majority of historical linguists regardless of nationality, it has been American linguists who have made the theoretical assumptions most explicit and who have tried most strenuously to relate them to assumptions about the nature of language generally, about the character of phonemic representation, and about the nature of phonetics, etc., which are the issues in which we are most interested.

AN ISSUE IN THE THEORY OF SOUND CHANGE

The present section is concerned with a straightforward question of linguistic fact which has, however, very deep and far-reaching consequences for any theory of phonological change and for phonology generally. The question is this. Are there quite regular and generally characterizable 'sound changes,' which describe the successive states of the linguistic history of any languages, that are not describable in purely phonetic terms? That is, are there systematic changes in the phonetic output whose positions of occurrence are unstatable in terms of any set of phonetic environments although the positions of occurrence are statable if reference is made to the morphophonemic and/or superficial grammatical structure of the relevant strings? This question is of interest for the following reasons.

Within modern linguistics, there is a widely accepted position on the nature of phonological change (I refer here to change which is independent of language contact) which claims that there are basically two subtypes; one, <u>regular phonetic change</u> which is describable in purely phonetic terms, or in phonological terms (autonomous phonemic) based only on phonetics and contrast;[2] and another kind, sporadic, unsystematic, etc. called <u>analogy</u>.[3] The position is that changes which are regular and systematic, i.e. which operate throughout the lexicon in generally specifiable conditions (where by 'generally specifiable' one means statable without giving a list of relevant morphemes), are necessarily purely phonetic, that is, phonetic changes which occur in phonetically specifiable environments. Although, as we shall see presently, this position is widely accepted in modern linguistics, indeed is essentially coextensive with the view that modern autonomous phonemics is the key to understanding phonological change,[4] the clearest and most extensive statements are probably

---

[2] For purposes of this discussion, there is no need to distinguish phonetic environments from autonomous phonemic environments, since autonomous phonemes are either uniquely defined as, or equivalent to, sets of phonetic segments in sets of phonetic environments. Hence any environment stated in terms of autonomous phonemes can be replaced by a normally more complex but equivalent environment in terms of a set of phonetic segment sequences.

[3] 'Analogy' is really an unfortunate term. There is reason to believe that rather than being some sharply defined process, analogy actually is a residual category into which is put every kind of linguistic change which does not meet some set of a priori notions about the nature of change. In particular, I think that the term 'analogy' has been used very misleadingly to refer to cases of perfectly regular phonological change in which part of the conditioning environment involves Surface Constituent Structure; i.e. changes which happen only in nouns, or only in verb stems, etc. I suspect that an analytic survey of cases which have been referred to as 'analogy' would yield many instances of regular phonological change with nonphonetic environments, that is, many cases bearing on the issues raised in the present section. For some further discussion cf. the references to work of Kuryłowicz and related comments in Chapter 12.

[4] I ignore here and throughout the distinction often drawn between phonetic change and phonemic change, that is, between phonetic changes which affect the system of autonomous contrasts and phonetic changes which do not and thus affect only the allophonic pattern.

still those of Leonard Bloomfield, especially in his *Language* (1933) (the following quotes are from pages 353, 353–354, 354, 363, 364, and 369 respectively):

Historically interpreted, the statement means that sound change is merely a change in the speakers' manner of producing phonemes and accordingly affects a phoneme at every occurrence, <u>regardless of the nature of any particular linguistic form in which the phoneme happens to occur</u>. (Emphasis mine: PMP)

The limitations of these <u>conditioned sound changes</u> are, of course, purely phonetic, since the change concerns only a habit of articulatory movement; phonetic change is independent of non-phonetic factors such as the meaning, frequency, homonymy, or what not, of any particular linguistic form.

A great part of this dispute was due merely to bad terminology. In the 1870's, when technical terms were less precise than today, the assumption of uniform sound change received the obscure and metaphorical wording 'phonetic laws have no exceptions.' It is evident that the term 'law' here has no precise meaning, for a sound-change is not in any sense a law, but only a historical occurrence. The phrase 'have no exceptions' is a very inexact way of saying that non-phonetic factors, such as the frequency or meaning of particular linguistic forms, do not interfere with the change of phonemes.

The neo-grammarian[5] hypothesis implies that sound-change is unaffected by semantic features and concerns merely the habits of articulating speech-sounds.

The neo-grammarians define sound-change as a purely phonetic process; it affects a phoneme or type of phonemes either universally or under certain strictly phonetic conditions, and is neither favored nor impeded by the semantic character of the forms which contain the phoneme.

Phonetic change, as defined in the last chapter, is a change in the habits of performing sound-producing movements.

An excellent selection of similar statements by Bloomfield from less well-known publications of the period before 1933 has been

---

[5] It is not at all clear that the position maintained by Bloomfield is really equivalent to that of the 19th century Neogrammarians, as is now widely assumed. This depends very much on how the older concept of 'regular analogy' is to be interpreted.

provided by C. F. Fries (1962a:199–202).

The whole of Bloomfield's discussion of sound change makes it clear, as do the statements of others who hold similar positions, that 'semantic character' in statements like these is to be interpreted to include not only semantic features in the strict sense, but also grammatical and morphophonemic properties of the forms, i.e. to exclude every possible type of environmental factor but phonetic.

More modern statements of this position of the purely phonetic character of regular sound change are not hard to find. Hoenigswald, for example, puts it as follows (1960:76):

In the case of phonemes there are no such bifurcations; the set of all discourse-long environments in which a phoneme occurs splits up into subsets such that the replacement for the phoneme in each subset is a different phoneme at the later stage and such that the subsets do not overlap: at the time when some of the instances of E *k* go to *k* (*clip* > *clip*) and others go to ø (*knot* > (*k*)*not*), there are no environments whatever in which the outcome is, at the given time and place, ambiguous; sound change is, in this sense, entirely REGULAR. In a somewhat different way this has already been said above . . . , where it was pointed out that phonemic split affects positional allophones; synchronically (here with reference to the earlier stage of a change), any environment, even if minimal, determines a definite positional allophone or range of positional allophones.

And for a restricted type of change[6] the case is put thus by W. Chafe (1959:482):

Zero is an acceptable reconstruction only if epenthesis is plausible as a historical explanation. Epenthesis is plausible whenever the environments in which it might have taken place are definable in strictly phonological (read autonomous phonemic, i.e. by footnote 2 phonetic: PMP) terms.

Gleason (1961:395) states it as follows:

There are two important characteristics of such a change that require comment. In the first place, what is shifting is not the pronunciation

---

6 This restriction is unimportant, especially so because one of our counterexamples to the position advocated is a case of epenthesis.

of a specific sound in a specific place, say a certain word. If it were, we might expect the same sound to change in a different way in some other place. Instead, the shift affects the statistical norm based on all occurrences of the given phoneme in a given environment—that is, on all occurrences of a certain allophone. In turn this norm controls the pronunciation of this allophone whenever it occurs. Phonetic change, therefore, affects allophones as wholes. Within the understanding that the effect is statistical, phonetic change affects any given allophone consistently. This is commonly expressed by saying that PHONETIC CHANGE IS REGULAR. This means that any phonetic change will affect all instances of the sound concerned in the positions in which it is operative. The same phonetic change may affect all the allophones of a given phoneme, or only a single allophone.

Martinet (1952:3) accepts basically the same view:

We shall, in what follows, center our attention on 'regular' sound changes, the type whereby all the performances of a given phoneme, everywhere or in a well defined context, are eventually affected. . . . In the frame of the present exposition, it is completely immaterial whether a change affects a phoneme in all contexts or only in phonemically well defined ones, whether what is eventually merged or kept distinct is two phonemes or two combinatory variants of different phonemes.

And again (1953:1):

It should be clear that diachronic phonemic theory is based upon the assumption that, apart from well defined cases, the meaning, function, or use of a given word cannot influence the phonetic evolution of its phonemic components. It is clear that if, in synchronic descriptions, we are able to ascribe all the sounds of a language to a definite number of phonemes, it is because all the realizations of a given phoneme in a given context are, as a rule, found to shift in the same direction and at the same rate of velocity.

And Waterman (1963:54) states it:

A more acceptable phrasing might be: 'Within certain limits of time and space, the same sounds, given the same conditions (read <u>phonetic conditions</u>: PMP) behave in the same way.'

And Fries (1962:51) asserts:

The following statement attempts to summarize briefly the chief features of what is meant by the heading of this section—'Phonetic Laws Without Exceptions' . . . we infer that there was a change in the native speaker's manner of pronouncing a particular 'sound,' and that this change

> (1) affected every occurrence of that 'sound' in essentially the same phonetic surroundings,
> (2) operated within a particular span of time and within a particular dialect or group of dialects,
> (3) was not interfered with by any nonphonetic factors such as meaning, homonymy, etc.

And this position is also strongly maintained by C. F. Hockett in his well-known text (1958). We shall not, however, quote any statement from there because Hockett has extended and reformulated his position in his recent Presidential Address to the Linguistic Society of America.[7] This work is the most extensive recent statement and attempt at justification of the position we are discussing here. We feel it deserves separate attention and have devoted an entire chapter (14) to its analysis.

The view under consideration is also strongly advocated by R. A. Hall, although a really good illustrative quote is difficult to find (1964:295):

> Phonological development is to be divided into two aspects: phonetic change and phonemic change. The former involves simply change in speakers' habits of making sounds; . . .

A similar remark holds for I. Dyen (1963:631), whose position is as follows:

> Now we can usefully describe what is ordinarily meant by *regular* phonetic change among comparative linguists in the following way. Let us take the words of the earlier stage and construct a set of rules by which the words are to be transformed into the words of the later stage. The rules permit that (1) for a phoneme sequence of the earlier stage there is one and only one phonemic transform everywhere, or that (2) for a phoneme sequence of the prior stage there are various transforms, but for each transform each set of environments of the

---

[7] 'Sound Change,' paper read before the meeting of the Linguistic Society of America, New York, December 1964. I am indebted to Professor Hockett for providing me with a copy of this paper.

phoneme sequence of the prior stage is mutually exclusive with the set of environments for each other transform of that phoneme sequence.

Dyen's discussion makes it quite clear that 'environment' must be understood here in terms of autonomous phonemics (i.e. phonetically). More than seven decades ago Hermann Paul (1891:58) wrote:

> If we, therefore, speak of the uniform operation of sound-laws, this can only mean that in the case of sound-change occurring within the same dialect, all the separate cases, in which the same sound-conditions occur, are treated uniformly. It must either happen, therefore, that where the same sound existed previously, the same sound always remains in the later stages of development as well; or where a separation into different sounds has occurred, there must be a special reason to be assigned; and, further, a reason of a kind affecting sound alone—such as the effect of neighboring sounds, accent, place of syllable, etc.—for the fact that in one case one sound has arisen and in another a different one. No doubt we must take into account in this all the different factors in the production of sound.

We thus see that modern linguistics is in general dominated by this traditional Neogrammarian conception of sound change. This view can be taken as the generally accepted view of the nature of sound change today, a view enshrined in our textbooks and manuals and underlying actual historical work undertaken within the framework of modern phonemics. The determination of the truth value of this conception is thus a matter of the greatest importance. If, for example, it could be shown to be false, a reconsideration of the mass of work in historical phonology for almost a century would be required, work which is often considered among the most solid and unimpeachable results of linguistic science.

In recent years, those working within the framework of generative grammar have claimed that correct synchronic phonological descriptions of natural languages are incompatible with the autonomous phonemic view of phonology which has developed in modern (post-1933) linguistics, both European and American. As we have seen in Part I, the chief property of autonomous phonemic descriptions is that phonological representations must be arrived at solely on the basis of phonetic facts plus knowledge of which utterance pairs contrast (i.e. are not free variants or repetitions) and hence independently of considerations having to do with grammatical structure and morphophonemic alternations. There is obviously a striking similarity between the principles which define modern autonomous phonemics and those which characterize the Neogrammarian position on sound change. Indeed the former can be looked upon as simply the result of making the claims of the latter synchronic. Whereas the Neogrammarian position asserts in effect that all the regular systematic statements or rules, the so-called *Lautgesetze,* which describe the change of phonological structure, must be purely phonetic in both operation and environment, modern autonomous phonemics asserts that all the rules which describe the relation between phonemic and phonetic representation must be determined purely on phonetic grounds, given knowledge of contrast. This contrasts with the phonological position of generative grammar, which recognizes many rules with nonphonetic environments in synchronic phonological descriptions and likewise claims that such rules may therefore be added over time and thus play a role in describing sound changes.

We can now see the importance of the simple factual question raised at the outset. Upon the answer to this question hinges the correctness of crucial aspects of the view of sound change which dominates modern linguistics of the pre-generative type. We may distinguish three distinct views of regular sound change with respect to the kinds of environments in which these occur:

(PI) Autonomy[8]—the view that *no* regular sound changes require reference to morphophonemic or superficial grammatical environments.

(PII) Non-Autonomy—the view that *some* regular phonetic changes take place in environments whose specification requires reference to nonphonetic morphophonemic and/or superficial grammatical structure.

(PIII) Inseparability—the view that *all* regular phonetic changes take place in environments whose specification requires nonphonetic information.

---

[8] For this three-way distinction and similar criticisms of the position developed in this regard by Ferguson, cf. Chomsky (1964b:110–111).

(PI) is, as we have seen, the dominant modern view. (PII) is the view suggested by phonological work done within the framework of generative grammar. (PIII) is a position which has never been held by anyone past or present. It is defined and discussed here briefly only because a failure to distinguish between (PII) and (PIII) has led to recent confusions about the evidence which could bear upon the relative merits of (PI) and (PII), the basic question to which the present investigation is addressed.

In his review of Halle's *The Sound Pattern of Russian*, the first modern study to reject explicitly the autonomous framework of phonology, C. F. Ferguson (1962:284–297) rightly assumed that the conflict between the view of Halle and others working within the generative framework (that phonology is not independent of grammar, and that phonological representation is determined in part by grammatical and morphophonemic facts as well as phonetic ones) and the dominant autonomous position which he maintains is properly argued in terms of historical as well as synchronic phonology. Ferguson argued that historical evidence refutes the position Halle maintained (exclusively on synchronic grounds). His remarks require full quoting:

The effect of Condition (3a)[9] is to set a careful line between phonology and grammar, and it is the abandonment of this condition and erasure of its dividing line which constitute the greatest break between the current approaches to phonological analysis and that of Chomsky and Halle. It may seem plausible, as they suggest, that the sound system of a language is so intimately tied up with its grammar, and functions so completely as a tool of the grammar, that any attempt to treat it separately from the grammar is fundamentally mistaken. The autonomy of phonology, however, is a concept arrived at as the result of over a century of linguistic research, and the concept is not to be discarded lightly: to discard it would surrender some of the most striking achievements of linguistic science.

Ferguson then attempts to document this latter claim with the following remarks:

---

[9] Condition (3a) is the requirement that, given a phonemic description, the phonemic representation of a form is uniquely determined by its phonetic representation.

First, the autonomy of phonology was forced upon investigators in historical linguistics in the nineteenth century by the facts of language change. The discovery of Verner's Law made clear that, in general, phonological change takes place under conditions and within limitations which are in phonological terms and not in grammatical or semantic terms. The conditions under which these particular changes took place involved features such as voicing or voicelessness of neighboring sounds and the position of accent with regard to the sound in question, and the changes took place not only not in terms of grammatical conditions but in many cases in direct opposition to 'natural' grammatical parallels and analogies.

On the basis of this factual summary Ferguson then concluded with the following summary dismissal of the position he was criticizing:

A synchronic analysis which ties phonology and grammar up in a neat bundle not only falsifies the current situation but makes it impossible to understand the diachrony. One area of flux which is of importance diachronically is the borderline between phonology and grammar, where the fit of the two segmentations shifts and structural change takes place.

Although Ferguson is certainly correct in assuming that historical evidence bears on the question of the truth values of the incompatible theories of autonomous phonemics and generative phonology, his argument against the latter is thoroughly vitiated by its failure to distinguish position (PII), the position implied by generative phonology, and (PIII). Let us note that (PI) is consistent only with the existence of regular sound changes with purely phonetic environments. (PII) is consistent with the existence of regular sound changes with both purely phonetic and with more abstract environments. The existence of a single sound change of the latter variety is not only consistent with (PII) but supports (PII) vis-à-vis (PI) with which any such change is incompatible. (PIII) is consistent only with the existence of changes whose environments are not fully phonetic. Hence the existence of a single purely phonetic sound change refutes (PIII) vis-à-vis (PI) and (PII).

Consider now Ferguson's criticism of Halle's position. The

evidence which Ferguson brings forth is the existence of purely phonetic sound changes, in particular Verner's Law. Such sound changes, which obviously exist and whose existence has surely not been denied by any reputable linguist for decades, thoroughly refute position (PIII), a matter of limited interest since no one maintains (PIII). However, such evidence has no bearing whatever on the relative correctness of (PI), which Ferguson believes, and (PII), the position implied in the phonological theory he was criticizing, since both (PI) and (PII) are consistent with the existence of purely phonetic sound changes. Hence by failing to distinguish (PII) from (PIII) through an appeal to the metaphor of 'tying up phonology and grammar in a neat bundle' Ferguson fails to deal with the problem he raised, and his rejection of the position of generative phonology on historical grounds is without basis. This is a good illustration of the fact that in serious discussion of rival linguistic theories, imprecise and metaphorical statements of the opposing positions cannot be tolerated.

The real problem for linguistics at the moment is not to evaluate position (PIII), an artifact no one does or could maintain, but to decide between (PI) and (PII). It is to this real question that the next chapters of this study are addressed by way of the factual matter alluded to at the beginning. Ferguson has argued that generative phonology 'makes it impossible to understand the diachrony.' I shall argue that the reverse is the case, and that on the contrary, it is autonomous phonemics with its historical corollary, position (PI), which has this property, for the quite simple reason that there exist sound changes inconsistent with (PI). I shall argue this chiefly on the basis of some examples from the Northern Iroquoian languages. This will extend the counterevidence to the principles of autonomous phonemics (cf. Part I) strongly into the area of diachronic linguistics, and will provide grounds for the assertion that the version of the Neogrammarian position on sound change so strongly advocated by Bloomfield and generally accepted thereafter is mistaken; i.e. it will provide grounds for the assertion that the theory of sound change must be formulated around position (PII), not around position (PI) as is the case today. I shall try to accomplish this principally by showing that there are quite regular and easily characterized sound changes which relate contemporary Mohawk and Oneida to proto-Mohawk-Oneida which are indescribable in purely phonetic terms, although they have quite elementary descriptions in terms of representations which would now most likely be called 'morphophonemic.'

11

SOME IROQUOIAN SOUND CHANGES

MOHAWK

Proto-Mohawk-Oneida[1] had consonant-resonant consonant clusters which included the following types [wr, nr, sr, tr, kr, tn, sn, kn, tw, sw, kw, sy].[2] With certain minor exceptions irrelevant to the present discussion (for example, proto [nr] is, in con-

---

[1] I should like to indicate here my indebtedness to F. G. Lounsbury for my knowledge of much of the following factual material, a large portion of which was originally uncovered by him. I am also grateful to him for providing all of the Oneida forms quoted below. This is not to say, however, that he necessarily endorses the arguments given here or agrees with any particular assertions made in this study.

[2] This class of clusters also included [sy], [ty], [ky], [ny], [ry]. These were, however, later eliminated from the narrow phonetic level in Mohawk by rules which turned the initial consonant palatal and dropped the following glide. In discussing protosequences I enclose the elements in phonetic brackets '[ ]'. This is not necessarily to indicate a claim about the most detailed phonetic form which these had in the protolanguage, but

245

temporary Oneida, pronounced [ndl]), these clusters still exist in Oneida. In Mohawk, however, these have, with one particular type of exception, been eliminated *on the phonetic level* by the introduction of the epenthetic vowel [e], identical in quality to other distinctive, nonepenthetic [e] vowels which derive from those which existed in the parent language. Hence any autonomous phonemic description of Mohawk must consider these epenthetic [e] vowels to be phonemic although they are easily predicted in systematic terms and are thus not part of the dictionary representations of forms. For instance, an item like [o'nerahte?] 'leaf' has a systematic representation which can be abbreviated #wa+o+nraht+?#. The effects of the epenthesis sound change on Mohawk are illustrated by the Mohawk-Oneida cognates in the following list:

	Mohawk		*Oneida*	
(11.1)	[onuta'keri?]	Mo. 'beer,' On. 'sugar'	(11.10)	[onuta'kli?]
(11.2)	[kâ':sereh]	'vehicle'	(11.11)	[kâ':slet]
(11.3)	[yê':teru?]	'she, someone resides'	(11.12)	[yê':tlu?]
(11.4)	[teninû':we?s]	'we 2 inclusive like it'	(11.13)	[tninû':wehse?]
(11.5)	[seninû':we?s]	'you 2 like it'	(11.14)	[sninû':wehse?]
(11.6)	[yakeninû':we?s]	'we 2 exclusive like it'	(11.15)	[yakninû':wehse?]
(11.7)	[tewanû':we?s]	'we several like it'	(11.16)	[twanû':wehse?]
(11.8)	[sewanû':we?s]	'you several like it'	(11.17)	[swanû':wehse?]
(11.9)	[sata'weya?t]	'come in'	(11.19)	[sata'wyaht]

Consider now proto [kw]. No examples of epenthetic [e] from [kw] are given above. But these are the crucial cases for

---

only to indicate their phonetically crucial properties. That is, such representations are used where most contemporary linguists would quote protoforms or sequences in autonomous phonemic writing. In quoting phonetic sequences, I give no more detail than is necessary to illustrate the point under discussion. In quoting full forms, however, narrower representations are given. Unlike the examples in Part I, voicing and tenseness in consonants are not marked except in affricates, the latter only for reasons having to do with my personal transcription habits. Like previous examples, aspiration is not marked. The accent mark of course indicates stress, the colon length, and a circumflex 'ʌ' over a vowel falling tone.

our discussion. For in fact, the rule of [e] epenthesis which Mohawk has added is indescribable in purely phonetic terms, just because of the behavior of proto [kw] under this addition. This follows since these vowels were introduced only between *some* but not *all* [kw]. Furthermore, and most significantly, those proto [kw] which were split by epenthetic vowels were in no way distinguishable in *phonetic* terms from those which were not, although, with one exception, they are *automatically* distinguished in morphophonemic terms. It can easily be shown that whether or not epenthesis took place in such cases was determined by two different sorts of factors: in some cases, the Surface Syntactic Structure was relevant, but more generally, the underlying phonological structure which differentiated phonetically like elements was a determining factor.

If we investigate the following Mohawk-Oneida cognate forms we find that we must distinguish four different types of [kw] sequence:

	Mohawk			*Oneida*
(11.19)	[kewi′stos]	'I am cold'	(11.26)	[kwi′stos]
(11.20)	[rawi′stos]	'he is cold'	(11.27)	[lawi′stos]
(11.21)	[yakwanû′:weʔs]	'we several exclusive like it'	(11.28)	[yakwanû′:wehseʔ]
(11.22)	[ya′kwaks]	'we several exclusive eat it'	(11.29)	[ya′kwaks]
(11.23)	[ra′kwas]	'he picks it'	(11.30)	[la′kwas]
(11.24)	[ru′:kweh]	'man'	(11.31)	[lukwe′]
(11.25)	[o′:kwireʔ]	'branch'	(11.32)	[o:kwi′leʔ]

In forms (11.21) and (11.22), we find [kw] sequences in contemporary Mohawk not broken by epenthesis and for the same reason. Irregularly, and for reasons which are inexplicable, [kw] simply did not undergo epenthesis when the [k] was the first person morpheme and the [w] the first element of the plural morpheme, despite the fact that this same [k] element plus *stems* beginning with w̲ did yield epenthesis, as can be seen in form (11.19), and despite the fact that when the w̲ which begins the plural morpheme was preceded by s̲ of the second person morpheme or the t̲ of the inclusive person sequence, epenthesis also occurred. (Compare forms (11.7) and (11.8) with form

(11.21).) Hence the irregularity in (11.21) and (11.22) is wholly a function of the sequence first person+plural. It should be emphasized that this irregularity is 'regular' in the sense that it happens throughout the language in both noun and verb prefixes regardless of stem or inflection whenever this sequence of morphemes is juxtaposed. Here then we have a case of a regular sound change being impeded in a particular grammatical environment, a situation definitely not countenanced by position (PI). Although significant, this case of failure of epenthesis with first person and plural is not the most essential argument which can be given against (PI).[3]

---

[3] Another case of grammatically conditioned sound change within the history of Mohawk and Oneida is known to me. I have not discussed it in the text because certain of the facts in Oneida, which I have not studied personally, are unclear. Mohawk has a rule which deletes word final [+Abrupt Onset] segments in *nouns* only (actually only nouns which are not reduplicating animal names). Thus compare the Mohawk noun-verb pairs:

Nouns		*Verbs*	
[kâ':sereh]	'vehicle'	[ke²serehtanû':we²s]	'I like vehicles'
[odzi'stoh]	'star'	[kdzistohkwanû':we²s]	'I like stars'
[o'shes]	'syrup, honey'	[keshestanû':we²s]	'I like honey'
[ka'tshe²]	'bottle, can'	[ketshe²tanû':we²s]	'I like cans'
[o'hšdžʌ²]	'bone'	[kšdžʌ²tanû':we²s]	'I like bones'

with the verbs:

[i':sek]	'eat it'
[rakâ':rut]	'let him make a hole'
[tke'htak]	'let me believe it'
[ke²nikû':rarak]	'let me be careful'

Oneida has a similar rule whose domain is, however, more limited in ways that are not completely clear to me. Thus compare Oneida noun forms like:

[o'shes]
[odzi'sto]
[o'šdyʌ²]

in which word final [+Abrupt Onset] segments drop, with Oneida noun forms like:

[kâ':slet]
[kanâ':talok]

A second type of [kw] sequence is shown in the perfectly regular forms like (11.19), in which epenthesis occurs as expected, i.e. as in tw̲, sw̲, etc., sequences. Next take form (11.23), which also does not̲ undergo epenthesis. The epenthesis rule does not operate in this case because the underlying representation of this [kw] is ko̲. Compare Mohawk forms like:

(11.33) [waha':koʔ] 'he picked it'

Given the fact that [ko] and [kw] alternate in Mohawk morphemes, it is not self-evident that the underlying or basic representation is ko̲. The arguments for this are, however, strong. First of all, there is a general rule in the language that within morphemes, no sequences of the type consonant+w̲ are allowed. Choice of the representation kw̲ for stems like 'to pick' would force a partial rejection of this regularity. On the other hand, ko̲ occurs within morphemes regardless of how the class of stems involving [kw]-[ko] alternations are treated. Second, choice of kw̲ would complicate the rule of [e] epenthesis which operates in the̲ environment: Any Consonant̲—Resonant Consonant,[4] but not in these cases. Finally, the rule which turns o̲ to [w] is the quite general one which operates in the environment ̲—Vowel (and is needed not only for stem final vowel plus aspectual suffix, but also for other cases, for example, those involving the objective morpheme). However, if w̲ is chosen as basic, the rule to turn this to [o] is not nearly as̲ simple. For this rule would have to operate in terms of both preceding the following environments, since w̲ normally drops instead of going to [o] in ̲—Consonant:

(11.34) [waho':taʔweʔ] 'he slept' waʔ+hra+o+itaʔw+ʔ
(11.35) [ro':taʔs] 'he sleeps' hra+o+itaʔw+s

---

in which they do not. We can see then that, regardless of details, Mohawk has in fact extended the rule of dropping in nouns to a further set of cases. But since this extra deletion is grammatically conditioned (only in nouns), is it another case of nonphonetic sound change whose environment is partially determined by Surface Syntactic Structure.

[4] One of the facts which leads to a [+Consonantal] systematic representation for phonetically [−Consonantal] [w] and [y] in Mohawk, as discussed in footnote 18 of Chapter 8, is their behavior as resonant or liquid consonants in this rule. Cf. footnote 6 of this chapter.

Hence the environment for this putative rule cannot be simply

$$\underline{\qquad} \left\{ \begin{array}{l} \text{Consonant} \\ \text{Glide} \end{array} \right\},$$

which is more complicated than the environment of the o to [w] rule anyway, but would have to involve preceding structure as well. There are thus very strong reasons for considering the underlying representation of the [kw] sequence in forms like (11.23) to be ko.[5] And it is simply a fact that [kw] sequences which derive from ko never permit epenthesis.[6]

Finally, in forms (11.24) and (11.25) there is no epenthesis because the [kw] sequence here must be considered the representative of the single morphophoneme p,[7] which also existed in

---

[5] The treatment of stem final [o]-[w] and [i]-[y] alternations in the Northern Iroquoian languages is an interesting and difficult one which has, I think, never been adequately managed in the past. Seduced by the phonetic parallelism here, all past treatments have assumed that either the full vowels are basic in both cases or the glides are basic. Lounsbury, for example, in his unpublished Master's Thesis (1946), treated w and y as basic. W. L. Chafe, in all of his work on Seneca, also assumed that w and y are basic here. In my Doctoral Thesis (1962), I assumed that o and i were basic. But I am now convinced that, at least for Mohawk, it is necessary to treat o as basic in the [o]-[w] cases, but y as basic in the [i]-[y] cases. This follows because the [w] in the former cases does not behave like the true consonantal, systematic w, behaves under a variety of rules, but the [y] in the latter cases does obey the rules which hold for consontal systematic y. This issue is discussed at length in Postal (to appear c).

[6] One might assume that this failure of epenthesis is accounted for by order of rules, i.e. that the epenthesis rule precedes the rule which yields the [w], thus preventing epenthesis. But this is not true, and the order of rules is the opposite. What prevents the epenthesis is the fact that the 'w' element which is introduced from o is not marked [+Consonantal], and hence does not define the proper environment for epenthesis. This 'w' element thus contrasts with systematic w which is marked [+Consonantal] at the point at which the epenthesis rule applies. In the final, most narrow representation, these elements fall together as a [−Consonantal] glide. What may seem here simply an ad hoc solution is in fact highly motivated and general. I have justified it in some detail in Postal (to appear c). Cf. also footnote 18 of Chapter 8.

[7] As pointed out in footnote 16 of Chapter 8, the labial character, which is both implied by the notation p and definitely claimed by the $\left[\begin{array}{l} \text{+Grave} \\ \text{+Diffuse} \end{array} \right]$ structure this is meant to abbreviate, has not been justified

the proto-language, although the falling together of the phonetic realizations of this single element with the [kw] which come from k+w and ko dates to a period before the separation of the Northern Iroquoian languages, i.e. to something on the order of three millennia ago. Again, the evidence which shows that in contemporary Mohawk the [kw] sequences in forms like (11.24) and (11.25) are representatives of a single systematic phonological element (morphophoneme) is overwhelming. First of all, this eliminates a set of exceptions to the rule of [e] epenthesis. Second, as was briefly discussed in Chapter 7, there is a rule in the language that stressed vowels are long before (systematically) single consonants. And there is length before these [kw] sequences but not before those in forms where the [kw] comes from k+w or ko (here absence of length is due to rule ordering). Hence recognition of a single element here also regularizes the description of length. Furthermore, although this is not obvious (Postal (to appear c)), recognition of systematic p simplifies the statement of the restrictions, briefly discussed in Chapter 8, that k and y do not occur within morphemes before i,[8] while p and w do not occur within morphemes before rounded vowels (o, u). Finally, the 'w' elements after velars behave differently in word final and prerounded vowel position than true w, which is represented by [f] in the former position and by [y] in the latter. In both of these positions p yields [k].[9]

---

in the present work. It is interesting, in this historical context, that Chafe (1964), in his recent work arguing for genetic relationship between Siouan and Iroquoian, finds [p]-[kw] differences distinguishing cognates. He thus sets up a Proto-Siouan-Iroquoian *p which became [kw] in most Seneca environments and [p] in Siouan. Hence to the extent that Chafe's conclusions can be accepted, it is fairly clear that what I claim is systematic p in contemporary Mohawk had a labial origin *historically*. What is controversial then is the claim that this labial character has been maintained in the underlying systematic representations of Mohawk, and probably contemporary Iroquoian languages generally, even though the labial elements have essentially been lost phonetically. Notice that it is only within the framework of a systematic phonemic theory embodying the Naturalness Condition that a claim of underlying labial character makes sense. Cf. footnote 11 of Chapter 4.

[8] There are a handful of exceptions to the former generalization with k, for example [ki'tkit] 'chicken.' This should only figure as one exception, incidentally, since it is a case of reduplication.

[9] Actually, I have run across a handful of related speakers who quite

Hence there is no doubt that in systematic phonemic terms, contemporary Mohawk has a single consonantal phoneme which is represented phonetically by [kw] and [k]. This is, on roughly similar grounds, also true of Oneida, and hence by direct inference was also the case in the proto-language. And cognate comparisons with other Iroquoian languages, for example Seneca, show that the merging of p̲ with ko̲+vowel and k̲+w̲ dates to before the split of the Northern Iroquoian languages. Compare:

A. For p̲

Seneca	*Mohawk*
(11.36) /tɛ:nɔhtahkwayɛɔˀ/	[wahtahkwara′kʌh]
'they bet on a shoe'	'white shoes'
(11.37) /hekä:hkwa:ˀah/	[tkarahkwi′nekʌˀs]
'afternoon=less sun'	'the sun rises'
(11.38) /kɛkwitekhneh/	[kʌkwitê′:neh]
'spring'	'spring'

B. For ko̲+vowel

(11.39) /yesa′eˀtä:kwas/	[rasaheˀta′kwas]
'she picks out the beans'	'he picks beans'
	[wahasahê′:ˀta koˀ]
	'he picked beans'
(11.40) /sæ:kweh/	[rara′kwas]
'you choose it'	'he chooses'
(11.41) /ˀɛkæ:koˀ/	[ʌhara′:koˀ]
'I shall choose'	'he will choose'
(11.42) /ˀɛɔti:wake′skwahse:k/	[rake′tskwas]
'they masc. pl. will get up the ceremony'	'he raises it'
(11.43) /ˀɛyɔtyaˀta′keskoˀ/	[ʌhake′tskoˀ]
'people will arise'	'he will raise it'

---

exceptionally pronounce p̲ as [kw] in word final position. Since the absence of [w] here in the standard dialects dates to protoIroquoian, this is another case of nonphonetic sound change; nonphonetic, because this [w] appears for these few speakers only after those [k] which come from word final systematic p̲ and not those from word final k̲. I have not utilized this example in the text because it is limited to a few speakers and because I have not as yet been able to study it in detail.

C. For k+w

(11.44) /akwahsiʔ taʔ/   [yakwahsiʔtâ':keh]
        'our feet'   'our feet'
(11.45) /waʔakwayɛ:ʔ/   [waʔakwa':yʌʔ]
        'we ex.pl. put down'   'we leave it, set it'

Seneca examples (11.36), (11.37), (11.38), (11.39), and (11.44) are from Chafe (1963:36, 38, 39, 35, and 12 respectively). Seneca examples (11.40) through (11.43) and (11.45) are from Chafe (1961:242, 250, 232, 246, and 168 respectively). Chafe's representations are of course autonomous phonemic rather than literally phonetic. They are, however, very close to phonetic.

Summing up, it can be seen that the sequences in Mohawk which correspond to phonetic [kw] in Oneida can be understood only in terms of at least four distinct underlying or systematic phonemic interpretations. Namely, as k+w irregularly marked as not undergoing epenthesis when representing first person+ plural, as ko, as a single element p, and as perfectly regular k+w. One need make only two assumptions to make the facts of change automatic consequences of the addition of the following schematically stated rule (this rule is discussed and stated precisely in Postal, to appear c) to the grammar of proto-Mohawk but not proto-Oneida, that is, to the grammars of some but not all speakers of proto-Mohawk-Oneida:

(11.46) null $\longrightarrow$ [e] in the environment: [Consonant]_____[Resonant Consonant]

The first assumption is that the three-way systematic contrast between k+w, ko, and p existed in proto-Mohawk-Oneida, which is hardly questionable. The second is that the added rule of epenthesis operated *not* on phonetic or autonomous phonemic representation, but on the much more abstract systematic phonemic representation, a structure which is independently motivated by a host of other phenomena. Actually, this latter statement is something of a simplification. For the rule of epenthesis would operate on the systematic representation of forms directly only if it were added as the first phonological rule, which was certainly not the case. More precisely then, this added rule operated on sub-represenations which were derived from the systematic structure by previous rules, but which were not identical to phonetic or autonomous phonemic representations. In this way the rule was able to distinguish the identical phonetic sequences which ultimately resulted from the grammar of proto-Mohawk-Oneida prior to the rule addition, despite the fact that *phonetic contexts* provided no unique specification of whether a proto-Mohawk-Oneida [kw] would or would not be affected by the new rule.

ONEIDA

As striking support of the claim that the Mohawk data just discussed concerning [e] epenthesis is not some kind of peripheral or accidental occurrence, or due to some overlooked or misinterpreted facts, there is the crucial evidence of a parallel development in Oneida. Just as one must postulate that Mohawk has added to the proto-grammar a rule which is unstatable in autonomous phonemic terms because of the varying structural characterizations of the phonetic sequence [kw], so also Oneida has added a quite different rule which is indescribable in such limited terms for exactly the same reasons.

In both languages the ancient rule of stress assignment still functions. The penultimate vowel in a multivowel word is strssed. This rule must, of course, be stated on a relatively abstract representation; one, for example, which does not include epenthetic vowels of various types, only one of which is that discussed earlier. This representation is hence neither phonetic nor autonomous phonemic. Oneida has, however, added a rule which Lounsbury (1946:58–59) refers to as the <u>Oneida Accent Shift</u>. The full details of this rule need not concern us, but one of its effects is to move the stress from the penultimate to the final nonepenthetic vowel of a word provided that only a *single consonant* intervenes. Thus compare the following Mohawk and Oneida forms:

<u>Mohawk</u>			<u>Oneida</u>	
(11.47)	[waha′:koʔ]	'he picked it'	(11.50)	[waha:kồ′]
(11.48)	[wakhuri′:yoʰ]	'I have a good gun'	(11.51)	[wakhuliyo′]
(11.49)	[waha′:kʌʔ]	'he saw her'	(11.52)	[waha:kʌ̂′]

But the striking thing is that those [kw] sequences in Oneida which represent systematic phonological or morphophonemic p̲, i.e. exactly those which correspond with those morpheme internal [kw] in Mohawk that are not derived from k̲o̲, permit the accent shift to take place, *but no others do*. This has in fact already been illustrated by the Oneida forms (11.29) through (11.32). In (11.29) the accent has not shifted because the [kw] represents k̲+w̲, in (11.30) it has not shifted because the [kw] represents k̲o̲ where the o̲ yields a [w] in the representation before the shift rule applies. But in (11.31) and (11.32) the accent does shift because in these forms there is underlying p̲, still a single consonant in the abstract representation at the point when the accent shift rule applies. Note that the final [e] in (11.32) is epenthetic and hence the penultimate rule places the stress originally on the initial [o].

The same fundamental and independently motivated analysis of morphophonemic structure accounts for the facts of accent shift with respect to [kw] in Oneida as accounts for the epenthesis facts with respect to [kw] in Mohawk. Surely nothing could show more clearly the depth and reality of the underlying structural differentiation in the proto-system of what were unquestionably phonetically identical [kw] sequences, or show more clearly the fundamental role that morphophonemic structure plays in perfectly regular and systematic phonological change.

ALTERNATIVES

Of course, at least for those not familiar with Iroquoian, it is reasonable at this point to suggest the possibility that, at the time when the antecedents of contemporary Mohawk and Oneida [kw] and [k(e)w] were differentiated by the epenthesis and accent shift sound changes, they were in fact phonetically distinct. However, comparison of the languages with each other and with other Iroquoian languages makes it clear that this is quite out of the question. The sound changes we are discussing are quite recent. Lounsbury (1946:58) dates the Oneida Accent Shift to the beginning of the 19th century at the earliest. The Mohawk epenthesis rule is perhaps a few hundred years older.

The exact age of this rule is difficult to determine. The oldest relevant material would seem to be the materials recorded in *The Voyages of Jacques Cartier*, dating to the 1530's. These contain several hundred recordings of Iroquoian words and expressions. Unfortunately, it is unclear exactly what languages are represented in these materials. It appears that they contain items from more than one Iroquoian dialect. Some of the forms do appear to be Mohawk, and in epenthesis positions one does not find the epenthetic [e] recorded. Thus one finds tigneny 'two' where contemporary Mohawk has [te'kenih]. If, therefore, these forms in the Cartier *Voyages* are in fact recordings of 16th century Mohawk, this places an upper bound of four hundred years as the maximum age of the Mohawk rule of [e] epenthesis between consonant and resonant consonant. For discussion and analysis of these forms, cf. Barbeau (1959).

On the other hand, a glance at the other Iroquoian languages shows that ko before a vowel and the single systematic element p have been phonetically [kw] for at least several millennia. This follows, for example, from the fact illustrated above that Seneca has cognate forms with [kw] in all the positions of Mohawk k+w, ko, and p and from the fact that the Seneca–Mohawk–Oneida split has been estimated by Lounsbury (1961:2) to have taken place approximately twelve to fifteen hundred years ago. Therefore, in order to postulate phonetic differences in Mohawk and Oneida during the present millennium, it would be necessary to say that ko, p, and k+w fell together in proto-Iroquoian, then redivided in Oneida and Mohawk, and then separately in both languages largely fell together again, obviously an inconceivable set of occurrences. Even worse for the view of purely phonetic sound change is the fact, pointed out to me by Eric Hamp, that if one compares form (11.22) in Mohawk with form (11.29) in Oneida, one finds that the postulation of phonetic differences leads to inconsistent assertions about the proto-language. For in Mohawk, in order to prevent epenthesis, one would like to say that the antecedent of the [kw] in (11.22) was a single phoneme in say 1400 to 1800, but in Oneida in order to prevent the accent shift one would have to say that the antecedent of (11.29) was a consonant sequence. But the antecedents of (11.22) and (11.29) are the same. Clearly any hypothetical phonetic differences between [kw] sequences in Mohawk and Oneida during this millennium are completely untenable.

My colleague R. P. Kiparsky has pointed out that in view of the apparent role played by relative chronology in these arguments about Mohawk [e] epenthesis and Oneida Accent Shift, it is advisable not to leave the impression that the chronologies are based purely on Stammbaum considerations. That is, the chronologies are not based simply on assuming that within a set of related languages the more widespread rule is necessarily older and that all instances of some rule within a family must have the same unique origin with only genetic transmission. While one cannot assume that wider distribution necessarily means greater age, and while one must admit that the same rule may arise within the same family independently, of course in general the probability of these happenings is smaller than that of the contrary assumption. This is especially the case when the rules in question are not of the type which commonly arise again and again. Nonetheless, one must allow for the existence both of 'drift,' i.e. independent origin of the same rule within separated members of a family, and for the possibility of rule borrowing. And it might be claimed, for example, that a rule of the form o̱ to [w] before vowels, which plays an important role in our arguments above, is sufficiently common as not to rule out the possibility of multiple origin.[10]

It should therefore be pointed out that anyone who disputes the relative chronologies assumed in the arguments above must face the following kinds of difficulties. I shall consider only the

---

[10] What is really common is the shift of high back rounded vowels to [w] before other vowels. This fact is one of several arguing that the *phonetically* mid back rounded vowels [o] of Mohawk are actually *systematically* high ([+Diffuse]) vowels. Other evidence for this derives from the fact that o̱ falls into a set with other diffuse vowels i̱, u̱ with respect to relevance for the gravity dissimilation of w̱ and p̱ discussed in Chapter 8. It seems then that these three vowels are divided from the other three Mohawk vowels a̱, ʌ̱, e̱ by being [+Diffuse], that i̱ differs from o̱ and u̱ in terms of Grave, and that o̱ and u̱ are distinguished, as are a̱ and ʌ̱, by nasality. Both ʌ̱ and u̱ have phonetic manifestations which are [+Nasal]. If this analysis is correct, it provides a rare instance where the nasality of nasal vowels is not predictable in systematic terms. The analysis is not entirely secure because there are rules which introduce both. [ʌ] and [u] in certain positions as a function of non-Nasal vowels. I have not, however, been able to justify any use of these rules to predict instances of lexical [ʌ] and [u]. For further discussion cf. Postal (to appear c).

assumed chronology: <u>o</u> to [w] before vowels, penultimate accent, Mohawk [e] epenthesis. In Mohawk, Oneida, and Seneca, the basic stress rule accents the penultimate vowel within a word. But each language has developed subsidiary accent rules which affect at least some stress positions. Seneca, in particular, has developed a highly complex system of rules which are such that phonetic stress is only in the most indirect way related to the original penultimate accent. However, in all cases the vowel count for penultimate accent placement does not count the vowel of the [o]-[w] alternations which motivate the <u>o</u> to [w] rule. Hence in Mohawk <u>hra+ko+as</u> is [ra'kwas]. This then argues strongly that the accent rule is later in each of these languages than the <u>o</u> to [w] rule. Further, the Mohawk epenthetic [e] rule in no case adds vowels which are counted in the accent placement. Therefore straightforward considerations show that [e] epenthesis is later than the <u>o</u> to [w] rule.

In order to object to this argument it would be necessary to deny that the fact that the accent rule ignores the <u>o</u> which switches to [w] means that the accent rule is later, or to deny that the fact that the accent rule ignores the vowels of the [e] epenthesis rule means that the epenthesis rule is later. But this can be done only at the cost of asserting that these rules were nonphonetic sound changes.[11] It thus appears that on grounds

---

[11] This ignores the logical possibility of setting up a large number of ad hoc changes which have no independent justification. For example, it might be hypothetically suggested that in fact [e] epenthesis addition is historically earlier than penultimate accent, but that these vowels are irrelevant for the stress count for the following reason. When first introduced they were rising-tone vowels, the subsequently added accent rule stressed only level-tone vowels. After a while, the rising-tone [e] fell together with other [e] as level-tone vowels. Such hypothetical accounts deserve no consideration whatever. For as noted earlier, if historical accounts are not constrained to pick the simplest solution and to accord with linguistic universals (which, for example, will specify rising-tone as Marked and thus highly unlikely to appear in an epenthesis rule), the claim that all rules are purely phonetic is empty. One can always construct a sufficiently long, ad hoc, chain of happenings which will reduce any set of changes to purely phonetic environments. The example given here is, of course, a straw man. But no other analysis conceivable to me really has any more justification. Epenthesis is clearly a unitary phenomenon which must be accounted for by a single rule. This means that it was either added to the grammar after the accent rule or was a nonphonetic sound change; etc.

independent of Stammbaum considerations, any quarrel with the relative chronologies assumed above is poorly founded and in any event irrelevant to the deeper point. For any change of the chronologies of the rules for o to [w], accent placement, and [e] epenthesis in Mohawk yields other nonphonetic sound changes. An analogous argument for Oneida yields the same conclusion for the rules of o to [w], accent placement, and Oneida Accent Shift. Similar arguments can be given for the other cases involving p and k+w. It is thus evident that the relative chronologies are supported not only by Stammbaum considerations, but also by internal arguments which can be disputed at best only by positing nonphonetic sound changes of exactly the sort whose existence is supported by the argument with the originally assumed chronology. Thus the situation is as follows: the chronologies assumed in our arguments are supported by Stammabum considerations, internal arguments, and limited textual evidence, all of which dovetail to support the same conclusions, which have never been questioned by students of Iroquoian (i.e. my chronological claims are completely uncontroversial). But more significantly, even if one should choose to deny the chronology, one would be led to the recognition of other nonphonetic sound changes so that the deeper point is maintained in any event.

It is also possible, I suppose, that someone will at this point wish to speak of analogy. It should be clear that all talk of this type is completely pointless and without foundation in these cases. As ordinarily understood, analogy only makes sense, if at all, to explain correspondences or lack of them which cannot be brought under general rules (that is, rules operating for the lexicon as a whole).[12] But in the cases we have considered, the correspondences *are* a result of general rules, although they are ones which violate the constraints imposed by the Neogrammarian view of sound change, which is thereby shown to be false. Notice further that in these cases there is nothing to analogize *to,* and indeed the force of analogy, had it operated, would have

---

[12] In his Doctoral Thesis, Kiparsky (1965) argues convincingly for the inadequacy of the proportional, allomorphy-regularizing view of analogy. He proposes instead that analogy is actually a perfectly regular type of sound change involving the simplification and reordering of phonological rules.

shifted the forms which violate the Neogrammarian constraint in such a way that they would not violate it. Especially in the case of the lack of epenthesis between first person and plural in Mohawk, all the force of analogy would be expected to have yielded epenthesis to bring the first person plural exclusive paradigm into line with the second person and inclusive paradigms. Clearly analogy can be invoked in these Iroquoian cases only as a kind of terminological magic wand.

12

FURTHER COMMENTARY ON NONPHONETIC SOUND CHANGES

In Chapter 11 it was shown that there are obvious and simple 'sound changes' which in part characterize the shift from Proto-Mohawk-Oneida to contemporary Mohawk and Oneida, that are easily described in terms of what would not be called 'morphophonemic' representations but which are indescribable in purely phonetic and hence autonomous phonemic terms. Cases like these falsify the version of Neogrammarian position on sound change which Bloomfield so strongly maintained, and which is so closely identified with the application of autonomous phonemics to historical phonology. We see that sound change cannot be looked upon as changes of articulation in phonetic environments.

The above conclusions are controversial, and the fact that the evidence thus far brought forward is from languages which are, to say the least, not widely known, certainly will not contribute to convincing linguists of their validity. Two different sorts of considerations strengthen these conclusions, however. First is the fact that the cases in Chapter 11 are in no sense isolated examples, unsupported by cases from other language families. Indeed, Kiparsky (1965) has uncovered a variety of such cases within the Indo-European and Finno-Ugric families, some of them as well-known as Lachmann's Law. These are discussed at some length, and it is shown that certain subtypes are really commonplaces.

W. O'Neil has pointed out to me that the case of Lachmann's Law was discussed by De Saussure (1959:167–168):

Old Latin apparently favors the analytical procedure. Here is obvious proof: quantity is not the same in *făctus* and *āctus* despite *făcio* and *agō*; we must assume that *āctus* goes back to *°agtos* and attribute lengthening of the vowel to the voiced consonant that followed; this hypothesis is fully confirmed by the Romance languages. . . . But *°agtos*, *°tegtos*, *°regtos* were not inherited from Proto-Indo-European, which certainly had *°aktos*, *°tektos*, etc.; prehistoric Latin introduced them, and this despite the difficulty of pronouncing a voiced consonant before a voiceless one.

All of the forms quoted by Saussure are intended to be phonetic. What has clearly gone on here is that the Latin rule of vowel lengthening before clusters beginning with voiced consonants was added to the grammar *before* the historically older rule of Indo-European consonantal voicing assimilation. Hence the order of rules in Latin grammar did not reflect the order of historical development. And quite crucially, the added rule of lengthening had to operate not on phonetic representations, in which the velar stops of <u>făctus</u> and <u>āctus</u> were not distinguished, but on the systematic representation in which the latter had a *structurally* voiced consonant, the former a *structurally* voiceless one. The merging to voicelessness resulted only after the rule of voicing assimilation had applied. Instead of adopting this simple explanation in which only one (to be sure nonphonetic) rule is required for Latin, Saussure made up, without independent justification, an additional 'analogic' change from *°*<u>aktos</u>, *°*<u>tektos</u>, etc., on the basis of stems <u>ag-</u>, <u>teg-</u>, etc., a change which even he noted was implausible because of its conflict with voicing assimilation. Saussure's only motivation for such a change was the fact that he was a firm believer in the otherwise disproved thesis (PI) (Cf 1959:143–144, 152). For the emptiness of (PI) if historical accounts are not required to meet the condition of being the simplest available set of changes to explain the facts, cf. below. The fact that Saussure, who was a firm believer in (PI), discovered a counterexample to it without drawing any negative conclusions about the truth of (PI) is highly relevant to the discussion in the text below.

Similarly, W. O'Neil has uncovered a very clear case in the history of English, one in which the facts are abundantly documented in the traditional manuals. Briefly described, this case is as follows. Chronologically, West Germanic consonant doubling *precedes* Proto-Old English breaking. The former is a rule which doubles a consonant other than r in the environment: <u>short vowel</u> _____<u>y</u>. Thus *tælyan > *tællyan, *sætyan > *sattyan, etc. The latter is a more complex rule which inserts an epenthetic vowel of a quality related to that of the vowel in the environment

$$\text{vowel}\underline{\qquad}\begin{Bmatrix}\underline{h}\\ \underline{r}+\text{conconant}\\ \underline{l}+\text{consonant}\end{Bmatrix}$$

Hence: *wærp > *wæarp; *werp > *weorp; *wirp > *wiurp, etc. The crucial fact which shows that this breaking violates (PI), and must be considered to have been added to the grammar in a position before the historically older West Germanic consonant doubling, is that <u>vowel</u>_____<u>l + consonant</u> acts as an environment for breaking only if it is *not* the result of the rule of consonant doubling. In other words, some instances of <u>vowel</u> _____<u>l + consonant</u> behave one way, and some the other, and the differentiating factor is the underlying morphophonemic difference, i.e. that one of them is not systematically ll. Thus *fællyan > *fæallyan (>fiellan), but *tælyan > *tællyan (>tellan) where the ll of fællyan is not the result of West Germanic consonant doubling. Notice that there is a subsidiary rule dropping y in the environment <u>consonant</u>_____<u>vowel</u>, where the consonant is not r. This case will be discussed at greater length and with more supporting evidence in a forthcoming monograph by O'Neil on the history of English. For the facts cf. Cambell (1959).

If now it be asked how decades of work assuming the validity of the principle of purely phonetic sound change could have failed to turn up counterexamples, my suggestion is that such work has not failed to do so. On the one hand certain scholars, in particular J. Kuryłowicz (1960:70, 260), have emphasized the existence of regular sound change conditioned by nonphonetic factors, including grammatical category. In fact this emphasis is perhaps one of the most notable aspects of Kuryłowicz's historical work. On the other hand, even in the work of those who accept (PI), one can find materials disproving it. Judging by the case within Iroquoian studies, many such counterexamples have been found, but have been either ignored or dealt with by ad hoc unjustified postulations of extra changes. Thus as noted in footnote 1 of Chapter 11, many of the facts of sound change relevant to the argument in that chapter were discovered by F. G. Lounsbury. In his Master's Thesis (1946:46, 59, 64, 70, 74) he gives examples which show that the Oneida Accent Shift treated some [kw] as single consonants and others as clusters. But, despite the fact that he devoted a whole section to 'special cases under the accent shift,'[1] he did not mention explicitly this behavior of [kw] sequences under the accent rule, nor did he draw any general conclusions from it. Similarly, W. L. Chafe in his historical work on the phonological development of Seneca reported a situation in which Proto-Seneca [t] and [k] dropped in a number of environments. He describes this as follows (1959: 486):

We can infer that °t and °k were lost before an °s that was followed by an obstruent or a word boundary, and that they were also lost in word-final position after an oral obstruent.

However, since in Seneca, other Iroquoian languages, and indeed no doubt universally, word boundaries cannot be fully characterized phonetically, since they may be optionally either a real pause or phonetically null, this loss of [t] and [k] reported by Chafe is another case of sound change in nonphonetic environments. However, instead of reaching this conclusion, Chafe added a footnote characterizing the word boundary:

---

[1] This section contains, incidentally, a number of cases illustrating the fact that sound changes in particular and linguistic rules in general have exceptions. Lounsbury notes, for example, that there are a few morphemes which unpredictably require accent shift across the cluster h̲n̲, one morpheme in which it irregularly shifts across l̲h̲, and a handful of cases where it irregularly shifts across h̲, etc.

At which there is always a potentiality of juncture, although the juncture is not always present. We may infer that the prejunctural forms have been generalized.

That is, instead of positing *one* historical change which took place in a nonphonetic environment, Chafe posited *two* changes. One of these occurred in a phonetic environment (prejuncturally). But curiously enough, the second change still fails to meet the condition of phonetic sound change although it is perfectly general, cross-lexical, exceptionless, etc. Chafe no doubt intended this to be a case, not of sound change, but of analogy ('generalization' in his terms). This terminological decision has, however, naturally no empirical force whatever. That is, it amounts only to naming an exception to the principle accepted. One can only conclude that, in order to get around the nonphonetic sound change which he had discovered, Chafe posited without independent grounds two rules instead of the one rule actually required. But even then he was forced to recognize a change of exactly the sort which is not supposed to happen.

Although Chafe has not accomplished it in this case, it goes without saying that by positing enough unmotivated changes any set of facts can be reduced to description in terms of purely phonetic environments. That is, if historical explanations are not constrained to pick the simplest description of the facts, and are not constrained to agree with linguistic universals, the claim that all changes occur in phonetic environments is empty since no possible facts could ever conflict with it.

Incidentally, since, as far as I know, word boundaries are in all languages realized phonetically sometimes as null, I would expect that the vast majority of sound changes which take place at word boundary are in fact counterexamples to position (PI) of exactly the type run into by Chafe. This difficulty was actually noted by Bloomfield (1935:371) who remarked:

When changes of this sort appear at the beginning or, more often at the end of words, we have to suppose that the languages in which they took place had, at the time, some phonetic markings of the word-unit.

Bloomfield's inadequate position thus forced him to postulate a situation in protolanguages which has never been observed in actually observed ones, namely, the presence of a unique phonetic marking for *every* word boundary occurrence. The desperate character of Bloomfield's assumption here is revealed by the fact that in the same book (1933:181) he himself recognized that languages do not uniformly mark word boundaries phonetically. However, the assumption that protolanguages had a feature never found in actually investigated languages ignored, of course, what must be a basic principle of historical work: descriptions of earlier languages must never violate universals which hold for actually observed languages. For an emphatic statement and discussion of this principle cf. Jakobson (1958). Again we see how exceptions to (PI) have been handled by illegitimate devices.

I conclude on the basis of Iroquoian examples and others that the strength with which modern linguists have in general accepted the incorrect thesis of sound change with purely phonetic environments has apparently prevented them from acknowledging counterexamples to this position, even when they have been found. If this conclusion really generalizes to other language families, one would expect that an analytic survey of the literature will reveal many instances of supposedly impossible regular sound change in nonphonetic environments. In fact this suspicion is already partly confirmed by the European language examples uncovered by Kiparsky and O'Neil, which we discussed earlier.

In a recent attack on systematic phonemics, F. Householder, (1965:29) remarked:

Halle . . . achieves the remarkable position of specifying distinctions which are present (apparently) only in the brains of speakers . . .

Notice that each case of nonphonetic sound change we have discussed is exactly an instance where a distinction was maintained mentally for long periods in spite of an absence of direct phonetic distinction. It is indicative of the deviance from linguistic reality represented by the autonomous phonemic position which Householder illustrates that far from rare linguistic facts seem absurd or impossible when viewed in terms of it.

In Chapter 10, I quoted a remark from Ferguson's review of *The Sound Pattern of Russian* in which he claimed in effect that the facts of historical sound change justify autonomous phonemics vis-à-vis systematic phonemics. I think that what has been said here already is sufficient to show that in fact the situation is the reverse of this. The relative merits of these two as a basis for diachronic phonology are the same as for synchronic.

I remarked above that two sorts of considerations supported the conclusions drawn in Chapter 11. One sort has just been considered. The other kind is more theoretical and relates directly to the general nature of sound change, a topic controversial enough to require separate discussion.

13

WHAT IS SOUND CHANGE?

THE MENTALISTIC CHARACTER
OF SOUND CHANGE

The second sort of factor strengthening the conclusions of Chapter 11 is as follows. The position which Chapters 11 and 12 falsify, namely, the purely phonetic character of sound change, is completely unmotivated and in most versions borders on outright incoherence. This position seems to have some initial plausibility because it is wrapped up with certain common mistakes, in particular a failure to recognize the logical status of the notion *grammar*, and a failure to distinguish between *language* and *speech*, i.e. between *linguistic competence*, or *knowledge*, and *linguistic behavior*, or *performance*. Crucial to these misunderstandings, indeed the pivot on which their relevance to the nature of sound change is based, is the almost complete failure within modern linguistics to recognize the correct status of phonetic representations. The principal motivation underlying all this is the widespread and tremendously harmful view that linguistics can and must avoid 'mentalistic' statements.

269

'Sound change' is unfortunately a very bad and misleading term for the phenomena to which it is supposed to refer for the simple reason that what really changes is not *sounds* but grammars. And grammars are abstract objects—sets of rules represented in human organisms. Grammars are thus logically analogous to computer programs, or to the rules of chess, or to complex cultural objects in general. The fact that such objects may be represented in physical systems or *performed in physical activity* obviously does not mean that they are identical with the physical systems in which they are represented or the *activity by which they are performed*. Notice that we may quite naturally speak of an *utterance* as a *performance of a sentence* in the same sense in which a *concert* is the *performance of a certain piece of music*.

What is sound change? In fact we have already given our answer to this question several times in Chapter 11 in the discussion of those sound changes which violated the modern version of the Neogrammarian constraint. We explicitly spoke there of sound change as *the addition of rules to grammars*. This was not meant as any sort of metaphor or abbreviatory remark. Following the explicit and insightful suggestion of M. Halle (1962), we wish to insist that sound change consists exactly of changes in the phonological parts of grammars, that is, changes in the sets of rules which map Surface Syntactic Structures into phonetic representations.

Again, following Halle, we agree that sound change is of at least two different types. First there is the addition of rules to the grammar. This, he posits, is the only way that the grammars of adults may change. However, since the addition of a rule R to a grammar G_1 may define a language of which the optimal grammar is not $G_1 + R$, it follows that children in the next generation will in such cases learn not this but the optimal grammar, in effect yielding a distinct type of sound change. Thus it is not fully the case, as concluded by Lounsbury (1962:294–295), that:

A logical consequence of the position of this new school of linguistics, it would seem, is that our notion of 'structural change' is an illusion, and that changes are—as they were treated in early historical linguistics —particularistic, with no further consequences except that they must be noted, i.e., added to the list of 'rules' of derivation which, operating on the construct forms, are to yield the forms as they actually occur.

This conclusion would follow only if, falsely, the language defined by adding a rule to a fixed grammar always had as its optimal grammar the original plus the rule. If rule addition were the only mechanism of change, that is, if reformulation by children did not take place, the number of rules would increase over time, obviously an untenable conclusion. It goes without saying that this reformulation imposes great constraints on the ability of the linguist to reconstruct past happenings, since unlike simple rule additions such changes need not leave a direct record.

What is right in Lounsbury's remark is the fact that many rule additions which would be considered to effect the autonomous representation of utterances do not affect their *systematic* representation at all. For example, the addition of the rule of [e] epenthesis in Mohawk is one of several phenomena which would force stress to be considered phonemic in autonomous terms, where previously it was automatic. But in systematic terms stress is still predictable. Hence in this regard the addition of [e] epenthesis is without structural effect.

We can perhaps clarify this conception of sound change and contrast it with the more usual view, say that of Bloomfield ("change in the habits of performing sound-producing movements") or Hockett (Chapter 14) with the following nonlinguistic example. Imagine a computer attached to a print-out device in the form of an ordinary electric typewriter. Suppose that the computer is programmed in such a way that the output of its operation is a certain string of symbols in the ordinary alphabet of the typewriter keys, and suppose that on receiving such a string the control box of the typewriter interprets it as the instruction to print the given string of letters in the given order. Suppose further that the computer program consists of the following set of ordered instructions governed by the meta-condition to carry out instruction j from 1 to n times and then precede directly to instruction $j+1$:

(13.1) Start with the sequence $\underline{S}$.
(13.2) replace $\underline{S}$ by $\underline{aSb}$
(13.3) replace $\underline{\overline{S}}$ by $\underline{\overline{b}}$
(13.4) replace $\overline{a}\,\underline{b}$ which is directly before $\underline{\,.\,}$ by $\underline{c}$

It is clear then that the computer program generates all sequences of the form $a^n b^n c$. and transmits these to the electric typewriter, which will type any sequence when instructed to do so.

Assume now that that part of the computer program consisting of the four ordered instructions is changed by the addition of a new instruction inserted between (13.3) and (13.4). Thus the new set of instructions consists of old (13.1) through (13.3) followed by:

(13.5) replace a b which is before b. by d
(13.6) = (13.4)

When this new program is put into operation with the same meta-conditions as before, it is clear that the electric typewriter will now receive sequences drawn from the set of the form $a^n b^{n-1} dc$. and will type out the result accordingly.

I maintain that the above description is analogous in significant respects to the rule addition type of so-called sound change. In each case there is an abstract object consisting of a set of partially independent subelements, in one case the computer instructions and in the other the grammatic rules, in particular, the phonological ones. And in each case the function of the independent subelements which are represented in a physical system of a certain sort is to derive successively a set of strings in some finite vocabulary, in one case the vocabulary of typewriter symbols and in the other the vocabulary of a universal phonetic alphabet. And in each case the abstract object is changed by the addition of a new subelement, instruction (13.5), or a new phonological rule, say Mohawk [e] epenthesis. Of course, as soon as this change in the abstract object occurs, the performance of the physical system is changed. In the computer case, the printed letter sequence produced by the typewriter changes. In the human case, the acoustic signal produced for a fixed input (sentence) changes. Why?

Quite clearly, changes in the abstract object, the computer program instructions in one case or the phonological rules in the other, ultimately yield a change in actual performance or behavior of the relevant physical system. This is because, in both cases, the function of the abstract computational system is to derive a certain formal object, namely, a string in some vocabulary, which the relevant physical system interprets as a set of instructions to set a certain effectively fixed physical apparatus into operation in a determinate way. In one case, it is the control of the electric typewriter interpreting the input string of letters. In the other case, it is the human vocal apparatus interpreting the input string of phonetic elements received from the central nervous system as the instruction to perform a certain sequence of articulatory movements. Hence addition of rules to the phonological parts of grammars yields a change in the actual acoustic signals which are produced just because such rule additions affect the ultimate phonetic string generated by the total grammar for a fixed sentence. And this ultimate phonetic output is interpreted by the human organism as a set of instructions about how to set a certain effectively fixed physical system into operation. The analogy: electric typewriter = human vocal apparatus, computer = human organism, computer program = grammar, output letter sequence = phonetic representation, typewriter operation = human articulation, is then quite instructive. One can see that there is no more justification for the terminology 'sound change' than there would be for the terminology 'typewriter printing change.' In each case, although the performance of the physical system changes, this is an automatic and derivative result of a change in the set of formal instructions which determine[1] the operation of this apparatus. That is, changes in the kind of complex systems manifested by humans and computers are not changes in behavior or performance per se, but changes in the underlying competence, knowledge, or 'programming' of the system.

Most importantly, the above discussion shows that phonetic transcriptions are not direct descriptions of either the acoustic signal or of the articulation which produces it. Rather, they must be interpreted as the instructions which indicate the way the physical system of articulation is to perform. The claim that there is a fixed, finite, universal phonetic system, which is central to

---

[1] Of course only in part. In humans, for example, actual speech behavior is obviously also determined by such parameters as age, sex, health, emotional state, past history, etc.

generative phonology, is almost always criticized on the grounds that the number of possible articulations, sounds, etc., are infinite, i.e. that performance is continuous. This well-known fact is, however, quite irrelevant, since phonetic transcriptions do not and are not intended to describe such data. Rather, they provide the ideal information about how the vocal apparatus is to behave. A discrete phonetic representation of a sentence is not a distorted description of some continuous performance, but an account of the derivative knowledge of how the sentence is to be pronounced which a speaker has by virtue of his knowledge of its syntactic structure and the rules of the phonology. The continuous and nondiscrete performance of the articulatory apparatus is then a *performance effect* and has no more bearing on the discreteness (and universality) of phonetic representation than the electric typewriter's continuous, though perhaps more exact, carrying out of its instructions has on their noncontinuous character. In other words, phonetic transcriptions are as 'mentalistic' as any other level of linguistic description.[2] They are part of the description of a highly complex abstract object which is represented in the human organism.

Once we look at language in this way, that is, once we correctly distinguish between the continuous linguistic performance of an organism and its underlying discrete linguistic knowledge, which includes a fixed account of the way a sentence is to be pronounced, any motivation for the position of purely phonetic sound change really vanishes. The underlying appeal of this position is that it seems to offer hope that sound change is really a physical or articulatory phenomenon. There is appeal in this if one views all statements about nonobservables as strangely mystical, obscure, and 'unscientific' as did Bloomfield. Bloomfield was, in his theoretical writings, totally unable to conceive of any aspect of language and speech besides utterances, the articulatory movements which produce them, the physical structure

---

[2] The mentalistic character of phonetic representations was in large part understood before the development of modern linguistics. Cf. Saussure (1959:11–12). The elimination of this insight and the reduction of phonetic structure to an arbitrary, unconstrained, ineffective distortion of physical reality is one of many definitely retrogressive movements discernible in modern linguistics.

of the organism, and the contexts in which utterances are produced. That is, he had no conception of an internalized abstract system. Transferring this view of humans to computers, one would refuse to grant that they had programs and would insist that in studying computer systems a 'scientist' can deal only with their physical structure and observable activity.[3] I cannot believe that in 1966 this position can stand explicit statement so I shall say little more about it. It is important to emphasize, however, that in large part what Bloomfield and many of his followers were rejecting when they rejected mentalism in linguistics was equivalent to a rejection of the claim that a computer has a program. Bloomfield made this quite clear in fact both in *Language* and in his article 'Language or Ideas.' In the latter, he explicitly denies that there is any abstract system ('ideas') beyond observable utterances and behavior (1936:95):[4]

It is our hypothesis that the terms 'concept,' 'idea,' and so on add nothing to this. We suppose that the person who says 'I was having an idea of a straight line' is telling us: 'I uttered out loud or produced by inner speech movements the words *straight line,* and at the same time I made some obscure visceral reactions with which I habitually accompany the sight or feel of a straight edge or the utterance or hearing of the word *straight.*' Of all this, only the verbal action is constant from person to person. If we are right, then the term 'idea' is simply a traditional obscure synonym for 'speech form,' and it will appear that what we now call 'mental' events are in part private and unimportant events of physiology and in part social events . . .

Because he could not accept the idea of an abstract object represented in a physicial system, elements of which were traditionally called (vaguely and obscurely to be sure) 'ideas,' 'concepts,' etc., Bloomfield was forced to the unsound view that this terminology

---

[3] Of course I am not denying here that in principle a purely physical approach (say by way of the neurophysiology of the brain) could account for the nature of language, although obviously the probability of this is vanishingly small. Rather I am emphasizing the fact that linguistic study need not depend upon nor wait for the ultimate development of a theory of the biological structure of the organism.

[4] For some discussion of mentalism, linguistics, Bloomfield's position, etc. cf. Katz (1964); Postal (to appear b); Chomsky (1965).

referred to internal physical events and external behavior. It is hardly surprising then that these 'very subtle' internal (visceral) events to which Bloomfield was driven were never discovered. It may seem pointless to belabor the inadequacy of this position of Bloomfield's. But as we shall see below, similar ideas continue to this day to prevent many from coming to grips with the real nature of many linguistic phenomena, sound change included.

Involved also in Bloomfield's and many others' attachment to the view that sound change is purely physical phenomenon is the curious belief that this and only this can explain the regularity of sound change. Indeed there is within this tradition a strong and thoroughly misleading tendency to *equate* the purely phonetic character of sound change with its regularity (cf. the first quote from Bloomfield as well as the quote from Fries in Chapter 10). There are several things to be said here. First, in the sense normally meant, sound changes are not necessarily completely regular, that is, there are exceptions.[5] We have noted

---

[5] The claim that phonological changes have exceptions is of course somewhat revolutionary. But, in view of the overwhelming evidence in favor of it, such a position cannot really be considered very controversial. Opposition to the existence of exceptions has often been of the empty or purely methodological sort. In particular, Bloomfield's rejection of exceptions is largely of this character (1933:355):

"The neo-grammarian sees in this a serious violation of scientific method. The beginning of our science was made by a procedure which implied regularity of phonetic change, and further advances like Grassman's discovery were based on the same implicit assumption. It may be, of course, that some other assumption would lead to an even better correlation of facts, but the advocates of sporadic sound-change offer nothing of the kind; they accept the results of the actual method and yet claim to explain some facts by a contradictory method (or lack of method) which was tried and found wanting through all the centuries that preceded Rask and Grimm."

There is, of course, no contradiction whatever between utilizing the search for regularity as a method and accepting that this regularity has its limitations. The value of the principle lies exclusively in picking the *most* general solution. More fundamentally, there can be no *methodological* argument for any empirical assumption. The only way to justify the view of no exceptions is to show that in fact every phonological change can be stated in terms of general rules which cover *every case*. This is impossible. Along these lines, however, Bloomfield does say more substantively (1933:356):

"If such things happened, then every language would be spotted over with all sorts of queer deviant sounds, in forms which had resisted sound-change

examples of this with respect to both Mohawk epenthesis and the Oneida Accent Shift. Secondly and more importantly, the notions of phonetic character and regularity are totally distinct. This is true not only empirically, as shown by the quite regular nonphonetic sound changes discussed above, but also logically. It is curious that linguists should have sought the most obscure and strained explanations for the regularity of sound change in terms of physics, biology, sociology, etc., without looking for a really linguistic explanation.[6] It is curious, that is, that they have not sought an account of the regularity of sound change in the nature of linguistic regularity generally. Surely the regularity of a change from proto-Mohawk [kn] to contemporary Mohawk [ken] is no more and no less in need of explanation than the regularity of the parallel and derivative phenomenon in contemporary Mohawk, i.e. the regularity of the fact that whenever systematic k̲ and n̲ combine in that order an [e] is inserted in the phonetic representation of the form. That is, the regularity of sound change is due to exactly the same causes as the regularity of the linguistic phenomenon of distribution (phonetic or otherwise) generally. Such phenomena are regular, that is, capable of general formulation across the lexicon, formulation other than listing of all the cases, just because they are the result of general rule, i.e. formal statements which apply to whole classes of (sequences of) lexical items in ways determined by their structure. We see then that the claim that sound change is a result of adding rules to grammars and subsequent reformulation of nonoptimal grammars accounts for the regularity of this phenomenon automatically without further addition. Further, it accounts for documented limitations on this regularity, that is, for the fact

---

or deviated from ordinary changes. Actually, however, a language moves within a limited set of phonemes."
But the wider implications of this comment are just false. Languages are in fact characterized by limited numbers of deviant phonetic sequences. Consider for example the few Mohawk forms which exceptionally have stressed vowels before glottal stops, the few which irregularly contain [hdz], the few exceptional Oneida forms which have accent on the final vowel after a consonant cluster, etc., etc. In short, in so far as Bloomfield's justification is methodological, it is both confused and empty. In so far as it is substantive, it is just wrong. Exceptions exist.

[6] For an essentially physical account cf. Chapter 14; for a basically sociological discussion cf. Dyen (1963).

that many such changes have exceptions. For this turns out to be a general feature of phonological (and in fact also transformational syntactic) rules as was noted before in Chapter 8. Finally, the explanation of sound change regularity as being due to rules accounts for the fact that there can be regular sound changes with nonphonetic environments as documented earlier, since of course most phonological rules have this kind of abstract environment.

Even assuming, counterfactually, that sound changes are without exception and occur in purely phonetic environments, the claims that sound change is a physical phenomenon of articulation change is still without basis from the point of view of regularity. For contrary to common assumption, no one has ever shown explicitly how such an assumption would in fact explain the regularity. That is, this assumption provides no basis for showing why such changes should happen in all relevant morphemes and not just one, a few, etc. We return to this topic in Chapter 14. Notice that exactly what is not explained by the physical assumption here is accounted for by the account of sound change as grammar change.

This rule account of the nature of sound change and its regularity is relevant to the discussion of whether sound changes are 'laws of nature' or merely historical happenings. In one of the quotes given earlier from Bloomfield, it was claimed that the term 'law' in connection with sound changes 'has no precise meaning' since sound changes are merely historical occurrences. This position denying the law character of sound changes now seems well established. Thus the following is a not untypical modern view (Hall, 1964:304):

Thus, 'Bartsch's law' is a statement of a phonemic change which took place under certain conditions, and at a certain time. . . . It is about as sensible to talk about 'Bartsch's law' as it would be to talk about 'the law of Gettysburg,' referring to the historic event of the battle of Gettysburg.

It is now general, that is, to assume that the assertions that sound changes are laws and that they are historical events are mutually incompatible. But this is just false. In fact they are clearly both. They are obviously historical events in that particular rules are added at particular times. But the rule is a law in a perfectly good sense; namely, it states in a general way (i.e. without listing the cases) the derivative properties of a large (in fact infinite) class of lexical items (sequences). Hence if, for example, a new form is added to Mohawk which contains the systematic sequence k+n, a Mohawk need not learn as a special fact that this form will contain phonetically an epenthetic [e]. For this is guaranteed by the 'law' of epenthesis which operates on the independently determined structure of the form. Obviously these properties of generalization and prediction of new facts on the basis of fixed structures have nothing in common with the Battle of Gettysburg, so that the analogy attempting to show that the view of sound changes as laws is ludicrous or absurd fails completely.

Once it is recognized that so-called sound change consists of changes in the grammars which provide the knowledge underlying speech, the claim that all sound changes take place in purely phonetic environments is the claim that new rules can be added only very near the end of the phonology, that is, only before rules whose combined operation does not radically change the character of the strings on which they operate. This view has a certain limited plausibility because the later in the sequence of rules a new rule is added, the less its overall effects on the final output. And obviously the addition of new rules is subject to the constraint that it not destroy intelligibility. Nonetheless, as the earlier examples in Chapter 11 show, the claim is false. That is, certain rules may be added relatively early in the grammar. For example, the Mohawk rule of [e] epenthesis has been added before the rules which turn p to [kw]. Although this rule has been added relatively early, it has not affected intelligibility too greatly (indeed, despite the mass of rules which differentiate Mohawk and Oneida they are still largely mutually intelligible and Mohawk speakers say about Oneidas that 'they speak our language'). It should be mentioned that in cases where, as here, rules are added to the phonology at a relatively early point, the methods of internal reconstruction and the so-called comparative method will give conflicting results with respect to the relative chronologies. The method of internal reconstruction depends in effect on assuming that the order of rules in a synchronic grammar at time t reflects the order in which these rules were added.

Thus, on internal grounds alone, one would conclude that the addition of the [e] epenthesis rule in Mohawk *preceded* the incorporation of the rules which turn p̱ to [kw]. But comparative evidence shows that in fact the reverse order is the real one historically. In short, the method of internal reconstruction can yield literally correct chronological inferences only in those cases where sound change has proceeded by the addition of very late rules. Where rules have been added at relatively early points, or where there has been reformulation of the grammar, the chronological inferences cannot be expected to be accurate.

Once it is seen that sound change is mentalistic, i.e. consists of changes in internally represented grammars rather than in speech performance directly, the claim that all sound changes occur in phonetic environments can be seen to have rather curious and untenable consequences. For it is evident that the majority of morphophonemic and phonological rules in a language at any one time do not have purely phonetic environments. If then one opts for a view of sound change which permits only the addition of rules with phonetic environments, one has in fact not allowed for any regular mechanism by which the majority of phonological rules can have been incorporated into languages. This would leave as the only mechanism for the development of such rules the combined effects of various analogies, losses, borrowings, etc. That is, it would claim strangely that such regularities can arise only from irregularities. But since the regular character of rules with nonphonetic environments is in no way different from that of rules with phonetic environments, this position is, to say the least, implausible. For example, there is in Mohawk (and other Iroquoian languages as well) the rule we discussed earlier in Chapter 8 that no *verb* can contain less than two nonepenthetic vowels. Thus if a verb would on other grounds contain less than two vowels, an initial prothetic [i] is inserted. But this rule does not apply to words which are not members of the category Verb. Similarly, there is the rule which drops word initial glides (w̱, y̱) off the front of nouns but not other words. And the same morphemes undergo this truncation in nouns but not in verbs. Clearly to claim that such regular rules as these could have entered the language only as the result of a complex set of accidents is absurd. These comments are not of course intended to demonstrate the falsity of (PI), which is argued already by the documented nonphonetic sound changes, exceptions, etc. Rather it is intended to show further that this position has no a priori plausibility, i.e. that its falsehood, far from behind surprising, is exactly what should be expected.

THE METHODOLOGICAL ARGUMENT

It should be emphasized that in completely rejecting the nonmentalistic conception of sound change held by Bloomfield and modern developers of his position, one does not by any means accept the approach to this topic against which Bloomfield argued. Similarly, the methodological justification offered for the so-called Neogrammarian position (PI) by Bloomfield and others in no sense supports this position vis-à-vis that developed in the present study. Quite the contrary. Modern supporters of (PI) have often argued that this is a methodological assumption which has proved its value in research. That is, they argue that the attempt to reduce all sound changes to regular shifts in phonetic environments has led to the discovery of many regularities and to the reduction to generalization of many facts which had seemed erratic or exceptional. However, this perfectly real justification is not a defense of the view that the environments of all sound changes are phonetic. To assume this is to restate the confusion between the *regularity* of phonetic change and its putative *purely phonetic character.* The justly valued results which are brought forward here to defend (PI) support not this but rather only *the attempt to reduce the facts of phonological changes to rule.* That is, what has been proved valuable here as elsewhere in linguistic description, both synchronic and diachronic, is the attempt to replace lists of exceptional forms by statements of linguistic rule which predict the properties of these lists. Once this is seen, however, it is evident that the very methodological arguments which have been brought forward to defend the necessarily phonetic character of sound change actually support the view developed above, namely, that sound change consists in changes in the form of grammars—changes in the rules which operate on sequences of abstract elements. For as we have seen, it is this approach which can reduce to rule cases which the purely phonetic assumption must treat as inexplicable and mysterious irregularities. That is, every rule of sound change which can be stated in terms of (PI) can be stated in terms proposed here, and many rules which are unstatable in those narrow terms are easily formulated in terms of the more abstract conception of phonological change given by (PII). And this extra power is in fact required on empirical grounds, as was shown. These historical facts are simply a special case of the more general principle that every rule which can be formulated in autonomous phonemic terms can be stated also in systematic phonemic terms, but not conversely.

Therefore, in adopting a view of sound change based on (PII), one is not accepting the kind of arbitrary, ad hoc, unconstrained (often semantic) pseudo-explanations of changes or lack of changes so typical of much of the writing on linguistic change which Bloomfield attacked and rejected. In the terms being advocated here, the discovery of rules of change is basic, and the postulation of the abstract, morphophonemic environments which many of these require is subject to the same kind of constraints as the postulation of all linguistic structure. It was to support this claim that a detailed discussion was presented in Chapter 11 to show that the underlying representations p, ko, k+w, which determined the differential behavior of identical phonetic [kw] on Mohawk-Oneida, were independently justifiable on a host of grounds.

Of course it goes almost without saying that in general it will be more difficult to discover and justify abstract systematic representations of the kind needed to explain nonphonetic sound changes than will be required simply to set up correspondences and define changes which occur at a very low level and are essentially phonetic. Much more of the structure of the language will be relevant, and the knowledge and time required of the investigator will be correspondingly greater. This is, again, simply a special case of the more general principle that it is difficult to discover and justify systematic representation, that is, it requires more knowledge, more analysis, etc., than normally required to undertake autonomous analysis. This is just what should be expected since, with respect to systematic descriptions, autonomous phonological descriptions are so superficial and involve such a relatively limited portion of phonological structure.

SOME REMARKS ON THE 'CAUSES OF SOUND CHANGE'

It is perhaps not inappropriate to ask what implications the view that sound change consists in changes in grammars has for the much discussed and controversial question of the causes of sound change. Why should a language, independently of contact with other languages, add a new rule at a certain point? Of course there are some scholars who hold that all linguistic change is a result of language contact, but this position seems too radically improbable to demand serious consideration today. Assuming then that some if not all phonological changes are independent of contact, what is their basis? It seems clear to the present writer that there is no more reason for languages to change than there is for automobiles to add fins one year and remove them the next, for jackets to have three buttons one year and two the next, etc. That is, it seems evident within the framework of sound change as grammar change that the 'causes' of sound change without language contact lie in the general tendency of human cultural products to undergo 'nonfunctional' stylistic change. This is of course to be understood as a remark about what we might call 'primary change,' that is, change which interrupts an assumed stable and long-existing system. It is somewhat more plausible that such stylistic primary changes may yield a grammar which is in some sense not optimal, and that this may itself lead to 'functional' change to bring about an optimal state. Halle's suggestion that children may learn a grammar partially distinct from that underlying the utterances they hear and thus, from the point of view of the adult language, reformulate the grammar (while adults may only add rules),[7]

---

[7] Halle (1962:344) has insightfully noted that this limitation in the ability of adults to alter their grammars is related to and supported by the obvious loss of ability in language learning which sets in with adulthood. Both can be viewed as due to loss of the ability to construct optimal overall grammars.

may be looked upon as a suggestion of this type. For as he noted, a grammar G^2 which results from the addition of a rule to a grammar G^1 may not be the optimal grammar of the set of sentences it generates. Hence one would expect that children learning the new language will internalize not G^2 but rather the optimal grammar G^3. It remains to be seen how many of the instances of so-called 'structural sound change,' discussed in the writings of scholars like A. Martinet, can be provided with a basis of this type.

It should be emphasized that the claim that contact independent sound change is due basically to the stylistic possibility for adults to add limited types of rules to their grammars does not preclude the fact that these changes may serve social functions, i.e. may be related to group differentiation, status differences, etc. That is, the claim that change is stylistic is not incompatible with the kinds of results reached by such investigators as Labov (1963). These latter matters concern more properly the social explanation for the *spread* of the change, a matter which seems more properly sociological than linguistic.

I have been careful above not to insist that all instances of what have been called sound change were necessarily independent of language contact. Although committed to the view that sound change *can* occur without contact, we can also accept the view that some changes result from borrowing. The view that sound change is grammar change in fact really eliminates much of the importance of this difference. For under the rule interpretation of change, the only issue is the forces which led to the grammar change. Studies of complex cases of phonological grammar change due to contact have actually been carried out recently within the framework of generative grammar. This work, to be reported in a forthcoming monograph (Keyser and Halle, to appear), shows quite clearly that English has borrowed a number of Romance phonological rules. In particular, English has incorporated essentially the Latin stress rule, that which softens Romance k̲ to s̲ in certain environments, etc. This work has important implications beyond the area of sound change and may affect radically concepts of genetic relationship, Mischsprache, etc., all of which will, I think, require reevaluation.

It should be clear that the view that primary sound change which is independent of language contact is basically stylistic in nature is hardly original. It is indeed maintained even by some who hold to (PI), and is apparently relatively ancient. Hall, for example, expresses just such a view and gives an excellent statement of it which he credits to Dante (1964:298):

Since, therefore, every human language . . . has been re-made in accordance with our whims since the confusion of the Tower of Babel . . . and since man is a most unstable and variable being, language cannot be long-lasting or stable; but like other human things, such as customs and dress, it has to vary in space and time.

14

HOCKETT'S PRESENT POSITION

In his presidential address to the 1964 winter meeting of the Linguistic Society of America, C. F. Hockett reformulated and extended his previous views on sound change. Hockett has long been a supporter of (PI). I think it is not unfair to anyone to say that he is at present its most outstanding supporter and defender. Hockett's recent study 'Sound Change'[1] is, to my knowledge, the most extensive attempt to state and justify (PI) since Bloomfield's time. It is thus an important and valuable study on this ground alone. Its importance grows, however, by virtue of Hockett's certainly correct perception that the nature of sound change, in particular the truth of (PI), is inherently bound up with a number of crucial theoretical issues including many of those raised earlier in the present study. These include the role of mentalism, the logical status of phonetic representations, the status of the notion *grammar*, and the adequacy of distinct proposals about the nature of phonological representation, in particular the relative merits of systematic and autonomous phonemics, one version of which Hockett supports. Since these are the issues with which, in effect, this whole monograph

---

[1] Published as Hockett (1965). All page references are to the published version.

is concerned, and since Hockett's position on them is essentially the opposite of the present work, it is certainly appropriate to consider his recent views in great detail.

Hockett's recent account of sound change is notable not only for its advocacy of (PI), but also for the maintenance of an extreme, physicalist account of the nature and causes of sound change.[2] These two positions are by no means necessarily coextensive. As we have seen, (PI) has a mentalistic interpretation, namely, as the claim that all rules of change are added very near the end of the phonological part of the grammar. Of course stated this way it seems rather unmotivated, since the requirement that intelligibility must be maintained does not entail this condition. Further, we have seen that even someone as close to Hockett as his longstanding colleague R. A. Hall maintains (PI) without a physical theory of the causation of sound change. There is, of course, a logical relation between (PI) and a physical theory of the causes of sound change. Namely, if (PI) were true, a physical interpretation of it together with a physical theory of causation would provide an explanation for this fact, whereas the mentalistic interpretation of (PI) together with a nonphysical view of sound change causation leaves this mysterious and inexplicable, as we have seen.

Hockett embeds his discussion in a treatment of the historical development of linguistics, not all of which is relevant to present concerns. He considers the nineteenth century or Neogrammarian

---

[2] This physical view of sound change is by no means a recent development in Hockett's thought. For example compare (1958:443–444):

"In order to see why we should believe that sound change, so defined, is constantly going on, we need only consider the vast multitude of factors which can contribute to the determination of the physical properties of any bit of heard speech. These physical properties depend only in part on the 'speaker's intention.' Before the sound reaches the inner ear of the hearer, other variables come into play. A list would have to include the following: the amount of moisture in the throat, nose, and mouth of the speaker, random currents in his central nervous system, muscular tics, muscle tonus, emotional state, a possible presence of alcohol or drugs, the care with which the speaker is enunciating, the amount and nature of the extraneous noise which reaches the hearer along with the speech signal, the condition of the hearer's outer ear (presence of wax or dirt), the amount of attention the hearer is giving to the speaker. The list could be extended. Since the physical properties of each actually heard bit of speech in turn condition the expectation distribution of the hearer—and thus his articulation and, ultimately, the expectation distribution of the whole community—every one of the factors we have named bears directly on sound change."

establishment of the notion of the 'regularity of sound change' as one of the great 'breakthroughs' in linguistics (he terms it the 'regularity hypothesis'). And he gives an account of how this regularity is to be interpreted. He feels that this hypothesis is composed of two parts, a heuristic technique for comparative research and a question as to why the procedure should be so successful together with an answer to this question. Discussing the views of the later nineteenth century, Hockett concludes that there was general acceptance of a basic distinction between borrowing, analogy, and sound change, noting however that there is obscurity as to whether these were kinds of change, causes of change, or mechanisms of change. Most importantly, Hockett remarks about this period (190–191):

Everyone agreed that forms may pass from one language or dialect to another. Everyone acknowledged instances of analogic reshaping. And everyone felt it fitting and proper, in setting forth the development of a daughter language or later stage from a parent language or earlier stage, to cast many statements in this form:

Par x > Dau y (in the env. z). "If the environment was specified, the statement described a *conditioned sound change*. . . . If environmental specification was unnecessary, the statement described an *unconditioned* or *general* sound shift."

Hockett also notes that these shifts were often referred to as 'sound laws,' but he does not completely agree with Bloomfield that the great confusion and conflict engendered by the Neogrammarians in the 1870's was a result of this. Rather, he believes it was due to confusion as to whether the term 'sound law' referred to a statement of the above form, to the events described by such a statement, or to 'some vague Platonic entity hovering between these two.' I think Hockett is largely right here but for reasons totally distinct from those which he accepts. We return to this below. Most importantly, Hockett finds that within the framework of agreement sketched above, there were two really controversial issues (191):

(1) What features or aspects of language design can legitimately be included in the specification of the environment for a 'conditioned sound shift'?
(2) Are attested sound shifts merely the statistically predominant results of analogy and borrowing (especially, perhaps, of a particularly

intimate form of the latter), or do they reflect the workings of a *mechanism* of linguistic change distinct from and not reducible to analogy and borrowing?

Hockett's major thesis consists of answers to these two questions (191):

The answer to the second question is more important than, and implies, the answer to the first. (1) In the statement of a sound shift, the environment z, like the source x, must be a sound or finite combination of sounds of the parent language. (2) There is a mechanism of linguistic change, hereafter to be called sound change, not to be confused with and not reducible to analogy or borrowing . . .

Hockett claims that it is really these answers that define what he calls the regularity hypothesis. Thus, like Bloomfield and a host of followers since, Hockett does not unravel the differences between a purported phonetic character for sound change and the regularity of this phenomenon in the literal sense, i.e. that sound changes can be described by rules without listing all of the morpheme (sequences) involved. Hockett basically attributes this position which he holds to the Neogrammarians of the 1870's, although he notes his own special formulation.

With Hockett's answer (2) we are in basic agreement (cf. the previous chapter) although there is radical difference as to the type of mechanism envisaged, as we shall see. His answer (1) is essentially a statement of what was called earlier (PI).[3]

Thus we know that his position cannot be correct because it has such factually intolerable consequences as that the incorporation of [e] epenthesis in Mohawk and the Oneida Accent Shift never could have happened. Hence what is of interest here is not so much the factual correctness of Hockett's position about the nature of sound change, which has in effect already been determined above. What is of significance is to unravel the unfortunately not unique structure of false argument, misapplied fact, and ignored data by which the position is defended and

---

[3] Actually it is a little stronger assertion than (PI), since (PI) referred only to the environment while Hockett's comment covers the elements which change as well (and is thus even more incorrect).

related to other important linguistic issues.

As Hockett emphatically recognizes, his physical view of the nature of sound change is crucially related to the nature of phonetics. Indeed this view of sound change as a physical phenomenon, strongly advocated by Bloomfield and others since, is based squarely on a complete failure to appreciate the nature and status of phonetic representations in linguistic description. Hockett's present version is simply the most recent and relevant statement of a doctrine which is in fact quite widely accepted. Namely, that the finite, discrete phonetic representation used by all linguists corresponds to no real aspect of the world, since of course actual speech signals and articulation are continuous, not discrete, and differ from each other not finitely but in an endless number of ways. The fact that almost every aspect of linguistic work, synchronic phonemics, dialect studies, historical phonology, etc., etc., depends directly on this 'unreal' discrete phonetics is a major embarrassment to defenders of this position about phonetics, one which they generally treat by not mentioning it.[4]

Hockett introduces his version of this position in relation to the comparativists of the 1870's. He remarks that they spoke of 'speech sounds' as if these were perfectly clear kinds of items. He then claims that this confidence was shaken by what he calls 'the discovery of phonetics.' That is, the work of men like Sievers, Sweet, Lundell, Rousselot, etc., showed that neither articulatory motions nor the resulting acoustic effects were discrete or finite. Most crucially Hockett concludes from this that (192):

In due time it was realized that there simply is no neatly definable finite set of 'speech sounds' available for use in languages. There is no end to the fineness of difference that can be observed, given appropriate apparatus and conditions. The number of points along the median line of the roof of the mouth that can be touched by a given point on the tip of the tongue, for example, is the same as the number of points along any line segment: a nondenumerable infinity.

Hockett thus apparently regards phonetic notions like alveolar, prepalatal, stop, vowel, etc., obviously crucial to all linguistic

---

[4] For a discussion of the dependence of any sort of phonemic analysis on a universal system of discrete phonetics, cf. Chomsky (1964b), Chomsky and Halle (1965).

practice, as illusory. He makes this even more explicit with his rejection of the claim of workers within generative grammar that there is a universal phonetic system (201–202):

The parameters of the speech signal (the coordinate axes) are universals, the same for all languages. But Chomsky and Halle are wrong when they assume that a single fine-grained quantization of acoustic space can yield a finite set of points of reference valid for all languages; . . .

He then relates this view (that discrete phonetic representation is an illusion) to the question of sound change (192):

The 'space' of all possible speech sound, either in articulation or acoustically, is a multidimensional continuum. What then of the neat discrete 'speech sounds' of the comparativists? Even more, what of their 'sound shifts'? If parental x and daughter y are both mere blurs, then what can '$x > y$' possibly mean?

Hockett believes that the solution to these difficulties lies in what he calls the 'quantization hypothesis' and which others have called the phonemic principle. He quotes a passage from Jespersen which he claims answers these difficulties, but claims that Jespersen did not really appreciate their significance so that he is not thought of as one of the inventors of phonemics. Hockett looks upon the development of the quantization hypothesis, rather fancifully in my view, as a response to the 'discovery of phonetics.' He states it as follows (194–195):

The quintessence of the quantization hypothesis can be stated as follows. In any speech community, only certain *differences* of speech sound are functional. This breaks the continuous multidimensional space of all possible speech sound into a finite number of regions; in at least some environments it matters, to hearer and thus to speaker, whether a given sound falls into one region or the next, but does not matter where it falls within a single region. Successive articulations aimed into the same region show a scatter, clustered around a *local frequency maximum*. The local frequency maxima are, or create, the 'sort of conception of an average pronunciation' of which Jespersen spoke. The frequency maxima, then, are the neat discrete functioning units of the phonological system of the language.

Hockett then attempts to show how this conception of phonetics and phonemics can provide a basis for understanding sound change. Before turning to these comments, I should like to consider the views sketched thus far.

Hockett's position about phonetics is not simply false, it is in fact in large part incoherent. And this incoherence arises directly from his refusal to countenance an underlying finite, discrete, mentalistic phonetic system.

One must not be misled when Hockett identifies his 'local frequency maxima' with the 'neat discrete functioning units' of the phonology. For he means these to be the allophones, not the phonemes. That is, he does not wish to claim that all allophonic variation is handled by the scatter within a fixed region. Even under this allophonic interpretation, however, the position is untenable. For he speaks of 'aiming into a region,' i.e. as if the articulation were target oriented. And his account implies that there are a discrete number of such consistent targets, namely, just those which account for the existence of a 'frequency maxima.' But now it is evident that even in Hockett's terms underlying the continuous variation of the speech signal and its causal basis, the articulatory wave, there is a discrete system of articulatory 'targets' which cause the acoustic allophones or 'frequency maxima.' But it is just this set of elements which the linguist who speaks about a discrete phonetic system is talking about. Of course, as earlier discussion in Chapter 13 (and Chapter 5) suggested, these 'targets' must actually be thought of as elements of the discrete code of articulatory instructions transmitted from the nervous system to the articulatory apparatus. And clearly these discrete instructions are not direct properties of the speech signal or of articulatory movement. Hence the continuous physical character of these phenomena has no bearing on the existence of such a level of linguistic structure. All of this is no more surprising than the fact that the instructions to the electric typewriter keys discussed in Chapter 13 are not directly represented in the movement of the typewriter parts or the resulting written letter sequences. The continuous and nonfinite character of both articulation and the resulting acoustic form are a function of the fact that one is dealing with the behavior of a physical system. But the language or linguistic knowledge underlying this behavior is not thereby of this character.

Obviously, part of what a speaker knows about a sentence is its ideal pronunciation . . . a discrete set of instructions specifying how the vocal apparatus should behave in order to produce a signal which will be a token of it. Hence discrete linguistic concepts like velar, vowel, stop, prepalatal, etc., are not illusory distortions of an actually continuous world of articulation and acoustics. They are rather part of the fixed code which partially determines the operation of the physical system whose behavior creates these observable continuous properties. In the production of an utterance, it must be assumed that the organism transmits this discrete representation to the vocal apparatus. And part of perceiving an utterance must be the construction of its phonetic representation. Thus the real question for linguistics is not the existence of a finite phonetic system, but rather the actual character of this system, a topic about which there is already a great deal of knowledge, albeit far from complete.

It is important to consider the arguments which Hockett gives *against* the existence of a finite phonetic system. These are two. First, he argues that both the speech signal and articulation are continuous and nondiscrete. Second, he notes an inadequate phonetic description from Miller and Chomsky.[5] Both of these are non sequiturs. The first for reasons just discussed. An erroneous phonetic description is as relevant to the existence of a discrete phonetic system as an erroneous phonemic description is to the existence of a discrete phonemic system.

One sees that underlying all of Hockett's discussion of phonetics is a simple failure, which has been endemic since at least Bloomfield's time, to draw the line between language and speech. Once this line is drawn, the linguist need no longer suffer from a philosophy which, at the same time, recognizes no level of discrete phonetics and yet involves a linguistics which requires a discrete phonetics at almost every point. This obvious inconsistency is one of the lingering heavy prices linguists like Hockett must pay for continuing futile and rationally unmotivated attempts to avoid recognition of the mentalistic character of natural language.

It is significant that Hockett implicitly recognizes that his

---

[5] (1963:280). The example was originally given in Miller (1958:397–398).

argument depends on maintaining the inadequacy of mentalism. Thus he brings up the recent paper by Katz (1964), who argued quite strongly that a causal account of linguistic phenomena must be mentalistic. It is symptomatic of the weakness of Hockett's position that, instead of dealing with Katz's arguments, he indulges in irrelevant comments about style ('tone strikes me as scurrilous'), which he does not even attempt to justify, and a curious retreat into meaningless metaphor ('It is as though a traveler, unable to see far enough ahead because a mountain obscures his view, were to try to clear the way with a few well-placed bombs.').[6] Hockett tries to make it seem as if Bloomfield's antimentalism was almost without content and unobjectionable to any reasonable reader (199):

Bloomfield's recommendation was that we remove irrelevant psychologizing from linguistics. Katz does not contradict this but goes another step, recommending *the introduction of relevant linguisticizing into psychology.*

I find this comment incomprehensible. Bloomfield made it clear again and again in his major publications that his antimentalism included a strong acceptance of the extreme positivistic or radical empiricist view of the philosophy of science which was so popular in the 1930's. He even devoted a whole article, namely 'Language or Ideas,' to arguing the identity of his antimentalist position and the radical empiricism of the Vienna Circle philosophers. We quoted not irrelevant portions of his discussion in the first part of Chapter 13. Since Katz points out this positivist aspect of Bloomfield's position and refuses to accept it, it is difficult to understand how Hockett can assert that Katz does not contradict Bloomfield's position. Involved in Bloomfield's view was, in particular, the claim that all valid scientific terms are either observation terms or terms definable on an observation

---

[6] In the same vein, Hockett concludes his paper with the following criticism of work in generative phonology:

"In the forays that they have so far made from their synchronic home territory into diachronic or contrastive linguistics, the generative grammarians have had to leave most of their precision tools behind, and what they have had to say has not yet been very enlightening or elegant."

Not only does Hockett fail to substantiate these claims, he does not even give any references indicating what he is criticizing.

term basis, using only the tools of logic and mathematics (1939b:-12–13). Thus following Bloomfield one could not utilize such concepts as rule, systematic phoneme, etc., since these cannot be so defined. It was, incidentally, not totally implausible for Bloomfield to maintain a radical empiricist philosophy of science during the 1930's, since this was widely accepted at the time by many among the best of philosophers. What proved unfortunate for the linguistics which followed was a failure to keep up with work in the philosophy of science, work which led to the abandonment of this radical empiricist position when it was found incompatible with the nature of actual scientific theories.[7] Hockett's claim that Bloomfield's antimentalism is right as far as it goes is thus completely unfounded.

The important point about mentalism here is that Hockett, like Bloomfield, can apparently not accept that language is an abstract object represented in a physical system, an object determining in part the behavior of the system. Like Bloomfield, Hockett can recognize only the physical system and its behavior, and his denial of the mental character of language is thus equivalent to denying that computer has an (obviously unobservable) program.[8]

To return to the main point of this discussion, Hockett's antimentalism is fatal because it leads to an erroneous conclusion about the nature of phonetic representation. The change schemata of the comparativists of the 1870's of the form Par $x >$ Dau y (in the env. z utilized discrete phonetic entities. And these were es-

---

[7] For an introduction to this movement within the philosophy of science, which completely destroyed the philosophic basis for antimentalism to which Bloomfield appealed, cf. R. Carnap (1936:419–471), (1937:10–40), and (1956); C. G. Hempel (1952), (1956); I. Scheffler (1963).

[8] I suspect that an important factor in Hockett's inability to come to grips with the fact that a language is an abstract object represented in neural tissue is his long-favored appeal to the notion of 'habit' (for example cf. 1965:31). The claim that a language is a set of habits, although extraordinarily common, is completely empty since there is no notion of habit in psychology or anywhere else which can serve as an explanatory basis for linguistic phenomena. Hockett himself never attempts to characterize precisely any notion of 'habit' in terms of which it would make sense to talk about language. Nonetheless, appeal to this concept may offer the appearance of having provided some link between observable behavior and the properties of the organism which determine this behavior.

sentially what they were thought to be, namely, discrete phonetic categories describing language. Perhaps the only thing not fully recognized was that these categories describe not the speech signal or articulation itself, but the ideal instructions which in large part determine the articulation.

With the thoroughly inadequate basis we have described, it is hardly surprising that Hockett's account of sound change should be unsound. He superficially accepts the idea of a generative grammar, that is, of a set of formal rules generating all the sentences. But fatally he fails to come to grips with the interpretation to be made of this grammar, that is, its relation to the organism. He does not regard it, as those who developed the notion intended it to be regarded, as a description of the internalized (hence mentalistic) linguistic knowledge of a native.

Following Lamb, Hockett regards phonemes as being bundles of 'distinctive features' (his equivalent of Lamb's phonons), and claims that the terminal strings of the grammar are strings of bundles of distinctive features. These features of Lamb's and Hockett's are, it must be noted (as we did in Chapter 5), *not* phonetic since by definition differing allophones of the same phoneme have the same representation in terms of them. It is thus obviously inconsistent for Hockett to assert that (201):

A speaker does not produce a succession of bundles of distinctive features. Although he *aims* at them in his articulation, what actually comes out is a continuous speech signal . . .[9]

---

[9] Most extraordinarily, Hockett (33) attributes to Chomsky the claim that a grammar should describe 'what people intend to say.' Then in a footnote he admits that this is a second-hand report of an oral remark and may not be accurate. In view of the fact that Chomsky has explicitly stressed over and over in print in a dozen or more places that in his terms a grammar is intended to describe the underlying linguistic competence of a speaker, it is more than a little odd that Hockett should bother with this kind of reference. This view not only fails to represent Chomsky's position, it is totally inadequate. Competence is clearly not what people *intend to say*. For example, although one knows that '*John is doctors' is not English, i.e. violates one or more syntactic constraints, one may on some occasion intend to say this for a variety of reasons. The task of describing 'what people intend to say' is clearly coextensive with that of describing the total psychological makeup of individuals and thus is beyond the bounds of any serious linguistic goal.

This would be true only if Hockett's distinctive features were intended to be part of a theory of discrete *phonetic representation*. And as we have seen this is explicitly not the case. This confusion is simply a further manifestation of the difficulties into which Hockett is led by a failure to grasp the logical status of a grammar and the ultimate phonetic representations which it generates.

Hockett then regards sound change as a function of the indeterminacy in the production of speech signals, caused by the fact that the speech apparatus cannot hit its intended targets in a completely determinate way. That is, he looks upon sound change as a function of the inability of performance to correspond completely to competence. The basic idea seems to be that variation in the performance of discrete articulatory 'intentions' statistically leads to drifting of the targets. To quote (201):

In the long run (measured in years), the time-dependent vector that is the speech signal for a given speaker—both for what he himself says and for what he hears from others—spends more time in some regions of acoustic space than in others. This yields a *density distribution* defined for all points of the space. The density distribution is also time-dependent, since the speech signal keeps moving. . . . Within acoustic space there will be a finite number of points at which the density distribution is a local maximum.

Remember that the local maxima are *acoustic allophones*. If allophone x is ever immediately followed by allophone y, then connecting these two points in the space there is a *most probable path,* the points on which are local maxima except relative to other points also on the path. The actual trajectory of the speech signal may only rarely coincide with either a local maximum or with points on the most probable paths, but by definition, it is more apt to pass close than far away. The speakers of a language have only their past experience as speakers and hearers as a basis for either their expectations as hearers or their acoustic aims as they themselves articulate.

And then (202):

Furthermore, in course of time in any one community, as the density distribution varies for all the speakers of the community in pretty much the same way, the local maxima slowly wander about. This drifting of allophones, and hence of distinctive features is *sound change*.

Hockett thus attributes sound change to the performance effect of statistical wandering of the results of articulation. Of course since this entails (PI) we know it is false. More than this, however, the view is really quite incredible. For this claim that performance deviations in the behavior of adults can lead to systematic change totally ignores the fact that there is linguistic knowledge underlying speech performance. No matter how someone may produce an intended [t] today or tomorrow, this cannot possibly affect the system of language which he has, for the quite simple reason that all such performance effects in no way change the underlying system of knowledge. To see how inadequate such an explanation is, consider that it is analogous to arguing that performance deviations in the playing of a symphony which someone has memorized can change the score, or that deviations in a computer's performance affect its program.

Hockett's false view of sound change is thus based firmly on a failure to distinguish between language and speech, a failure to recognize that there is any language underlying speech. In all this he follows the inadequate position of Bloomfield's *Language* quite closely.

Hockett relates his statement of sound change to his previous discussion (202):

The regularist hypothesis can now be restated as follows. Sound change can affect the design of a language in that, in the course of the wandering, two allophones, or just their projections on a particular axis, can coalesce, and in that, as traversed by *different most probable paths,* a single allophone may be split into two.

Although some readers may be surprised, it is in fact no accident that in this remark Hockett has emasculated the class of all documented sound changes and deals only with coalescing and split. He also recognizes epenthesis in a footnote which I find difficult to interpret (202):

Another thing that can surely happen is for a point on a most probable path, which is not (at a certain time) an allophone, to become (subsequently) a local maximum relative to other points on the path as well as relative to the rest of its neighborhood, thus becoming an allophone. This is the historical phenomenon of epenthesis.

If I understand this at all, it means that epenthesis comes about from, for example, trying to produce proto-Mohawk [kn], but producing instead [ken]. I say it is no accident that Hockett deals basically only with merger and split because his view of sound change has even superficial plausibility only for phonetic changes of the type [u] > [U], or [p] > [f], etc. When it comes to phonemena like epenthesis, or more complex and highly structured cases like accent shift (cf. the Oneida Accent Shift),[10] metathesis, and truncation, even this vanishes. Even if, counterfactually, the Accent Shift in Oneida did take place in phonetic environments as Hockett requires, are we really to believe that this came about through performance limitations, i.e. for example that in attempting to pronounce [wakhuli′:yo] proto-Oneida accidentally produced instead [wakhuliyo′] with shift not only of stress but length? And that this accidental pronunciation somehow became the regular one? Notice, for example, that a statistical wandering view of sound change should claim that metathesis of the type [xy] > [yx] should occur with a frequency which is orders of magnitude less than M, where M is the probability of [x] > [y] multiplied by the probability of [y] > [x]. I say orders of magnitude less since the multiple of the two probabilities simply gives the probability that within the same language the two changes will happen simultaneously. But to get metathesis it is necessary further that the changes happen *only* to contiguous [x] and [y], obviously far less probable. It is not surprising that Hockett does not discuss metathesis. In general, the fact that documented sound changes reveal all of the types of processes which must be represented by rules in synchronic grammars is among the strongest evidence showing that sound change is rule change and not the performance effect claimed by Hockett.

---

[10] The accent shift example would seem to be a special case of a general type of possible change, one in which the feature specifications of two different segments are changed for the same feature. I know of no terminology for this; perhaps feature jump might do. Many cases of this can be found in Iroquoian languages; cf. for example Chafe (1959). The features involved seem to be of the type generally called 'prosodic,' so that the possibility of occurring in rules of this type may contribute to defining this category of feature. For discussion of the formal properties of such rules cf. Postal (to appear c).

Bloomfield in effect noted the incompatibility of phenomena like the shift of dental to uvular [r], metathesis, dissimilation, etc. with the view of sound change as gradual drift in performance. Instead of admitting that these were counterexamples to the view, he simply appealed to terminology and declared they were not sound change in remarks like 1933:390-391):

A replacement of this sort is surely different from the gradual and imperceptible alterations of phonetic change.

Probably this type of change is entirely different from ordinary phonetic change.

Changes like these are very different from those which are covered by the assumption of sound-change; it is possible that they are akin rather to types of linguistic change which we have still to consider —analogic change and borrowing.

But, since these types of changes are as systematic, regular, cross lexical, etc. as other changes, this terminological attempt amounts to nothing more than the naming of a class of exceptions to the view that sound change is performance change and to the view (see below) that sound change is necessarily gradual and imperceptible. In short, the view which Hockett propounds without defense today has in fact been known to be false for these reasons for decades.

If one must note the incompatibility of Hockett's view with such phenomena as metathesis, feature jump, etc., it is also evident that his conception of sound change is strangely impervious to the fact that an enormous number (undoubtedly the overwhelming majority) of documented changes are not individual shifts of one phonetic type to another, but rather involve whole sets of changes among related phonetic categories. That is, to state sound changes generally it is necessary to refer to features of segments, not to unanalyzable segments. Thus voiced stops may become voiceless, high vowels become backed, dental consonants become palatalized, etc. Yet given Hockett's performance deviance conception, there is no mechanism whatever to relate such sets of changes as [p] > [b], [t] > [d], [k] > [g]. Under Hockett's assumptions such occurrences, far from being the typical linguistic developments they are, should be exceedingly rare since they can only result from incredibly improbable statistical accidents. That is, there is no basis within Hockett's theory for explaining why a simultaneous set of changes such as that illustrated above should be any more likely than a simultaneous set of changes like [p] > [b], [n] > [ŋ], [x] > [h]. Conversely, the assumption that sound change is grammar change provides a direct explanation for this. The rules of any adequate phonology must apply to complexes of phonological and phonetic features. But, if stated in terms of features, a rule which applies to whole classes of items is simpler, given the natural metric of simplicity, than a rule which applies to a single segment. That is, in feature terms it is cheaper to say: <u>all voiced stops in environment X becomes voiceless</u> than to say: <u>d in the environment X becomes voiceless</u>. One would therefore expect sound changes in general to be of the less restricted type, as they are.[11] Since the fact that sound changes are typically rules which affect whole classes of related segments is illustrated by the most well-known sound shifts, including those which form the basis of Indo-European linguistics, for example, Grimm's and Verner's Laws, Hockett's construction of a theory of sound change in 1965 which is incompatible with them almost defies comment.

However, the inadequacy of Hockett's position is really even deeper. For in fact his theory cannot actually account for any sound changes, not even those where a single isolated segment becomes some other related segment. This ultimate limitation is related to an assertion made earlier in the first part of Chapter 13. There it was claimed that the view that the *regularity* of sound change is to be interpreted as identical to the *phonetic character* of sound change is quite strange since no one has even shown how a phonetic character would explain the regularity, i.e. the possibility of cross-lexical generalization. It is important that Hockett provides no account of this crucial point. Indeed in his terms sound change should have the very opposite properties. The very randomness of variation, entailed by the view that sound change is the result of the inability of individual acts of pronunciation to meet fixed conditions exactly, should mean that each linguistic form will go its own way. For there is no explicit mechanism to relate the deviation in performance of linguistic

---

[11] For important discussion of the role of phonological features and simplicity in the description of phonological change, reconstruction, chronology, etc., cf. Halle (1961), (1962).

form j to that of linguistic form k. In fact, there isn't even any mechanism to relate the deviation in performance n of linguistic form j to that of performance m of form j. And this is no accident. The emptiness here is a direct result of the failure to relate performance rationally to an underlying abstract system of knowledge internalized by the speaker. It is not at all a minor nor peripheral flaw which can be patched up by some simple addition. In short, Hockett's account of sound change is totally without significant linguistic content, and this is why I said above that it cannot really handle any sound changes. It is curious that Hockett should not have tried to show more explicitly just how a performance deviation approach can explain the general (if incomplete) cross-lexical regularity (so easily handled by the rule account) since this is after all the crux of the whole problem.

Although at this point it may seem superfluous, we shall consider some further intolerable consequences of the position developed by Hockett in this recent paper. We shall attempt to show that it is incompatible with a variety of other facts of different types.

Those well documented facts of sound change which are ignored by Hockett in the attempt to preserve the plausibility of his physical, performance-drift theory are not exhausted by such phenomena as metathesis, truncation, feature jump, etc. On an entirely different level, Hockett ignores those cases in which sound changes affect not the population of a dialect as a whole, but only certain subgroups in it. I am thinking especially of those cases where a sound change is limited by sex. Boas (1911:79), for example, reported a case in certain Eskimo dialects in which final p, t, k, and q were pronounced by the women as the corresponding nasal. Sapir (1949) discussed several such cases in Yana, an Indian language of northern California, including one where women's forms have final devoicing of vowels. Jakobson (1962:332) noted a substitution of j for liquids in certain women's styles in northern Siberian dialects of Russian. Cases like these are completely incompatible with the view that sound change is the result of statistical accident in performance,[12] and are ex-

---

[12] Compare Hockett's remark quoted above that 'the density distribution varies for all speakers of the community in pretty much the same way. . . .'

ceedingly strong grounds for asserting the mentalistic character of sound change. That is, they greatly support the view that sound change consists in the addition of rules to grammars. It goes without saying that such cases contribute also to showing that the causes of sound change lie totally outside of performance effects, structural factors in language, etc., and must be looked for in nonfunctional stylistic possibilities. Sound changes must be viewed, in other words, as due to the existence of limited freedom to modify grammars which is available to individuals and which, when occurring, may, like other cultural differentia, come to serve various social functions.

Hockett's statistical view of sound change commits him to the view that all sound changes are necessarily gradual. In fact there is no documented instance of gradual sound change, although quite rapid shifts are known in accordance with the view that sound change is rule change. It is again curious that Hockett makes no attempt to defend this entailment from his position in view of the fact that strong criticisms of it can be found in many of our standard texts. We have already seen that Bloomfield gives, in effect, many types of changes which he notes cannot be considered gradual. One might expect, therefore, some discussion on Hockett's part which would provide some substantive grounds for distinguishing these changes from 'real sound changes.' Similarly Hoenigswald, for example, argued convincingly as follows (1960:72-73).[13]

Among its weaknesses is the fact that, in spite of an appearance to the contrary, it fails to explain the phonemic reinterpretation of the lexicon material which makes a change proper out of the alteration and which is by nature sudden (since phonemes are discrete entities): no matter how gradually the [k] in *knot* vanished, the act of letting *knot* become homonymous with *not* has nothing gradual about it. Another difficulty has to do with a class of sound changes (e.g., metathesis, certain dissimilations; the—largely subphonemic—replacement of lingual by uvular r in many European languages) for which a continuous articu-

---

[13] The realization that there are sound changes which cannot be interpreted as gradual dates, of course, at least to the nineteenth century period about which Hockett writes. In view of this it is doubly surprising that he makes no attempt to support the claim that all changes are gradual. Cf. Sturtevant (1947:76).

latory shift cannot well be imagined, but many of which occur never-
theless with the same regularity that characterizes other sound changes.

Instead of defending his view, Hockett gives only some imaginary
anthropological observations to support it, and this in spite of
the fact that not too long ago (1958:439) he agreed that sound
change happened so slowly as to be unobservable directly (1965:-
202).

When this happens, people say 'I beg your pardon?' more often, and
speakers either repeat with more precise enunciation or else find para-
phrases that are more redundant and hence unambiguous in the presence of a higher level of channel noise, or both.

Hockett's gradual shift theory of sound change also commits
him to the view that sound changes cannot be 'jumps,' i.e. for
example, that there can be no direct change from [u] to [ɔ] in a
language which has [o]. Counterexamples to this claim are also
known. For example, the shift of older English [x] to [f] (Ger.
'lachen,' Eng. 'laugh') is such a case. Similarly the shift of velars
to labials in Rumanian is also counterevidence (Jakobson, 1962:
275). Note how both of these cases support the postulation of the
distinctive feature Grave which assigns common properties to
velars and labials. Most interestingly, the so-called 'Great Vowel
Shift' in English seems to have been a very complex case of this
character. This controversial claim will be argued in Halle and
Chomsky (to appear). Within a grammar there will be many
phonological rules which shift an element to another 'across' an
intervening one so that from the point of view of sound change
as rule addition such facts are perfectly natural and expectable.

   A most important additional type of fact showing the rule
character of sound change may be derived from a consideration
of phonological dialect differences. Such differences, which must
of course be attributed in general to sound change, are naturally
characterized in terms of exactly the kind of ordered phonological
rules required for the description of single dialects. Most crucial
here is the existence of cases where two dialects have the same
rules but with partially different orders. Such a case was discovered by M. Joos for Canadian English and discussed by Halle
(1962). Similar examples from American dialects supporting the

same conclusions are discussed by Keyser (1963). Keyser showed, for example, that there are four different dialects, one of which has only rule a; one only rule b; one both with the order a, b; and a final one with both in the order b, a. A number of similar highly complex cases from European dialect areas are analyzed by Kiparsky (1965) and most recently, additional evidence has been presented by S. Saporta (1965) for Spanish dialects. The existence of dialectal differences which can only be accounted for by underlying grammars with differing rule orders shows clearly that the sound changes responsible for such differences cannot be random shifts in performance due to behavioral limitations but must instead be highly specific, structurally constrained alterations in the grammars of the dialects. Such facts show, in other words, that sound changes are limited types of alterations in systems of internalized linguistic knowledge.

The inadequacy of Hockett's view that sound change is a phenomenon of statistical drift in speech is demonstrated finally by the fact that he himself does not maintain it consistently. Thus he remarks (204):

Just as Saussure insisted a half century ago, linguistic change finds its seeds not in the formal design of a language but in the activity of its use. . . . A coalescence or split is a modification in what generative grammarians call the 'terminal alphabet' of the language . . .

But since the terminal alphabet of generative grammarians is, as Hockett elsewhere recognizes, a formal system under concatenation intended to describe language structure and not use, i.e. a discrete phonetic system, it follows that this implies the opposite of what Saussure is said to have maintained.

It is rather curious that in 1965 Hockett should present a physical view of sound change with so little supporting argument or justification in view of the fact that the dangers of such an account were pointed out by Sapir more than forty years ago in a passage whose moral is thus demonstrably still relevant (1921:-183):

Many linguistic students have made the fatal error of thinking of sound change as a quasi-physiological instead of as a strictly psychological phenomenon, or they have tried to dispose of the problem by bandying such catch-words as 'the tendency to increased ease of articulation' or 'the cumulative result of faulty perception' (on the part of children, say, in learning to speak). These easy explanations will not do. . . . 'Faulty perception' does not explain that impressive drift in speech sounds which I have insisted upon. It is much better to admit that we do not yet understand the primary cause or causes of the slow drift in phonetics, though we can frequently point to contributing factors. It is likely that we shall not advance seriously <u>until we study the intuitional bases of speech</u> (emphasis mine: PMP). How can we understand the nature of the drift that frays and reforms phonetic patterns when we have never thought of studying sound patterning as such and the 'weights' and psychic relations of the single elements (the individual sounds) in these patterns?[14]

Modern linguists have generally claimed that autonomous phonemics is the proper answer to this demand of Sapir's to study sound pattern. I suggest that just as this is a mistake in synchronic phonology, because Sapir's phonology was basically systematic,[15] it is a mistake in diachronic phonology because, as we have seen, the very dangers which Sapir warned against are in fact just what has resulted from the attempt to cast historical phonology in the antimentalist mold of autonomous phonemics.

Hockett's discussion is the most extensive modern attempt to provide a nonmentalistic account of the phenomenon of sound change. I have tried to show that the complete failure of this attempt is due not to superficial or peripheral factors, but rather exactly to the nonmentalistic assumptions. The inadequacy is based on a failure to recognize the existence of *language* underlying speech, in particular on a failure to recognize that part of this language is a discrete phonetic system whose representations describe not the speech signal or articulation directly, but the instructions governing the ideal behavior of the speech apparatus. Central to the limitations of Hockett's discussion is a misapprehension of the status of a grammar, which is simply intended to be a precise representation of the internalized linguistic knowledge of the native.

---

[14] One can accept these basically insightful remarks of Sapir's without agreeing with his slow drift theory and while noting that, although his usage is vague, he seems in fact to accept the purely phonetic environment view. For the latter cf. for example (1921:178).

[15] For some too brief discussion of this cf. Halle (1959); Postal (1964a), (to appear b).

Hockett's description of sound change as the result of random deviations in performance completely ignores the fact that there is an underlying mental system of rules unaffected by deviations in performance. His position commits him to the dubious doctrine of the gradualness of sound change, which he supports only with speculations. In order to maintain the plausibility of his position, he is forced to ignore a wide variety of kinds of sound change including metathesis, truncation, feature jump, etc., and thus does not in fact even attempt to provide a theory of the full range of known sound changes. Similarly, he ignores facts showing the severe social limitations (nonrandom) of certain sound changes. The falsehood of his position is shown strongly, of course, by the fact that it is inconsistent with the existence of sound changes in nonphonetic environments and with the fact that many sound changes have exceptions, i.e. that some morphemes behave in unpredictable ways with respect to them. Most surprising, however, is the fact that Hockett's conception is incompatible with the mass of perfectly phonetic sound changes since it does not account for the fact that changes typically affect classes of items. And even worse, his description provides no basis for the regularity of sound changes. Finally, the position is internally inconsistent involving equivocation over such notions as 'distinctive feature,' 'local maxima,' and 'terminal vocabulary.'

With the partial goal of keeping his description nonmentalistic, Hockett has been led to construct a theory of a linguistic phenomenon in terms which really ignore *language* and deal only with *speech*. In so doing, he is forced to a position which is in part radically at odds with easily documented linguistic fact, in part empty, and in crucial ways internally incoherent. The failure of this antimentalistic account thus contributes negatively to the demonstration of the mentalistic character of sound change. For as was emphasized throughout, the positions taken by Hockett are by no means all unique. We have heard for a long time of the evils of mentalism and the need for radical empiricism, positivism, behaviorism, etc., in linguistics. The results reached here are only some of many showing that the terms of this argument have somehow become strangely reversed.

15

CONCLUSION

CONCLUDING REMARKS ON SOUND CHANGE

I have argued above that sound change is a mentalistic phenomenon, i.e. that what really changes is part of the internalized linguistic knowledge of individuals represented in the form of a set of rules and structural elements we call a grammar. It was argued, following Halle, that these changes appear to be of at least two types: the addition of phonological rules by adults, and the reformulation of previous grammars by children in order to yield an optimal grammar. Mentalistic sound changes have physical effects just because such changes alter the final phonetic representation generated by the phonological component for fixed sentences. And this final or universal phonetic representation is interpreted as a set of instructions about how the speech production system is to function.

As evidence for the mentalistic or rule property character of sound change we brought forward cases where the changes which took place happened in nonphonetic, morphophonemic environments thus falsifying a very old and widespread view about the nature of possible regular sound changes. Three such cases from Iroquoian languages were discussed at length, and two further Iroquoian cases were mentioned more briefly. Two other cases from Indo-European languages were briefly discussed and references were given to others. In addition it was pointed out that so-called 'regular sound changes' often have exceptions and again supporting data was given. This conflicts with the physical or nonmentalistic view of change and is in accord with the general fact that phonological rules generally are found to have exceptions. In further support of the mentalistic nature of sound change it was pointed out that the class of rules needed to describe the set of well-documented sound changes appears to be coextensive with those needed to describe languages synchronically. That is, those rules needed to represent phonological changes appear to be exactly those which must be posited as parts of synchronic grammars. Finally, it was argued that various other diverse factors support the mentlistic view, in particular certain extreme social limitations on certain sound changes (sex-linkage, for example), the existence of rapid sound changes, the existence of changes which jump, i.e. which are not moves in a continuous phonetic space, etc.

As a corollary of the mentalistic character of sound change, it was shown that position (PI), a view which is the natural and actual historical implication of the application of autonomous phonemics to diachronic phonology is false. This contributes to the justification of the conception of systematic phonemics which can handle all those cases handled within the framework of (PI) (mentalistically interpreted), as well as all those brought forward showing the inadequacy of this more restricted view. Although acceptance of (PI) is today closely related to the application of autonomous phonemics to diachronic phonology, the historical view is, of course, much older and dates to the nineteenth century. What is common to most of those accounts which include (PI) is the attempt to view sound change as a physical, phonetic phenomenon having to do with the performance process of articulation. I suggest that it is this error, motivated by underlying physicalist, positivist, behaviorist, and antimentalist tendencies, which is the chief factor that has obscured the rule character of sound change. That is, it is this which has obscured the fact that sound change, like the other phenomena of both synchronic and diachronic linguistics, is essentially bound up with unobservable, internalized linguistic knowledge or competence which is traditionally and naturally referred to as 'mentalistic.'

GENERAL CONCLUSION

The central concern of this monograph has been to consider those aspects of phonological theory where systematic phonemics and autonomous phonemics differ. In comparing these two opposed conceptions of phonological structure, I have treated two variants of the autonomous position: a generalized variant, an amalgam of many particular views, which has become rather standard, and the more recent and socially much more restricted stratificational view. It has been my intention to clarify to the greatest extent possible the nature of the systematic-autonomous disagreement and to specify in detail the systematic position, its implications, and justification.

Autonomous phonemics and systematic phonemics are not completely opposed, but they differ in the overwhelming body of assertions they make. Their agreements are limited to little more than a recognition that there is a notion free variation/contrast, that some phonetic features are predictable, and that there is some kind of representation of sentences between that of morphemes and phonetics. I have tried to contribute to past demonstrations that, in both synchronic and diachronic domains, wherever the two theories make conflicting claims the autonomous theory is mistaken. This is a stark judgment, but as far as I can see it is borne out by the facts in every way. I further tried to show that the newer or stratificational variant of autonomous phonemics in no way avoids the limitations of earlier varieties. Most of the empirical inadequacies of traditional autonomous phonemics are found also in the stratificational variety. And, as was shown, the latter incorporates in addition a variety of mistaken assumptions of the most fundamental sort which in many ways render it less adequate than traditional versions of autonomous phonemics.

Theoretical positions are defined largely by the questions they ask. The great limitations of autonomous phonemics are due to asking the wrong ones. The fundamental question which autonomous phonemics has asked is, essentially, how may a description systematically distinguish those phonetic features which differentiate contrasting forms from those which do not. Metaphorically 'how are utterances kept apart by sound.' This question turns out to be wrong because it involves many implicit assumptions which turn out to be false, assumptions which exclude complete overlapping, which entail the nonlogical truth that phonetic contrasts directly yield phonological contrasts, and which insist that phonological structure is independent of grammar and completely based on phonetic considerations.

Most interestingly, the fundamental question of autonomous phonemics turns out to be quite deviant from those of such phonological pioneers as Boas and Sapir and the traditional phonological investigators who preceded and coexisted with them. Study of work by men like Boas and Sapir and of those they influenced reveals that they were concerned with a quite different question as basic to phonological inquiry. This may be formulated, more precisely than they ever succeeded in stating it, but still not unfaithfully: How is the pronunciation of sentences determined by the inherent phonological properties of their parts and the general pronunciation laws of the lauguage? If, as is claimed here, current systematic phonemics has been able to incorporate what is right in autonomous phonemics,[1] to avoid its

---

[1] In view of the generally negative position taken in this work on autonomous phonemics, it is fair to indicate what I take to be its real contributions. If we compare the phonological ideas and descriptions of Boas and Sapir, for example, with those of standard autonomous phonemics, I think we can see the following genuine improvements. First, the notion of free variation/contrast was, for all practical purposes, discovered, analyzed, and described in a vast number of languages. Of course, as we have emphasized in Chapter 9 the transitive account given was not correct, but previous linguistics had by and large ignored the notion entirely. Secondly, although the claims of 'rigor' made for autonomous phonemics are greatly exaggerated, there is at least one respect in which there is a real advance. Pre-1930 descriptions did not make a serious attempt to study the combinatory restrictions and distribution of phonetic elements within morphemes and words. Such descriptions abound with imprecise remarks like 'such and such a segment generally occurs before vowels' or 'normally does not occur after glottal stop,' with no attempt made to explicate concepts like 'generally,' 'normally,' etc. It was the autonomous phonemic concern with principles like complementary distribution which laid the basis for the elimination of toleration of this sort of thing and the requirement for the complete study and precise statement of distributional properties. Related to this is the autonomous concern with 'phonotactics' which added a whole new dimension of concern to phonological descriptions. Also, it was autonomous phonemics, particularly in certain versions such as Bloomfield's practice and Harris's theories, which moved phonological

manifold mistakes and limitations, and to incorporate a vast range of insights and generalizations necessarily excluded by autonomous ideas, it is only because systematic phonemic inquiry has returned to this evidently more valuable traditional question. In other words, autonomous phonemics is not only a largely erroneous theory of phonological structure. It is also a historically deviant movement[2] and not at all the natural scientific development and improvement of previous conceptions which its advocates often claim.

The developers of systematic phonemics have been able to improve the traditional 'morphophonemic' approach to phonology of scholars like Sapir for a number of obvious reasons. First, they have had the advantage of a vastly expanded base of factual

---

theory and description in the direction of providing a formal account of the nature of linguistic descriptions. Particularly in Harris's concern with formal principles of compactness and simplicity we see the beginnings of a serious concern with the question of formal properties of phonological descriptions. Finally, and possibly in the long run most significantly, it was autonomous phonemics, at least of the early Praguian and Jakobsonian varieties, which contributed fundamental aspects of the notions of phonetic and phonological features, neutralization, archiphoneme, feature hierarchy, and Markedness. An enormous substantive contribution to our knowledge of the right class of phonetic-phonological features is involved here. Nothing stands out more clearly as an inadequacy in the descriptions of Boas and Sapir than their failure to utilize any explicit notion of feature and their limitation to segmental entities. One must note, however, the extraordinary extent to which many varieties of autonomous phonemics have failed to move beyond the unanalyzable segment position even to his day. In each of these areas, one can find real contributions which are due to the work and concern of autonomous phonemicists. Unfortunately, many of these were purchased at the price of a loss of previous insights (such as the morphophonemic character of phonological structure, the role of grammatical structure, of rule ordering, etc.). And in addition, almost none of these positive features of autonomous phonemic notions was, as such, correctly formulated or developed as we have previously seen to a significant extent.

[2] The historical deviancy of autonomous phonemics is not of course isolated from the general deviancy of the whole movement of modern taxonomic linguistics. That is, just as the phonological aspect of generative grammar, systematic phonemics, is properly looked upon as a return to questions of traditional phonological interest which had been largely abandoned, so generative grammar as a whole with its syntactic and semantic aspects is properly looked upon as a return to traditional questions of syntactic and semantic interest which modern taxonomic linguistics largely abandoned. For discussion (cf. Chomsky 1964b, 1965).

knowledge about particular languages and about the nature of universal phonetics. Secondly, and even more important, they have had the advantage of vastly increased insight into notion of 'linguistic description' or 'grammar.' They have been able to utilize the precise formal conception of a linguistic description as a generative grammar. On the one hand, they have had the conception of a linguistic description as a precise formal system generating the class of significant linguistic objects, i.e. the conception of a 'generative grammar.'[3] On the other hand, they have had the substantive results of inquiry in generative syntax which has provided a significant, if far from complete, account of the kind of linguistic elements which serve as the input to the phonology, i.e. an account of Surface Syntactic Structures.

These advantages have permitted systematic phonemics both to state the traditional questions more precisely and, in significant part, to provide viable answers. In present terminology, the basic question of preautonomous phonological investigation can be put as follows:

(15.1) How does the Surface Syntactic Structure of a sentence determine its pronunciation, that is the set of phonetic representations which are associated with it?

This question breaks down into crucial subquestions which include the following:

(15.2) What is the proper form of representation for the inherent phonological properties of dictionary entries?

(15.3) What is the right universal phonetic system? That is, what are the right set of phonetic features, what are their possible values, what are their possible combinations into phonetic segments, what are their possible sequential combinations?

(15.4) What are the possible types of phonological rules? What kinds of grammatical information may such rules appeal to and how? How are phonological rules interrelated, i.e. are they ordered, if so what kinds of ordering exist, etc.

---

[3] For exactly analogous reasons, work in generative syntax has been able to more precisely reformulate significant traditional syntactic questions, such as those about grammatical relations, and to take fundamental steps toward answering them.

(15.5) How may phonological properties like <u>free variation/contrast, possible morpheme</u>, etc. be characterized by grammars?

(15.6) What is the empirically correct evaluation procedure for phonological segments of grammars, that is, what technique does the prelinguistic infant use to pick the right phonological description for the language on the basis of an arbitrary and limited sample?

(15.7) How may the phonological parts of grammars change over time and differ in space?

Answers to these questions would provide a complete phonological theory amounting to a supported hypothesis about the inherent structure of the human infant which permits the determination within a relatively short time of the phonological structure of an arbitrary language on the basis of highly limited, fragmentary, and largely irrelevant and/or actually wrong information.

Questions like the above have motivated past work in systematic phonemics and will continue to spur future research. The contributions of this approach are a direct function of their investigation, and these results have been obtained by relatively few people over a relatively short span of time. This cannot fail to suggest the profits which might ensue if such real questions could replace, for many of those studying phonological structure, the much too limited and largely stultifying questions which have for the most part been imposed on phonological investigation by acceptance of the distorted and limited framework of autonomous phonemics. If the present monograph makes any contribution to such a development, it will have done more than serve its purpose.

Bibliography

Allen, H. B.

1958 ed., *Readings in Applied English Linguistics,* New York, Appleton Century-Crofts.

Barbeau, M.

1915 *Classification of Iroquoian Radicals with Subjective Pronominal Prefixes,* Memoir 46, Ottawa, Canada Department of Mines, Geological Survey.

1959 *The Language of Canada in the Voyages of Jacques-Cartier,* Bulletin No. 173, Ottawa, National Museum of Canada, Contributions to Anthropology.

Bloch, B.

1941 'Phonemic Overlapping,' *American Speech,* **16,** 278–284.

1948 'A Set of Postulates for Phonemic Analysis,' *Language,* **24,** 3–46.

1950 'Studies in Colloquial Japanese IV: Phonemics,' *Language,* **26,** 86–112.

1953 'Contrast,' *Language,* **29,** 59–61.

Bloomfield L.

1933 *Language,* New York, Henry Holt and Co.

1936 'Language or Ideas,' *Language,* **12,** 89–95.

1939a 'Menomini Morphophonemics,' *Travaux du Cercle Linguistique de Prague,* No. 8.

1939b 'Linguistic Aspects of Science,' *International Encyclopedia of Unified Science, Vol. 1, No. 4,* Chicago, University of Chicago Press.

Boas, F.

1911 ed., *Handbook of American Indian Languages,* Washington, Bureau of American Ethnology Bulletin No. 40, Pt. 1.

Cambell, A.

1959 *Old English Grammar,* Oxford, Oxford University Press.

Carnap, R.

1936- 'Testability and Meaning,' *Philosophy of Science,* III, 419–
1937 471 and IV, 1–40.

1956   'The Methodological Character of Theoretical Concepts,' in Feigl and Scriven (1956).

Carroll J.
1953   *The Study of Language*, Cambridge, Harvard University Press.

Chafe, W. L.
1959   'Internal Reconstruction in Seneca,' *Language*, **35**, 477–495.

1961   *Seneca Thanksgiving Rituals*, Washington, Bureau of American Ethnology Bulletin No. 183.

1963   *Handbook of the Seneca Language*, Albany, New York State Museum and Science Service Bulletin No. 388.

1964   'Another Look at Siouan and Iroquoian,' *American Anthropologist*, **66**, 852–862.

Chao Y. R.
1933   'The Non-Uniqueness of Phonemic Solutions of Phonetic Systems,' *Academia Sinica, Bulletin of History and Philology*, **4**, 363–397.

Chomsky, N. A.
1951   *Morphophonemics of Modern Hebrew*, Philadelphia, University of Pennsylvania Master's Dissertation.

1955   *The Logical Structure of Linguistic Theory*, Cambridge, mimeographed.

1957a   review of C. F. Hockett, *A Manual of Phonology*, *International Journal of American Linguistics*, **23**, 223–234.

1957b   review of R. Jakobson and M. Halle, *Fundamentals of Language*, *International Journal of American Linguistics*, **23**, 234–242.

1959   review of B. F. Skinner, *Verbal Behavior Language*, **35**, 26–58.

1961a   'Some Methodological Remarks on Generative Grammar,' *Word*, **17**, 219–239.

1961   'Explanatory Models in Linguistics,' in Nagel, Suppes, and Tarski (1961).

1962   'A Transformational Approach to Syntax,' in Hill (1962c), also in Fodor and Katz (1964).

1964a   'The Logical Basis of Linguistic Theory,' in Lunt (1964).

1964b   'Current Issues in Linguistic Theory,' in Fodor and Katz (1964).

1965   *Aspects of the Theory of Syntax,'* Cambridge, MIT Press.

1966   *Cartesian Linguistics,* New York, Harper & Row.
to appear a 'Topics in the Theory of Generative Grammar,' in Fergu-
        son (to appear).

Chomsky, N. A., and M. Halle
1965   'Some Controversial Questions in Phonological Theory,'
        Journal of Linguistics, **2,** 95–138.

Chomsky, N. A., M. Halle, and F. Lukoff
1956   'On Accent and Juncture in English,' in Halle, Lunt, and
        MacLean (1956).

Chomsky, N. A., and G. Miller
1963   'Introduction to the Formal Analysis of Natural Lan-
        guages,' in Luce, Bush, and Galanter (1963).

Dyen, I.
1963   'Why Phonetic Change is Regular,' *Language,* **39,** 638–
        648.

Feigl, H., and M. Scriven
1956   eds., *Minnesota Studies in the Philosophy of Science I,*
        Minneapolis, University of Minnesota Press.

Fenton, W. N.
1961   ed., *Symposium on Cherokee and Iroquois Culture,* Wash-
        ington, Bureau of American Ethnology Bulletin No. 180.

Ferguson, C. F.
1962   review of M. Halle, *The Sound Pattern of Russian, Lan-
        guage,* **38,** 284–297.

to appear   ed. *Current Trends in Linguistics, Volume III,* The Hague,
        Mouton and Co.

Fodor, J. and J. Katz
1964   eds., *The Structure of Language,* Englewood Cliffs, N.J.,
        Prentice-Hall, Inc.

Foley, J. A.
1965   *Spanish Verb Morphology,* Cambridge, MIT Doctoral Dis-
        sertation.

Fries, C. F.
1962a 'The Bloomfield School,' in Mohrmann, Sommerfelt, and
        Whatmough (1962).
1962b *Linguistics and Reading,* New York, Holt, Rinehart and
        Winston.

Gleason, H. A.
> 1961   *An Introduction to Descriptive Linguistics,* 2nd edition, New York, Holt, Rinehart and Winston.
> 1964   'The Organization of Language: A Stratificational View,' in Stuart (1964).

Hale, K.
> 1965   'Some Preliminary Observation on Papago Morphophonemics,' *International Journal of American Linguistics,* **31,** 295–305.

Hall, R. A.
> 1964   *Introductory Linguistics,* Philadelphia, Chilton Books.

Halle, M.
> 1959   *The Sound Pattern of Russian,* The Hague, Mouton and Co.
> 1960   review of R. I. Avanesov, *Fonetika Sovremennogo Russkogo Literaturnogo Jazyka, Word,* **16,** 140–152.
> 1961   'On the Role of Simplicity of Linguistic Descriptions' in Jakobson (1961).
> 1962   'Phonology in a Generative Grammar,' *Word,* **18,** 54–73.

Halle, M., and N. Chomsky
> to appear   *The Sound Pattern of English,* New York, Harper & Row.

Halle, M., H. Lunt, and H. MacLean
> 1956   eds., *For Roman Jakobson,* The Hague, Mouton and Co.

Halle, M., and V. Zeps
> to appear   *Latvian Morphophonemics.*

Hammel, E. A.
> 1965   ed., *Formal Semantic Analysis,* Special Publication, *American Anthropologist,* **67.**

Harris, Z. S.
> 1951   *Methods in Structural Linguistics,* Chicago, University of Chicago Press.

Hempel, C. G.
> 1952   'Problems and Changes in the Empiricist Criterion of Meaning,' in Linsky (1952).
> 1956   'The Theoretician's Dilemma,' in Feigl and Scriven (1956).

Hill, A. A.
> 1958a   'Linguistics Since Bloomfield,' in Allen (1958).

1958b   *Introduction to Linguistic Structures*, New York, Harcourt, Brace and Co.

1962a   'Various Kinds of Phonemes,' *Studies in Linguistics*, **16**, 3–10.

1962b   ed., *Second Texas Conference on Problems of Linguistic Analysis in English*, Austin, The University of Texas.

1962c   ed., *Third Texas Conference on Problems of Linguistic Analysis in English*, Austin, The University of Texas.

Hockett, C. F.

1942   'A System of Descriptive Phonology,' *Language*, **18**, 1–21.

1951   review of A. Martinet, *Phonology as Functional Phonetics*, *Language*, **27**, 333–342.

1954   'Two Models of Grammatical Description,' *Word*, **10**, 210–231.

1958   *A Course in Modern Linguistics*, New York, The Macmillan Company.

1961   'Linguistic Elements and Their Relations,' *Language*, **37**, 29–54.

1965   'Sound Change,' *Language*, **41**, 185–205.

Hoenigswald, H. M.

1960   *Language Change and Linguistic Reconstruction*, Chicago, The University of Chicago Press.

Hoijer, H.

1946   ed., *Linguistic Structures of Native America*, New York, Viking Fund Publications in Anthropology Number 6.

Householder, F.

1965   'Some Recent Claims in Phonological Theory,' *Journal of Linguistics*, **1**, 13–34.

Jakobson, R.

1958   'Typological Studies and Their Contribution to Historical Comparative Linguistics,' in Sivertsen (1958).

1961   ed., *Structure of Language and Its Mathematical Aspects*, Providence, R. I., American Mathematical Society.

1962   *Roman Jakobson Selected Writings I: Phonological Studies*, The Hague, Mouton and Co.

Katz, J.

1964   'Mentalism in Linguistics,' *Language*, **40**, 124–138.

to appear   *The Phiolsophy of Language*, New York, Harper & Row.

322   *Bibliography*

Katz, J., and J. Fodor
    1963   'The Structure of a Semantic Theory,' *Language*, **39**, 170–211; (also in Fodor and Katz, 1964).

Katz, J., and P. M. Postal
    1964   *An Integrated Theory of Linguistic Description*, Cambridge, MIT Press.

Keyser, S. J.
    1963   review of H. Kurath and R. McDavid, *The Pronunciation of English in the Atlantic States, Language*, **39**, 303–316.

Keyser, S. J., and M. Halle
to appear   *Evolution of English Stress*.

Kiparsky, R. K. P.
    1965   *Phonological Change*, Cambridge, MIT Doctoral Dissertation.

Koch, S.
    1963   ed., *Psychology: A Study of a Science*, Volume 6, New York, McGraw-Hill Book Co.

Kurtyowicz, J.
    1960   *Esquisses Linguistiques*, Warsaw, Palska Akademia Nauk.

Labov, W.
    1963   'The Social Motivation of a Sound Change,' *Word*, **19**, 273–310.

Lakoff, G.
    1966   *The Nature of Syntactic Irregularity*, Bloomington, Indiana University Doctoral Dissertation.

Lamb S.
    1962   *Outline of Stratificational Grammar*, Berkeley, University of California.
    1964a 'The Sememic Approach to Structural Semantics,' in Romney and D'Andrade (1964).
    1964b 'Notes on Alternation, Transformation, Realization and Stratification,' in Stuart (1964).
    1965   'Kinship Terminology and Linguistic Structure,' in Hammel, ed., (1965).

Langendoen, D. T.
    1964a Review of *Studies in Linguistic Analysis, Language*, **40**, 305–322.
    1964b *Modern British Linguistics*, Cambridge, MIT Doctoral Dissertation, (to appear, MIT Press).

Lees, R. B.
    1957   review of N. Chomsky, *Syntactic Structures, Language,* **33,** 375–408.
    1961   *The Phonology of Modern Standard Turkish,* The Hague, Mouton and Co.

Li, F. K.
    1946   'Chipewyan,' in Hoijer (1946).

Lieberman, P.
    1965   'On the Acoustic Basis of the Perception of Intonation by Linguists,' *Word,* **21,** 40–55.

Lightner, T. M.
    1965   *Segmental Phonology of Contemporary Standard Russian,* Cambridge, MIT Doctoral Dissertation.

Linsky, L.
    1952   ed., *Semantics and the Philosophy of Language,* Urbana, University of Illinois Press.

Lounsbury, F. G.
    1946   *Phonology of the Oneida Language,* Madison, University of Wisconsin Master's Dissertation.
    1963   *Oneida Verb Morphology,* New Haven, Yale University Publications in Anthropology No. 48.
    1960   'Iroquoian Place Names in the Champlain Valley,' *Report of the New York–Vermont Commission on the Lake Champlain Basin,* New York State Legislative Document No. 9.
    1961   'Iroquois–Cherokee Linguistic Relations,' in Fenton (1961).
    1962   'Language,' in Siegel (1962).
    1963   'Linguistics and Psychology,' in Koch (1963).

Luce, R. D., R. Bush, and E. Galanter
    1963   eds., *Handbook of Mathematical Psychology, Volume II,* New York, John Wiley and Sons.

Lunt, H.
    1964   ed., *Proceedings of the Ninth International Congress of Linguists,* The Hague, Mouton and Co.

Lyons, J.
    1962   'Phonemic and Non-Phonemic Phonology: Some Typological Reflections,' *International Journal of American Linguistics,* **28,** 127–134.

324   *Bibliography*

McCawley, J. D.
    1965a *The Accentual System of Standard Japanese,* Cambridge,
         MIT Doctoral Dissertation.
    1965b 'Statement Vs. Rule in Linguistic Description,' paper pre-
         sented at the annual conference of the New York Lin-
         guistic Circle.

Mandelbaum, D. G.
    1949 ed., *The Selected Writings of Edward Sapir,* Berkeley,
         University of California.

Marckwardt, A.
    1962 ' "On Accent and Juncture in English"—A critique,' in
         Hill (1962b).

Martinet, A.
    1952 'Function, Structure and Sound Change,' *Word,* **8,** 1–32.
    1953 'Concerning the Preservation of Useful Sound Features,'
         Word, **9,** 1–11.

Matthews, G. H.
    1965 *Hidatsa Syntax,* The Hague, Mouton and Co.

Miller, G. A.
    1958 'Speech and Communication,' *Journal of the Acoustic So-
         ciety of America,* **30,** 395–401.

Mohramann, C., A. Sommerfelt, and J. Whatmough
    1962 eds., *Trends in European and American Linguistics 1930–
         1960,* Utrecht, The Netherlands, Spectrum Publishers.

Nagel, E., P. Suppes, and A. Tarski
    1961 *Logic, Methodology and Philosophy of Science; Proceed-
         ings of the 1960 International Congress,* Stanford, Stan-
         ford University Press.

Paul, H.
    1891 *Principles of the History of Language,* (trans. H. A.
         Strong), London, Longmans, Green, and Co.

Pike, K. L.
    1947 'Grammatical Prerequisites to Phonemic Analysis,' *Word,*
         3, 155–172.
    1952 'More on Grammatical Prerequisites,' *Word,* **8,** 106–121.

Postal, P. M.
    1962 *Some Syntactic Rules in Mohawk,* New Haven, Yale Uni-
         versity Doctoral Dissertation.

1964a 'Boas and the Development of Phonology: Comments Based on Iroquoian,' *International Journal of American Linguistics,* **30,** 269–280.

1964b *Constituent Structure: A Study of Contemporary Models of Syntactic Description,* Bloomington, Publication 30 of the Indiana Research Center in Anthropology, Folklore, and Linguistics.

to appear a review of R. Dixon, *Linguistic Science and Logic, Language,* **42.**

to appear b review of A. Martinet, *Elements of General Linguistics, Foundations of Language,* **2.**

to appear c *Mohawk Phonology.*

to appear d *Towards a Grammar of Exceptions.*

Romney, A. K. and R. G. D'Andrade

1964 eds., *Transcultural Studies in Cognition,* Special Publication of the *American Anthropologist,* **66.**

Sapir, E.

1921 *Language,* New York, Harcourt, Brace and Co.

1925 'Sound Patterns in Language,' *Language,* **1,** 37–51.

1933 'The Psychological Reality of Phonemes,' in Mandelbaum (1949).

1949 'Male and Female Forms of Speech in Yana,' in Mandelbaum (1949).

Saporta, S.

1965 'Ordered Rules, Dialect Differences, and Historical Processes,' *Language,* **41,** 218–225.

Saussure, F.

1959 *A Course in General Linguistics,* (trans. Wade Baskin), New York, Philosophical Library.

Schane, S.

1965 *The Phonological and Morphological Structure of French,* Cambridge, MIT Doctoral Dissertation.

Scheffler, I.

1963 *The Anatomy of Inquiry,* New York, A. A. Knopf.

Siegel, B. J.

1962 ed., *Biennial Review of Anthropology 1961,* Stanford, Stanford University Press.

Sivertsen, E.
  1958   eds., *Proceedings of the Eighth International Congress of Linguists,* Oslo, Oslo University Press.

Stanley, R.
to appear   'Phonological Redundancy Rules,' *Language.*

Stuart, C. I. J. M.
  1964   ed. *Monograph Series on Languages and Linguistics No. 17,* Washington, Georgetown Institute of Languages and Linguistics.

Sturtevant, E. H.
  1947   *An Introduction to Linguistic Science,* New Haven, Yale University Press.

Swadesh, M.
  1934   'The Phonemic Principle,' *Language,* **10,** 117–129.

Swadesh, M., and C. F. Voegelin
  1939   'A Problem in Phonological Alternation,' *Language,* **15,** 1–10.

Trubetzkoy, N. S.
  1936   'Die Aufhebung der Phonologischen Gegensätze,' in Vachek (1964a).
  1939   'Grundzüge der Phonologie,' *Travaux du Cercle Linguistique de Prague,* No. 7.

Vachek, J.
  1964a   ed., *A Prague School Reader in Linguistics,* Bloomington, Indiana University Press.
  1964b   'On Some Basic Principles of "Classical" Phonology,' *Zeitschrift für Phonetik, Sprachwissenschaft und Kommunikationsforschung,* **17,** 409–431.

Wang, W. S-Y.
  1962   'Stress in English,' *Language Learning,* **12,** no. 1, 69–75. Copyright 1962 by Research Club in Language Learning.

Waterman J. T.
  1963   *Perspectives in Linguistics,* Chicago, University of Chicago Press.

Wells, R.
  1947   review of K. L. Pike, *The Intonation of American English, Language,* **23,** 255–273.